KU-228-429

ENGINES OF PRIVILEGE

Britain's Private School Problem

FRANCIS GREEN AND
DAVID KYNASTON

BLOOMSBURY PUBLISHING
LONDON · OXFORD · NEW YORK · NEW DELHI · SYDNEY

BLOOMSBURY PUBLISHING
Bloomsbury Publishing Plc
50 Bedford Square, London, WC1B 3DP, UK

BLOOMSBURY, BLOOMSBURY PUBLISHING and the Diana logo are trademarks of
Bloomsbury Publishing Plc

First published in Great Britain 2019
This edition published 2019

Copyright © Francis Green and David Kynaston, 2019

Diagram design © Phillip Beresford, 2019

Francis Green and David Kynaston have asserted their right under the Copyright, Designs and
Patents Act, 1988, to be identified as Authors of this work

For legal purposes the Acknowledgements on p. 313
constitute an extension of this copyright page

All rights reserved. No part of this publication may be reproduced or transmitted in any form or
by any means, electronic or mechanical, including photocopying, recording, or any information
storage or retrieval system, without prior permission in writing from the publishers

Bloomsbury Publishing Plc does not have any control over, or responsibility for, any third-party
websites referred to in this book. All internet addresses given in this book were correct at the time
of going to press. The authors and publisher regret any inconvenience caused if addresses have
changed or sites have ceased to exist, but can accept no responsibility for any such changes

A catalogue record for this book is available from the British Library

ISBN: HB: 978-1-5266-0126-1; PB: 978-1-5266-0127-8; eBook: 978-1-5266-0124-7

2 4 6 8 10 9 7 5 3 1

Typeset by Newgen KnowledgeWorks Pvt. Ltd., Chennai, India
Printed and bound in Great Britain by CPI Group (UK) Ltd, Croydon CR0 4YY

To find out more about our authors and books visit www.bloomsbury.com
and sign up for our newsletters

A Note on the Authors

Francis Green is Professor of Work and Education Economics at the UCL Institute of Education. He is the author of ten books and 150 papers, and is a recognised authority on the economic and social effects of private schooling in the past and present. He also works as an occasional adviser to the European Foundation for Living and Working Conditions, the OECD and the World Bank.

David Kynaston has been a professional historian since 1973 and has written twenty books, including on the City of London and cricket, as well as a series aiming to cover the history of post-war Britain (1945–79), 'Tales of a New Jerusalem'. He is currently an honorary professor at Kingston University.

C334411829

Contents

Preface

Engines of Privilege has two underlying premises: that the existence in Britain of a flourishing private school sector not only limits the life chances of those who attend state schools, but also damages society at large; and that it should be possible to have a sustained and fully inclusive national conversation about the subject. Whether one has been privately educated, or has sent or is sending one's children to private schools, or even if one teaches at a private school, there should be no barriers to taking part in that conversation. Everyone has to live – and make their choices – in the world as it is, not as one might wish it to be. That seems an obvious enough proposition. Yet in a name-calling culture, ever ready with the charge of hypocrisy, this reality is all too often ignored.

For the sake of avoiding misunderstanding, we should state briefly our own backgrounds and choices. One of our fathers was a solicitor in Brighton, the other was an army officer rising to the rank of lieutenant-colonel; we were both privately educated; we both went to Oxford University; our children have all been educated at state grammar schools; in neither case did we move to the areas (Kent and south-west London) because of the existence of those schools; and in recent years we have become increasingly preoccupied with the private school issue, partly as citizens concerned with Britain's social and democratic wellbeing, partly as an aspect of our professional work (one as an economist, the other as a historian).

In an important sense, none of this matters. Rather, what matters infinitely more is the issue itself. *That* is the subject of this book. Britain's private schools – including their fundamental unfairness – remain a major elephant in the room, perhaps the biggest of all. It would be an almost immeasurable benefit if this were no longer the case. And our hope is that this book, by discussing in a sober, historically aware and evidence-based way both the problem itself and possible remedies, will contribute to a new openness for objective, guilt-free debate. It is, after all, high time.

July 2018

What Is the Problem?

Education is different. Its effects are deep, long-term and run from one generation to the next. Those with enough money are free to purchase and enjoy expensive holidays, cars, houses and meals. But education is not just another material asset: it is fundamental to creating who we are. If we buy an expensive and exclusive schooling for our children, we influence how they grow, the sort of people they will become and what they will do. On top of that, the qualifications they gain haul them further up the ladder to scarce, rewarding places, first at our elite universities and then later in life. So by making that purchase, we are at the same time buying significant positional advantage for our children – at the expense of other children's futures. Put plainly, the purchase of private education by a minority of us is incompatible with the pursuit of a fairer, more cohesive society: an inconvenient truth, but the truth nonetheless. Education, to repeat, is different.

What particularly defines British private education – as provided by 'prep' (that is, preparatory) schools at the primary stage and 'public' (that is, private) schools at the secondary – is its extreme social exclusivity. Only about 6 per cent of the UK's school population attend such schools; although, because some children switch to private schools during childhood, some 9 per cent of adults have been educated privately at some point.[1] The families accessing private education are highly concentrated among the

affluent (see Figure 1). At every rung of the income ladder there
are a small number of private school attenders; but it is only at the
very top, above the 95th rung of the ladder – where families have an
income of £120,000 – that there are appreciable numbers of private
school children. At the 99th rung – families with incomes upwards
of £300,000 – six out of every ten children are at private school.

FIGURE 1 Percentage in private school at each rung of the income ladder

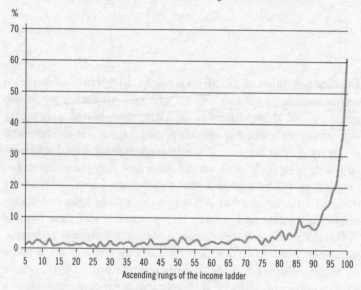

Source: Data from Family Resources Survey; see Green, F., J. Anders, M. Henderson and G. Henseke (2017), *Who Chooses Private
Schooling in Britain and Why?*, Centre for Research on Learning and Life Chances (LLAKES), London, Research Paper 62. The base
population is all children aged five–fifteen living in private households in Great Britain, between 2001/2002 and 2015/2016. The
income rungs are the percentiles of their families' gross weekly income.

A glance at the annual fees is relevant here. The press focus tends
to be on the great and historic boarding schools, such as Eton
(basic fee £40,668 in 2018–19), Harrow (£40,050) and Winchester
(£39,912), but it is important to see the private sector in the less
glamorous round, and stripped of the extra cost of boarding. In
2018 the average day fees at prep schools are, at £13,026, around
half the income of a family on the middle rung of the income

ladder.[2] For secondary school, and even more so sixth forms, the fees are appreciably higher. In short, access to private schooling is, for the most part, available only to wealthy households. Indeed, the small number of income-poor families going private can only do so through other sources: typically, grandparents' assets and/or endowment-supported bursaries from some of the richest schools. Overwhelmingly, pupils at private schools are rubbing shoulders with those from similarly well-off backgrounds.

They arrange things somewhat differently elsewhere: among affluent countries, Britain's private school participation is especially exclusive to the rich.[3] In Germany, for instance, it is also low, but unlike in Britain is generously state-funded, more strongly regulated and comes with modest fees. In France, private schools attract higher participation (some 16 per cent of all pupils) and are thus less socially exclusive. They are mainly Catholic schools permitted to teach religion: the state pays the teachers and the fees are very low. In the USA there is a very small sector of private schools with high fees, but most private schools are, again, religious, with much lower fees than in Britain; while in Sweden fee-paying schooling is confined to a handful of boarding schools with fees a fraction of their British equivalents, educating less than half a per cent of the population. Britain's private school configuration is, in short, distinctive.

1997–2018: a brief, expensive history

And what, then, does Britain look like in the twenty-first century? As the millennium approaches, New Labour under Tony Blair (Fettes) sweeps to power. The Bank of England under Eddie George (Dulwich) gets independence. The chronicles of Hogwarts School begin. A nation grieves for Diana (West Heath); Charles (Gordonstoun) retrieves her body; her brother (Eton) tells it as it is. Martha Lane Fox (Oxford High) blows a dotcom bubble. Charlie Falconer (Glenalmond) masterminds the Millennium Dome. Will Young (Wellington) becomes the first *Pop Idol*. *The Wire*'s Jimmy McNulty (Eton) sorts out Baltimore. James Blunt

(Harrow) releases the best-selling album of the decade. Northern Rock collapses under the chairmanship of Matt Ridley (Eton). Boris Johnson (Eton) enters City Hall in London. The Cameron–Osborne (Eton–St Paul's) axis takes over the country; Nick Clegg (Westminster) runs errands. Life staggers on in austerity Britain mark two. Jeremy Clarkson (Repton) can't stop revving up; Jeremy Paxman (Malvern) still has an attitude problem; Alexandra Shulman (St Paul's Girls) dictates fashion; Paul Dacre (University College School) makes Middle England ever more *Mail*-centric; Alan Rusbridger (Cranleigh) makes non-Middle England ever more *Guardian*-centric; judge Brian Leveson (Liverpool College) fails to nail the press barons; Justin Welby (Eton) becomes top mitre man; Frank Lampard (Brentwood) becomes a Blues legend; Joe Root (Worksop) takes guard; Henry Blofeld (Eton) spots a passing bus. The Cameron–Osborne axis sees off Labour, but not Boris + Nigel Farage (Dulwich) + Arron Banks (Crookham Court). Ed Balls (Nottingham High) takes to the dance floor. Theresa May (St Juliana's) and Jeremy Corbyn (Castle House) face off. Prince George (Thomas's Battersea) and Princess Charlotte (Willcocks) start school.

Life's gilded path

The statistics also tell a story. The fullest, most authoritative survey of the extent of the dominance of the privately educated in twenty-first-century Britain has been published by the Sutton Trust, a highly respected educational charity concerned with social mobility. *Leading People 2016* tracked the educational backgrounds of the prominent, rich and influential figures in seven key areas of public life (see Figure 2). The proportion of prominent people in every area who had been educated privately is striking, in some cases grotesque. From judges (74 per cent privately educated) through to MPs (32 per cent), this snapshot depicts a society where bought educational privilege also buys lifetime privilege and influence.[4]

None of this should surprise. 'The dogged persistence of the British "old boy"' is how a 2017 study describes the traditional

FIGURE 2 Percentage privately educated among the rich and powerful

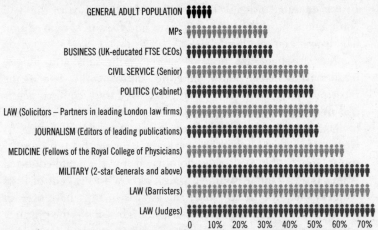

Source: Kirby, P. (2016), *Leading People 2016*, the Sutton Trust, London.

dominance of private school alumni in British society.[5] This reveals the fruits of exploring well over a century of biographical data in *Who's Who*, that indispensable annual guide to the composition of the British elite. For those born between the 1830s and 1920s, roughly 50 to 60 per cent went to private schools; for those born between the 1930s and 1960s, the proportion was roughly 45 to 50 per cent. Based on those figures, it is tempting to conclude (as the *Daily Telegraph* did in its report of the survey) that the British elite has very gradually started to open up; and, indeed, taking the twentieth century as a whole, that would be a fair point, though with the emphasis on 'very gradually'. Yet, among the new entrants to *Who's Who* in the twenty-first century, the proportion of privately educated has remained constant at around 45 per cent. Going to one of the schools in the prestigious Headmasters' and Headmistresses' Conference (HMC) still gives a thirty-five times better chance of entering *Who's Who* than if one has not attended an HMC school; while those attending the historic crème de la crème, the so-called Clarendon Schools (Charterhouse, Eton, Harrow, Merchant Taylors', Rugby, St Paul's, Shrewsbury, Westminster, Winchester), are ninety-four times more likely to join the elite than any ordinary British-educated person. 'It is a mirror to the trends of the day,' comments a *Who's Who* spokeswoman, 'and the aim of each edition has always been to reflect society.'[6]

Elites, though, are not just about politicians and judges, let alone newspaper editors and the commentariat. Two of the most piquant aspects of the Sutton Trust survey concern actors and musicians. Over the past quarter-century, some 60 per cent of British winners of Oscars and 42 per cent of British BAFTA winners have been privately educated; as for the field of popular music, once almost totally dominated by the state-educated (think Beatles, think Rolling Stones), almost 20 per cent of Brits winners since the inception of the awards in 1977 have been at private schools.[7] So, too, with sport. In rugby union, the privately educated share of England's 2007 World Cup squad hit 60 per cent; in cricket, an England team at Lord's in 2011 comprised eight privately educated and just three state-educated; and a third of the British medallists at the Rio Olympics in 2016 came from private schools, as had the medallists from the four previous Olympics combined.[8] Overall, revealed an Ofsted report in 2014, one-third of contemporary England sporting internationals were privately educated.[9]

Even if one's child never achieves sporting or cultural celebrity, sending him or her to a private school is usually a shrewd investment – indeed, increasingly so, to judge by the relevant longitudinal studies of two different generations. Take first the cohort born in 1958: in terms of those with comparable social backgrounds, demographic characteristics and early tested skills, and different *only* in what type of school they attended when they were eleven, by the time they were in their early thirties (around 1990) the privately educated were earning 7 per cent more than the state-educated. Compare that to those born in 1970: by the same stage (the early 2000s), the gap between the two categories – again, similar in all other respects – had risen to 21 per cent in favour of the privately educated.[10] Some ten years later (in 2012), the earnings premium within that 1970 cohort for those who had

been privately educated when they were sixteen was 35 per cent
for men and 21 per cent for women; and the chances of those
in the cohort reaching the top socio-economic group – higher
management and professional occupations – were 1.6 times greater
for the privately educated.[11] Another study with this same 1970
cohort, carried out for the Social Mobility Commission, shows that
the effectiveness of British private schooling holds, regardless of
children's prior abilities. In other words, even children who began
school with rather low cognitive skills attainment at the age of five
were substantially advantaged by a private schooling.[12]

There is also the marriage dividend. Social scientists around the
world have a term – 'educational homogamy' – for the practice of
marrying someone with the same level of schooling. In Britain's
case, educational homogamy is reflected also in a 'school-type
homogamy'. Because marriages more often arise among those with
shared values and social networks, going to a private school makes
it much more probable such people will marry someone who is
privately educated, university educated or both. Such a spouse is
also likely to be economically successful, often in a high-status
occupation. According to one estimate drawn from a representative
sample of UK families, husbands of privately educated women
earn 15 per cent more than the husbands of otherwise similar
state-educated women. The marriage dividend thus adds to the
economic benefits of attending a private school, and contributes
further to inequality between families.[13]

How do they do it?

Given the apparently irrefutable link between private schools and
life's gilded path, the obvious question arises: *how* do they do it?
In our view, the only realistic starting point for an analysis lies
with the assertion that, in the modern era, most of these schools
are of high quality, offering a good educational environment.
They deploy very substantial resources; respect the need for a
disciplined environment for learning; and give copious attention
to generating a positive and therefore motivating experience. This

argument – the resources point aside – is not an altogether easy one for the left to accept, against a background of it having historically been undecided whether (in the words of one Labour education minister's senior civil servant in the 1960s) 'these schools are so bloody they ought to be abolished, or so marvellous they ought to be made available to everyone'.[14] We do not necessarily accept that *all* private schools are 'marvellous'; but by and large we recognise that, in their own terms of fulfilling what their customers demand, they deliver the goods.

Above all, private schools succeed when it comes to preparing their pupils for public exams – the gateways to universities. In 2017 the proportion of private school students achieving A*s and As at A level was 48 per cent, compared to a national average of 26 per cent; while for GCSEs, in terms of achieving an A or 7 or above, the respective figures were 63 per cent and 20 per cent.[15] At both stages, GCSE and A level, the gap is invariably huge – last August, this August, next August.

There are, of course, some very real contextual factors to these bald and striking figures. It is undoubtedly true that the bulk of the private school intake is from well-off families with substantial cultural capital and a high degree of parental support and motivation. Accordingly, the great majority are likely to be well behaved in the classroom and aspirational, thereby creating a mutually encouraging and competitive atmosphere. It is also true that many private schools – particularly the best-known – are highly selective academically in determining their intake, with an ability to pay the fees often being only the first hurdle to jump. One estimate is that in London and the South-east the top private schools are so oversubscribed that applicants have only a one-in-eight chance of getting in.[16] Nevertheless, a significant proportion of non-selective private schools – as many as one in two – remains available to those with deep enough pockets. What all this means is that, in order to find out whether the private schools *themselves* make any difference to the children's academic progress, we need to drill down further. Any study must take account of where the children are coming from, both in terms of their family and their academic ability.

At the primary level, evidence comes from tests of verbal skills and numeracy, if only because children do not take public exams. For the generation who went to school in the 1970s, the children who were at prep school skipped five percentage points up the maths ranks and seven points up the reading ranks, compared with similar children at primary schools. For the later generation at school in the 2000s, the children at prep school again made better academic progress than their state-educated counterparts, though not spectacularly so, shifting a few percentage points up the reading score ranks.[17] At the lower secondary level, leading up to GCSEs, a 2016 Durham University study commissioned by the Independent Schools Council (ISC) reports an average gain in each GCSE subject of nearly two-thirds of a grade; however, that study does not have the best controls for the children's family background, so perhaps the gain is somewhat exaggerated.[18] A 2018 study using excellent controls finds rather smaller, though still positive, effects on a composite of students' maths, science and English grades at GCSE, once the students' characteristics, backgrounds and prior achievements up to the age of eleven are accounted for.[19] Then, at the sixth-form level, a 2014/15 study of the 'value added' between GCSEs and A levels reveals private school pupils continuing to outperform those in the state sector; on average, private school pupils' value-added is elevated by 0.12 of a grade, meaning that for every 100 A levels taken in a private sixth form, twelve are lifted by one grade – e.g. from B to A.[20] More evidence from a different 2018 study also shows that private sixth-form schooling moves pupils significantly up the A-level rankings.[21] Taken together, the picture presented by these studies is one of relatively small but still significant effects at every stage of education; and over the course of a school career, the *cumulative* effects build up to a notable gain in academic achievements.

Yet academic learning and exam results are not all there is to a quality education, and indeed there is more on offer from private schools. At Harrow, for example, its vision is that the school 'prepares boys ... for a life of learning, leadership, service and personal fulfilment'. It offers 'a wide range of high level extra-curricular activities, through which boys discover latent talent, develop individual character and gain skills in leadership and teamwork'. At Eton, meanwhile, 'fostering self-confidence, enthusiasm, perseverance, tolerance and integrity' are among the educational aims on offer. Lesser-known schools trumpet something similar. Cumbria's Austin Friars, for example, highlights a well-rounded education, proclaiming that its alumni will be 'creative problem-solvers ... effective communicators ... and confident, modest and articulate members of society who embody the Augustinian Values of Unity, Truth and Love ...' While these sorts of visions are by no means absent from state schools, the difference lies in the amount of resources and school time that are devoted to pursuing these broader objectives. With their additional facilities and staff, extra-curricular activities are far more extensive in the private sector. Many private schools like to emphasise how they can inculcate both teamwork and leadership skills, in part through extensive cultural education and sport, but also through military training activities (the Combined Cadet Force).

Such activities, contributing to the education of the 'whole child', are not only valuable in themselves, but reinforce what happens in the classroom. They build qualities which aid educational progress. An internal 'locus of control' (psychology's term for how far people sense they are in control of what happens around them), which is found in greater measure in private school children, is known to stimulate hard work, persistence, better academic performance and good educational choices. While private school children tend at the start to have a greater internal locus of control, stemming from their more affluent background, the schools themselves add to it, especially the prep schools. Similarly, private schools raise the bar for pupils' aspirations for what they might achieve in later life.[22]

If on the whole Britain's private schools provide a quality education in both academic and broader terms, we must now pose a further question – *how* do they deliver that? In Chapter 4 we give a fuller, more detailed picture of the reality of private schools in the twenty-first century, but four areas stand out.

First, especially small class sizes are a major boon for pupils and teachers alike. Second, the range of extra-curricular activities and the intensive cultivation of 'character' and 'confidence' are important. Third, the high – and therefore exclusive – price tag sustains a peer group of children mainly drawn from supportive and affluent families. And fourth, to achieve the best possible exam results and the highest rate of admission to the top universities, 'working the system' comes into play. Far greater resources for diagnosing special needs, challenging exam results and guiding university applications mean that, in these and other ways, the private schools can provide a level of expert services that the majority of their parental customers understandably see as part and parcel of what they are paying for.[23] Taking all four areas as a whole, the package on offer to those who can afford it amounts to a formidable armoury of competitive advantage on an uneven playing field. Underpinning all these areas of advantage are the high revenues from fees: Britain's private schools can deploy resources whose order of magnitude for each child is approximately three times what is available at the average state school.[24]

The relevant figures for university admissions are thus almost entirely predictable. Perhaps inevitably, by far the highest-profile stats concern Oxbridge, where between 2010 and 2015 an average of 43 per cent of offers from Oxford and 37 per cent from Cambridge were made to privately educated students, and there has been no sign since of any significant opening up; in a typical year during this decade, not only have some 1,600 state schools not had *any* sixth-formers going to Oxbridge, but more pupils from Westminster School have gone to Oxbridge than have pupils qualifying for free school meals from *everywhere* in Britain.[25] Yet for all the understandable media focus on Oxbridge, the equally important but often under-reported fact is that the path to the elite Russell Group of universities – Britain's most prestigious two dozen, out of some 130 universities and university colleges – is also a gilded one. By 2018 the ISC's own figures revealed that of the 94 per cent of privately educated pupils who went on to university, only 6 per cent went to Oxbridge – whereas 54 per cent went to

Russell Group universities, with, for example, Bristol, Durham, Exeter, Leeds, Nottingham, UCL and Newcastle all taking more privately educated pupils than Oxford and Cambridge.[26] Overall, government figures in 2015 showed pupils from fee-paying schools to be five times as likely as pupils from state schools to go to Oxbridge; and twice as likely to attend a Russell Group university.[27] Top schools, top universities: the pattern of privilege, in short, is systemic, and not just confined to the dreaming spires.

Going to a top university, it hardly needs adding, signals a material difference, especially in Britain where universities are quite severely ranked in a hierarchy. A stark light was shone by a report in 2014 on the future life chances (and influence) of Oxbridge students: three in four senior judges had been there, almost three-fifths of the Cabinet and of permanent secretaries, a half of all diplomats, nearly a half of our newspaper columnists, one-third of the shadow Cabinet, and virtually one-quarter of MPs.[28] Subsequently, a 2016 study of young adults' incomes confirmed the significant advantages associated with going to a top, as opposed to a lower-ranked, university, especially for those doing maths and computer sciences, engineering, technology and law subjects.[29] And the *Who's Who* study of 2017 confirmed that Oxbridge graduates continued to comprise 30–40 per cent of new entrants to that guide to top people.

Of course, it is while *at* university that the privately educated and the state-educated at last find themselves on an even playing field (apart from quality of parentally provided laptops and quality of parentally provided accommodation, not to mention the frequent need for students from less affluent backgrounds to find paid work even during term time). At which point, on that approximately level turf, it is the state-educated who outperform the privately educated. 'State school students tend to do better in their degree studies than students from independent schools with the same prior educational attainment', concluded a 2014 report from the Higher Education Funding Council. 'For example, a male student who gained BBB at A-level from a state school has the same probability of gaining an upper second or higher as a similar student who gained ABB ... from an independent school.'[30] Striking though this revelation is, not least its implication of the top universities missing out on some of the most talented people, on reflection it is hardly surprising. After all, such are the resources being thrown at private school pupils when they are still at school that inevitably there is a significant proportion who over-achieve and are subsequently in effect 'over-promoted' beyond their intrinsic capabilities. Yet, as in all walks of life, relatively few of the over-promoted (and their families) would wish it otherwise.

There is one final aspect to the private school dividend. Counter-intuitive though it may sound – at least to anyone who does not know Britain – a privately educated man (but not woman) leaving university with exactly the same degree as a state-educated man will later enjoy a pay gap of some 7 to 15 per cent (studies vary in their exact findings) in his favour. No single explanation accounts for this premium. Such factors as aspirations, self-confidence and leadership – or, in a phrase, 'polish and push' – seem plausible, but so far the empirical evidence has not found this to be a major factor.[31] Social networks (often deliberately cultivated by the schools themselves, including systematic use of 'old boys') almost certainly play a part in accessing well-paid jobs, notwithstanding modern employers' more meritocratic recruitment procedures. How much of a part is hard to tell, but it is perhaps suggestive that the chances of an 'old boy' of one of the elite Clarendon Schools entering the elite of *Who's Who*, even in the modern age, are more than twice as high if he also belongs to a top London private members' club; while the tendency of privately educated males to gravitate towards the financial services industry (especially in the highly remunerative City of London) also contributes.

Nevertheless, when all is said and done, the main reason for the material successes of modern-day privately educated women and men, despite suffering at university a modest setback compared to their state-educated peers, is that they have *already* achieved so much at school – in both an academic and extra-curricular sense – that usually they arrive at the workplace much more highly qualified than their state-educated peers. The figures on the

FIGURE 3 Proportions of twenty-five-year-olds with degrees in 2015 in England, according to type of school attended

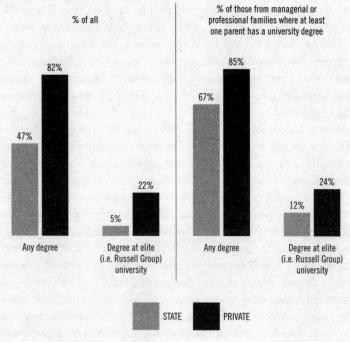

Source: Authors' analysis of data from *Next Steps*, University College London. UCL Institute of Education. Centre for Longitudinal Studies, *Next Steps: Sweeps 1–8, 2004–2016* [computer file]. 13th Edition. Colchester, Essex: UK Data Archive [distributor], June 2017. SN: 5545, http://dx.doi.org/10.5255/UKDA-SN-5545-5.

academic side are salutary (see Figure 3): for those aged twenty-five in 2015, at or near the start of their working lives, the privately educated are much more likely to be educated to degree level; specifically, they are more than four times as likely to have been at an elite university. Even if we restrict the comparison to those from professional or managerial backgrounds, the privately educated are still twice as likely to start their working lives on the back of an elite university degree. Private schools, to repeat, are for the most part good schools, often very good indeed; and theirs is a gift that to the fortunate recipients keeps on giving.

The Problem Explored

Ultimately, does any of this matter? Why can one not simply accept that these are high-quality schools that provide our future leaders with a high-quality education? Given the thorniness – and often invidiousness – of the issue, it is a tempting proposition. Yet for a mixture of reasons – political and economic, as well as social – we believe that the issue represents in contemporary Britain an unignorable problem that urgently needs to be addressed and, if possible, resolved. The words of Alan Bennett reverberate still. 'Private education is not fair,' he famously declared in June 2014 during a sermon at King's College Chapel, Cambridge. 'Those who provide it know it. Those who pay for it know it. Those who have to sacrifice in order to purchase it know it. And those who receive it know it, or should. And if their education ends without it dawning on them, then that education has been wasted.'[32]

The rest of this chapter explores further the malign and pervasive consequences of our educational apartheid. A starting point is the economic aspect, specifically the hugely distorted use of our national resources, both material and human. Consider these three fundamental facts: one in every sixteen pupils goes to a private school; one in every seven teachers works at a private school; one pound in every six of all school expenditures in England is for the benefit of private school pupils.[33]

The crucial point to make here is that although extra resources for each school (whether private or state) are always valuable, that value is at a diminishing rate the wealthier the school is. Each extra teacher or assistant helps, but if you already have two assistants in a class, a third one adds less value than the second one. Given the very unequal distribution of academic resources entailed by the British private school system, it is unarguable that a more egalitarian distribution of the same resources would enhance the total educational achievement. There is, moreover, the sheer *extravagance* – looked at from a strictly educational point of view – on the part of the private sector. Multiple theatres, large swimming pools and beautiful surroundings with expensive upkeep are, of course, nice to have and look suitably seductive on sales brochures. But how much they add to the educational experience, as distinct from a luxury experience, is at best a moot point (quite apart from the fact that, although a private school with five football pitches might benefit from an extra one, it would be nothing like as much as for an equal-sized state school that has only one). Richer schools spend notably more on non-teaching staff. Looked at from a larger standpoint – Britain's *overall* educational needs – it would be a more effective use of what we spend, as well as equitable, if more of those substantial, non-academic resources (in addition to some of the academic ones) were directed to where they could do the most good.

Further inefficiency arises from education's partially 'positional' character. The private sector's extra resources do help, as we have stressed, to deliver for their children a good-quality education which broadly elevates their capacities in intellectual, artistic and sporting domains. Yet the resources also lift up children in areas where their rank position on the ladder of success matters, such as access to scarce places at top universities. To the extent this happens, the privately educated child benefits but the state-educated child loses out. This lethal combination of private benefit and public waste is nowhere more apparent than in the time and effort that private schools devote to working the system, to ease access to those scarce places. Such investments have a private value, but no social value whatsoever.

Another area where resources could be better deployed more evenly relates to private school pupils themselves and their parents. 'Fee-charging schools,' observes Peter Wilby (veteran education commentator and co-founder of the *Journal of Education Policy*), 'deprive the mass of children of talented and advantaged peers who would raise standards across the board ... Too many schools, deprived of even a few such children, struggle with multiple disadvantages.'[34] As for private school parents, the point has been often and legitimately made about how the state system has suffered from a scarcity of these affluent and engaged advocates for school improvement. Although parental pressure can be a burden for teachers, well-directed parental support, which tends to be stronger in private schools, can be highly beneficial. Tellingly, private school parents are three times more likely than state school parents to lend a hand with fund-raising and join the Parent Teacher Association.[35] Nor is that all. Writing about 'the workings of social capital' in a school context, the novelist and commentator Tim Lott notes how this 'means having parents who are educated, interested in education, connected within the professions and happy to use those connections – what you might call cultural nepotism'.[36] Overwhelmingly, such parents are disproportionately to be found in the private rather than state system.

What about the implications for our polity? The Social Mobility Commission's 2014 report on British public life lamented 'the degree of domination', noting that 'few people believe that the sum total of talent in Britain resides in just 7 per cent of pupils in our country's schools'. To which we would add that the way the privately educated have sustained semi-monopolistic positions of prominence and influence in the modern era has created a serious democratic deficit.[37] Whereas once, long ago in Victorian times, it was perhaps just about possible to believe in the privately educated as being like Plato's virtuous 'guardians' of society, offering not only superior knowledge but also dedication and incorruptibility, now such lofty moral claims seem in our money-driven society almost risible. The unavoidable truth is that by and large the increasingly privileged and entitled products of an elite private education have – almost inevitably – only a limited and partial understanding of, and empathy with, the realities of everyday life as lived by most people. One of those realities is, of course, state education. Even allowing for complete selflessness and public-spiritedness on the part of our privately educated rulers (often educating their own children at private schools), how can they possibly know what such an education, so very different from their own, is truly like? It marked some kind of apotheosis when in July 2014 the appointment of Nicky Morgan (Surbiton High) as education secretary meant that every minister in her department at that time was privately educated.

Above all, there is the severe democratic impoverishment involved. At the heart of a healthy democracy is the notion of an active, participatory citizenry exercising influence on their own lives and the communities they inhabit. If in practice most of the key decisions – whether political or economic or social – are being taken by a privately educated minority drawn from the most affluent sections of society, who may or may not have got to that position on genuine merit, then the inescapable conclusion is that we have a deeply flawed and unrepresentative democracy.

We also, compounding the problem, have a much more unequal society than half a century ago, especially at the top. A family at the 90th rung of the income spectrum – i.e. richer than 90 per cent of the population, less rich than 10 per cent – enjoys roughly twice the income of a family on the middle rung (the median); back in the mid-1970s, when private schools were still at a relatively low ebb, this advantage was only 1.7.[38] At the very top the riches of the richest 1 per cent, which accelerated from the mid-1990s onwards, have become bewildering if ever we get to glimpse them. In the late 1970s, the richest 1 per cent enjoyed a 6 per cent share of our national income; by the time of the great crash in 2008/9 this share had risen to 15 per cent.[39] Accordingly, for those on middle or upper incomes, being socially mobile has become especially salient: an inability to climb up the ladder has become more of a deprivation, in monetary terms, for those held on the middle and lower rungs – just as, at the same time, protection against slipping down the ladder has become all the more important to those who start higher up.

So where, looking at the sweep of modern British history, are we now in the social mobility saga? The popular wisdom is that the golden age was the 1950s and 1960s, those immediate post-war decades. Expanding middle-class job opportunities, John Braine's *Room at the Top* (film as well as novel), the last great hurrah of the grammar schools before the comprehensives took over, the expansion of higher education, the youth and pop revolutions, the Conservatives abruptly ending their run of Old Etonian leaders – it is not difficult, nor was it difficult then, to construct a plausible picture. Yet in truth it is and was a seriously exaggerated one. The veteran sociologist John Goldthorpe has conclusively shown that, when it came to the crucial yardstick of *relative* social mobility (i.e. the relative life chances of children from less advantaged backgrounds compared to those from more advantaged), there was little if any intergenerational progress during that period; while as for the 1970s onwards, relative social mobility has either declined or simply stalled at a lowish level (by international comparisons), showing in recent years no real signs of improvement.[40] And there is little dispute that the significance of poor social mobility has been heightened by the increasingly unequal society that we live in.

Not that the problem has gone unnoticed. There has been an abundance of apparently sincere, well-meaning rhetoric, not least from some of the leading politicians of the past decade. In 2012 Nick Clegg proclaims his determination 'to fight for a society where the fortunes of birth and background weigh less heavily on prospects and opportunities for the future'.[41] Three years later it is David Cameron's turn: 'Britain has the lowest social mobility in the developed world. Here, the salary you earn is more linked to what your father got paid than in any other major country. We cannot accept that.'[42] In 2016 Jeremy Corbyn declares his movement will 'ensure every young person has the opportunities to maximise their talents' and will 'tackle the grotesque inequality that holds people back', while Theresa May follows on: 'I want Britain to be a place where advantage is based on merit not privilege; where it's your talent and hard work that matter, not where you were born, who your parents are or what your accent sounds like.'[43] Rather like corporate social responsibility in the business world, social mobility has become one of those motherhood-and-apple-pie causes which it is almost rude not to sign up to and utter warm words about.

Yet the mismatch between such sentiments and policy-makers' practical intentions is palpable. The Social Mobility Commission, with cross-party representation, reported regularly on what government should do, but in December 2017 all sitting members resigned in frustration at the lack of policy action in response to their recommendations. The effectiveness and exclusivity of Britain's private schools rarely intrude on the social mobility policy agenda, except occasionally in a relatively minor way, such as the promotion of private–state 'partnerships'. Even reports that are explicitly set up to look at inequality in education somehow manage to avoid talking about the issue. Moreover, the focus – whether from politicians, the Social Mobility Commission or policy-shapers more generally – is almost entirely on stimulating *upward* social mobility. But the awkward truth is that for social mobility to work anything like properly, it has to be a two-way street. 'The only way you can have more upward mobility in a relative perspective,'[44] Goldthorpe bluntly informed an interviewer in 2013, 'is if you have more downward mobility at the same time.' In relation to the problem of Britain's private schools – those unrivalled alpha-achievers and beta-blockers of our time – the implications of this *two*-way social mobility are, if social mobility is really to mean anything beyond pious platitudes, profound.

The underlying reality of our private school problem is stark. Through a highly resourced combination of social exclusiveness and academic excellence, the private school system has in our lifetimes powered an enduring *cycle of privilege*. Let us explain what we mean.

The first part of the cycle is the way in which a family's high income and wealth enable their children to attend a high-cost private school. The extreme exclusiveness is evident in our diagram at the beginning of this chapter; despite efforts to enhance bursaries and other access programmes, no one can seriously doubt that private schools are largely for the rich. Then, in the second part of the cycle, the advantages of the high-quality private schooling show up in the enhanced performance in public examinations by children of all abilities, disproportionate access to top universities and eventually to high-earning and influential jobs. Upward mobility for those at state schools, while not prevented, is thus inhibited. As for downward social mobility and the overall lack of it, certainly near the top of the ladder, the undergraduate evidence of the 'over-promoted' privately educated being outperformed – but nevertheless getting their degrees, and thus attractive career prospects, from the prestigious universities that overwhelmingly they attend – is eloquent testimony to how private schools often operate: in effect as crucial, well-paid safety nets for their somewhat less able pupils, not to mention a significant proportion of their outright nice-but-dims.

Taking the cycle as a whole, the overall consequence is that the income and status differences of one generation are very likely to be copied into the next. In short, the obstacle that the private schools present to British social mobility – inhibiting the many from going up, ensuring that the few do not descend – is formidable, systemic and wilfully ignored by our leaders.

In the jargon of sociologists, this cycle of privilege is the 'reproduction of social class'; and it is hard to imagine a notable improvement in our social mobility while private schooling continues to play such an important role. Allowing, as Britain still does, an unfettered expenditure on high-quality education for only a small minority of the population condemns our society in seeming perpetuity to a damaging degree of social segregation and inequality. This hands-off approach to private schools has come to matter ever more, given over the past half-century the vastly increased importance in our society of educational credentials. Perhaps once it might have been conceivable to argue that private education was a symptom rather than a cause of how privilege in Britain was transferred from one generation to the next, but that day is long gone: the centrality of schooling in both social and economic life – and the Noah's flood of resources channelled into private schools for the few – are seemingly permanent features of the modern era. The reproduction of privilege is now tied in inextricably with the way we organise our formal education.

Ineluctably, as we look ahead, the question of fairness returns. If private schooling in Britain remains fundamentally unreconstructed, it will remain predominantly intended and destined for the advantage of the already privileged children who attend. It is they who every day, by paid-for right, enjoy a range of facilities which would astonish visitors from any normal neighbourhood. It is they who get to grow up in an inspirational environment, alongside a concentration of other children from similarly well-off families. It is they who later in life gain for themselves an outsize share of the high-status, high-paid and influential jobs. Other social injustices surrounding the culture or organisation of education are visible around the world, often across gender or ethnic divides. But in Britain the starkest school segregation and the greatest social injustice lie in the enormous material separation between the two sectors – and the way that this locks in privilege across the generations.

The Choice in an Age of Choice

In the end, for all the practical complexities of the issue, it is a simple enough choice. Do we prioritise the right of those who can afford to educate their children privately to do so? Or do we find a way to harness the good qualities of these schools for the benefit of the many, prioritising the right of every child, including the poorest, to as even a start in life as possible? In effect, it is that eternal tension that the philosopher Isaiah Berlin identified with his famous two concepts of liberty: the tension between on the one hand the negative liberty of not being interfered with or constrained, on the other hand the positive liberty of being a full citizen enjoying the same potentialities as all one's fellow citizens. Negative liberty for the very few? Or positive liberty for the vast majority? Ultimately, it is a value judgement about what sort of society we want for ourselves – and for our children.

2

Roads Not Taken

The politics of education have always been complicated and often highly personal. Policies have been determined at least as much by matters of background and temperament as by more objective criteria. In 1978, examining Britain's 'uniquely serious gap' between the state sector and 'the feelings of politicians and social leaders towards it', the educationalist Maurice Kogan had this highly suggestive passage:

> Look at the choices they themselves have made. Four Prime Ministers in the twentieth century, Lloyd George, MacDonald, Wilson and Callaghan [plus Thatcher and Major later in the century], did not go to a public school. But their own children or grandchildren have repaired that omission of social good sense. The British have taken a divided, some would say divisive, education system for granted. Nor has the political intelligentsia done any differently even when associated with fashionable radical views. Many of the Labour intellectuals who have supported Labour at the national level have children in private schools. Until quite recently this was not a source of embarrassment or even comment.[1]

This chapter – a historical look at the politics of the private school question and how we got to where we are now – is largely a story of missed opportunities for reform, broken up by lengthy periods of relative silence or inaction; and for all the formidable power of more impersonal factors at work, it is a story that only really makes sense if the human factor is also taken into account.

Before 1939: No Violent or Precipitate Legislation

The first of three decades of major might-have-beens, of potential turning points that failed to turn, occurred as long ago as the 1860s (the other decades being the 1940s and 1960s). It featured two commissions of inquiry – the Clarendon Commission of 1861–4, the Taunton Commission of 1864–8 – that, in tandem with the legislative aftermath of their respective reports, effectively sealed the elevated place of fee-paying schools in the British social as well as educational order. What exactly did Clarendon and Taunton do? Just as importantly, what did they fail to do? And why?

Appointed by Parliament to investigate increasingly publicised financial abuses (including misappropriation of endowments) at Eton and elsewhere, and also charges of unruly and even violent behaviour, Lord Clarendon and his men focused on the nine already socially prestigious and long-established 'public schools', from Eton downwards, that in time would be known as the 'Clarendon Schools'. What they recommended, as duly embodied in the Public Schools Act of 1868, was essentially twofold: firstly, improving significantly the internal governance of the schools, thereby simultaneously making it harder for headmasters to succumb to the temptations of avarice, but easier for them to impose discipline on the pupils; and secondly, changing ancient endowments so that scholarships would not go to local boys but instead be awarded on the basis of competitive exams theoretically open to all from anywhere in the country – while at the same time confirming that the bulk of the schools' financial resources would come from fee-paying parents.[2] As for the much wider inquiry headed by Lord Taunton, eventually leading to the Endowed Schools Act of 1869, it broadly produced the same outcomes, at least as far as it concerned the two or three dozen endowed schools which were more recent foundations than the Clarendon nine but had become, or had the potential to become, 'public schools'. Crucially, by the end of the decade a firm hierarchy was now in place:

> The division within secondary education, which the Clarendon Commission established between the nine investigated schools and the rest [notes the historian Colin Shrosbree], was followed by further divisions within secondary education ... The division that came from the Taunton Commission was between those schools which charged high fees, provided a largely classical education for university entrance, catered for the upper middle classes and were, in consequence, successful, and those which did not do these things and were not successful. The successful schools all aspired to the status conferred on the original nine by the Clarendon Commission and, in time, joined with them in the Headmasters' Conference.[3]

The Headmasters' Conference (HMC) began in 1869 as the umbrella organisation representing what was sometimes called 'the public school movement'. It was a movement that involved an increasingly close alliance between the once opposed upper and middle classes; and by the time of Queen Victoria's death in 1901 it would include over a hundred public schools, most of them boarding and virtually all of them socially exclusive.[4] 'So the elders met, and so the tribes were unified into a nation,' reflects Jonathan Gathorne-Hardy in his history, *The Public School Phenomenon*. 'It was also somewhere for a new school to aim at and provided standards by which that aim could be realised. It became the tuning fork to test "tone". And the Conference was a great help in fighting the outside world ...'[5]

How might the dispensation coming out of the 1860s have been different? Three possibilities were not wholly unrealistic.

The first was of scholarships being awarded on a means-tested rather than mainly academic basis, so that the awards were not just made (as proved to be almost entirely the case) to those who had been to expensive private tutors and/or preparatory schools. A second possibility would have been a mechanism imposing on the schools much greater public accountability, whereas in practice for very many years there would be almost none. But it was the third possibility, involving the implication of the Taunton Commission's detailed research into some 800 endowed schools of one sort and another, that was the most radical and tantalising. Gathorne-Hardy (writing in 1977) again:

> Though often individually quite small, in sum the total of endowment money was colossal. If all these endowments were put together and redistributed on a national scale, they could form the financial core of a great new national system of secondary education. The [Taunton] Commission drew up detailed plans for this: the control to be central via Parliament, a national exam system, regular inspection, a modern curriculum including science. But more than this, the system was to be for everyone: those too poor to pay would be educated free, those who could afford to pay would do so, augmenting the merged endowments. For a moment the heart leaps. Supposing this had been done, just supposing those bastions of class and privilege, the new public schools, had been swept ruthlessly away into a national and classless system, and that proper secondary education for everyone had started to come thirty years before (much less sweepingly) it did [through the 1902 Education Act] – how different our country might have been ...[6]

The process by which this inspiriting plan was 'castrated' (Gathorne-Hardy's word) has yet to be fully explored by historians, but castrated it was. What is clear, moreover, is that the forces behind a high degree of continuing social exclusiveness were formidable. Take a trio of heartfelt contributions to the House of Lords debate in 1865 about the Clarendon report. Lord Houghton, opposing competitive exams for entrance by 'the sons of persons in narrow circumstances', declared himself 'anxious to see these schools [the

Clarendon nine] made available to the largest portion of the upper classes of this country'; Lord Lyttelton was equally adamant that – given the 'ample provision' for the education of 'the lower classes' (a truly ludicrous assertion) – 'these great schools ought to be reserved for the upper classes, for whose benefit they now existed'; while as for the marginally more egalitarian Archbishop of Canterbury, his main concern was that the foundation places at Harrow be kept for 'persons of moderate means among the upper classes'.[7] Among the politicians, William Gladstone would preside over the great Liberal reforming ministry of 1868–74; but when it came to the public schools, such was his deep and abiding loyalty to his old school, Eton, that he had no wish to see access to it and the others placed on a more authentic equal-opportunity basis. Gladstone also seems to have genuinely believed in their traditional class function, arguing that they should be allowed to go on with their prime task of 'rearing the English gentleman, and fitting him for the discharge of those various duties which in this country have always been inseparable from his position in life'. Accordingly, concluded Gladstone in the Commons in 1865 with justifiable optimism, 'I feel confident that there will be no violent or precipitate legislation upon the subject'.[8]

In fact, during the nineteenth century as a whole, none of the mainstream parties had a recognisable policy as such about the public schools. Nor did that really change during the early decades of the twentieth (just the 113 Old Etonians in the House of Commons in 1911), despite the advent of the Labour Party.[9] 'The public schools,' notes Rodney Barker, the historian of Labour and education, 'were secure in their rural seclusion from the vulgar gaze of socialists and proletarians', as instead the party concentrated, at a local as well as national level, on seeking to spread secondary education to all children.[10] Indeed, class warfare was conspicuous by its absence. 'I have no objection to the public schools' level at all,' one working-class Labour MP told the Commons in 1922. 'I do not begrudge them education, far from it – I congratulate them upon the fact that they have got education, and I would be very glad to have it myself.'[11] Instead, the major critique came not from a politician but from the notable historian and adult educator R. H. Tawney. It was, he declared in his 1931 tract *Equality*, 'the social division between the schools of the well-to-do and the schools of the mass of the population' that was the most 'pernicious' aspect of English education, one that 'works havoc with its intellectual standards and spiritual values, and, by coarsening both, coarsens the intelligence and spirit of the nation as a whole'. Accordingly, 'the English educational system will never be, what it should be, the great uniter, instead of being, what it has been in the past, a source of disunion, until children of all classes of the community attend the same schools'. Indeed, argued Tawney, 'while it continues to be muddied by absurd social vanities, it will never even be efficient as an educational system', given that it was 'only when all parents are equally interested in its progress' that there would be 'a common effort to improve it'. Still, he was not without hope. 'The time will come when the scheme of English education, which hitherto has followed and heightened the lines drawn by social divisions, will be the symbol and cement of social unity, and the idea that differences of wealth should produce differences of educational opportunity will seem as grotesque and repulsive as that they should result in differences of personal security and legal status.'[12]

During the rest of the 1930s there were some signs on the left, though still from intellectuals rather than politicians, of an increasingly hostile mood. 'The class division created by the public school system arouses resentment and disunity,' claimed Charles Douie, a Rugby old boy, in the *Journal of Education* in the summer of 1939. 'I cannot believe that the England of tomorrow will tolerate privilege in education.'[13] Yet in practice some of that hostility was undercut by a growing assumption on the part of the left-leaning intelligentsia that the public school system itself was so inherently antediluvian, and destined for the rubbish heap of history, that it hardly needed to be systematically attacked. 'Doomed' was Graham Greene's succinct prophecy in 1934, and he went on: 'Whatever the political changes in this country during the next few years one thing surely is almost certain: the class distinctions will not remain unaltered and the public school, as it exists today, will disappear.'[14]

In fact, the greater pressures to change the relationship between the schools and society as a whole came from within the system. In 1919, with the sector facing a temporarily difficult financial situation in the immediate aftermath of the Great War, the heads of Charterhouse, Eton and Marlborough, led by Charterhouse's Frank Fletcher, offered to take a proportion of ex-elementary schoolboys in return for government financial support for the less well-off public schools. The offer came to nothing – with the minister concerned, the great liberal historian H. A. L. Fisher, politely insisting there was no demand from that lowly part of society for such places – but the initiative was nevertheless a straw in the wind.[15] Fletcher was a genuine visionary, as was Harrow's Cyril Norwood, who also found it hard to make any practical impact. 'Most thinking men and women,' declared Norwood in the *Spectator* in 1926 shortly after the General Strike, 'must feel that one of the chief dangers, if not the chief danger, for the future of our country arises from the segregation of its social classes, and in particular from the utter separation of the children of the well-to-do during the whole course of their education from all other children.'[16] Or as Fletcher would defiantly put it in his 1937 autobiography: 'I have no wish to see the characteristic features of our public schools disappear from our education ... But I emphatically do *not* regard social distinction or wealth as one of those essential characteristics.'[17]

Still, the obvious question arises: were such men as Fletcher and Norwood, with their strong social consciences and willingness to set out the bigger picture, the exceptions rather than the norm? Almost certainly they were, since for the most part the schools continued to all appearances their undisturbed, largely inward-looking way – or at least until something of a perfect storm (falling middle-class birth rate, higher taxation, increased competition from state schools) hit in the late 1930s and numbers dropped alarmingly.[18] What to do? It was at this point, owing little or nothing to idealism on the part of the schools themselves, that the Board of Education (most of whose senior officials had been to public school) stepped in and in effect began to open a path to the establishment of a commission that might enable, à la Fletcher's initiative, a socially broader intake as the politically acceptable price for a government bail-out of the endangered sector. That deal was still in embryonic shape when war broke out in September 1939; and war, everyone knew, was a potential game-changer.[19]

1939–51: The Public Schools Are Saved

For the first time, the public schools found themselves under intensive scrutiny and serious attack. 'We can hardly continue to contemplate an England where the mass of the people coming on by one educational path are to be governed for the most part by a minority advancing along a quite separate and more favoured path,' argued the prominent educationalist Fred Clarke early in 1940 in his seminal *Education and Social Change*. 'There is no honest defence, no democratic defence, indeed no genuine *aristocratic* defence for the continuance of their present position.'[20] The twenty-three-year-old Edward Heath apparently agreed. Demanding that the state-educated schoolboy be allowed to compete on a level playing field with the public school boy, the future Conservative leader declared in the *Spectator* in April 1940 that the solution was to 'establish equality of opportunity' by 'abolishing inequality of education'.[21] A few months later saw the publication of T. C. Worsley's *Barbarians and Philistines* – a high-impact insider's account premised on the assumption that 'the idea of a separate class-system of education reserved for the well-to-do' was 'incompatible with any true meaning of democracy' – so that by January 1941 it was unsurprising that Rugby's head, Hugh Lyon, publicly confessed that the schools 'thrive upon, and tend to perpetuate, a class system which is undemocratic and unjust'.[22] Then the following month came George Orwell. 'There are certain immediate steps that we could take towards a democratic educational system,' that Old Etonian announced in his celebrated *The Lion and the Unicorn*. 'We could start by abolishing the autonomy of the public schools and the older universities and flooding them with State-aided pupils chosen simply on grounds of ability.' And though worried that 'some of the older schools, which will be able to weather the financial storm longest, will survive in some form or another as festering centres of snobbery', he still looked ahead hopefully to how 'the war, unless we are defeated, will wipe out most of the existing class privileges' – and, indeed, to how 'the Eton and Harrow match will be forgotten'.[23]

It was an extraordinary moment. 'Though engaged in a death struggle with Hitler, England is literally seething with plans for the reform of the public schools, from which almost anything can result after the war,' reflected Edward Mack in April 1941 as he concluded his exhaustive two-volume study of public schools and how they had been viewed since the late eighteenth century. What lay ahead? No revolutionary himself, Mack could not but concede the serious possibility of 'the complete absorption of the public schools into the national system'.[24]

As would be the case throughout the war, Labour's response to all this was fairly feeble, nicely described by Rodney Barker as having 'the air of being taken unawares by the whole matter'. In many ways, as he explains, this was down to a particular mental furniture: 'The preoccupation with the tangible benefits and immediate potential of the public [i.e. state] system, an experience of education formed through contact with local affairs and constituency politics, a suspicion of the public schools as playgrounds of the rich, a feeling that the home was the proper place for the adolescent – all these combined to convince many Labour MPs that they wanted nothing to do with co-operation or integration.'[25] Indeed, when in 1940 the Commons debated the issue, the most radical voice belonged to a veteran Liberal MP. 'The public school is a symbol of the feeling that there is a class character in our education, and that a privileged few have opportunities which are denied to the masses,' declared Sir Percy Harris on behalf of his Bethnal Green electorate. 'I believe that it would be to the advantage of the old public school if it could be dovetailed into the general education system.' And he added, tellingly if perhaps optimistically, 'I believe that we are all more or less agreed upon that.'[26] It is possible that one of those who *did* agree with Harris was a distinguished Old Harrovian. Early in 1941, Winston Churchill was reported by the press as arguing in favour of public schools using their endowments to benefit poor scholars; a year later, he told a Labour politician that he 'wanted 60–70 per cent of the places to be filled by bursaries', adding that 'the great cities would be proud to search for able youths to send to Haileybury, to Harrow and to Eton'.[27] Certainly Churchill liked bold strokes; and back in November 1939, another Tory of flair, Robert Boothby, had identified him as the only politician possessing 'sufficient imagination' to do away with 'our "caste" system of education'.[28] By this time, however, the PM had much else on his mind, and ultimately it would be another, younger Conservative politician who played the decisive role.

This was the liberal, reform-minded R. A. ('Rab') Butler, President of the Board of Education from July 1941 and aptly described by his biographer Anthony Howard as 'never a worshipper at the public school shrine', indeed as 'quite enough of a rationalist to see the advantages of ending "the great divide" in British education'. But in the end, as Howard regretfully notes, 'his nerve failed him'. Why? Partly no doubt because he could not be sure of sufficient political support – on either side of the aisle – for fundamental change; partly also because he needed for his other educational purposes the support of the Church of England bishops, many of whom had intimate connections with the public schools; but perhaps most of all because he took as gospel the advice of Will Spens, his old mentor at Cambridge's Corpus Christi (where Butler had been a Fellow), that 'there was no easy solution' and that 'any solution on the lines of free entry' would 'upset and destroy the spirit and character of the public schools'.[29] Accordingly, well aware that the financially straitened schools had little alternative but to agree to the idea, he sought to square the circle by setting up in the summer of 1942 an official inquiry (under a Scottish judge of sound views, Lord Fleming) into 'means whereby the association between the public schools and the general educational system of the country could be developed and extended'. A vague enough aspiration, and old hands could already detect the smell of the long grass, but the excitable press reaction caught the larger, expectant mood of change in the air. 'Public and Secondary Schools to be merged'

declared the *Evening Standard*; 'Public Schools for All Plan' hailed
the *Daily Mirror*; and even the *Daily Telegraph* accepted that
'Boarding Schools may open for all after the War'.[30]

Butler's decision to appoint an inquiry into the public schools
meant that over the next two years they were marginalised – in
practice excluded – from the larger educational story, which was
the shaping of what became the momentous 1944 Education
Act, giving free secondary education to all, including at grammar
schools for those who passed the eleven-plus. During those two
years (July 1942 to July 1944), Butler only occasionally spoke of
the public school question. In June 1943 the Soviet ambassador
Ivan Maisky recorded him saying – sincerely or otherwise – that
'the education system should be democratized, i.e. almost all *public*
schools should be abolished (though Butler would like to keep two
or three of them)', with Maisky claiming that Butler 'undoubtedly
reflects the mood of the ruling Tory elite', though that may well
have been wishful thinking; soon afterwards, on the publication of
the Coalition government's White Paper on education as a whole
(excluding the public schools, apart from a generalised statement
about the wrongness of quality of education being determined by
the parental purse), Butler blandly told the press that 'plans are in
hand for associating the public schools with the National system',
but that 'the means of doing so must await the report of an inquiry
which Lord Fleming and his Committee are conducting and which
they are unlikely to conclude for some months'.[31] Some months
indeed: when in January 1944 the Commons had a two-day debate
on the Education Bill, the Marlborough-educated Labour MP John
Parker spoke with a rare focus and cogency on the missing issue:

> We do not feel that the Bill goes far enough. We take the
> view that we should have a National all-inclusive system of
> education and we very much regret the fact that the position
> of independent or so-called 'public' schools is left on one side
> for a report from the Fleming Committee. We believe that
> unless the position of these schools is dealt with in this Bill
> it will not be dealt with for many years to come. Whatever

the recommendations of the Fleming Committee on this point they will be controversial, and to bring in a separate Bill after this one to deal with that point will obviously not be practical politics …

This Bill will still keep a particular form of education available to a section of the people because of their ability to find the money to pay for it. That is what we object to, and so long as we have a position in which specially favoured schools are only available because parents can find the money to pay for their children's education we still have not got rid of this position of the two nations in this country.[32]

Parker's reference at the end was to Benjamin Disraeli's famous subtitle to his novel *Sybil* of a century earlier, with 'The Two Nations' being, of course, the rich and the poor. He might also have cited what Disraeli had observed towards the end of his life – that 'too late' were the saddest words in politics. And, indeed, with an unmistakable irony, the publication of the Fleming report in July 1944 would almost exactly coincide with the arrival of the Education Act. It was as if Butler had successfully stage-managed the whole thing. 'Though Labour members breathed a certain amount of ritual fire and fury about social exclusiveness and privilege, the appointment of the Fleming Committee had temporarily removed the fuse,' he recalled with satisfaction three decades later. 'Or, in a railway metaphor, the first-class carriage [i.e. the public schools] had been shunted on to an immense siding.'[33]

The central recommendation of the report itself – the product of a body that included five public school heads (including those of Charterhouse and Roedean), and from which the socialist intellectual G. D. H. Cole had had to retire early because of ill health – was ultimately tame: that a mixture of central and local government money should make it possible for public schools to open up to non-fee-payers as many as 25 per cent of their places, if the demand was there and if the schools themselves were willing to embrace this plan.[34] Press reaction was mixed. 'An unparalleled opportunity of cementing unity in a society which is as never before disposed for it' was how *The Times* portrayed Fleming's gift to the public schools, but *The Economist* took the line that the report had done nothing to address the fundamental two-nations issue: 'The distinction is not that one is better educated than the other, but that one has a higher social prestige than the other.'[35] From the left, the *New Statesman* was also largely sceptical: the inquiry had failed to break free from its narrow terms of reference and examine the first-order question of whether the public schools should continue; its recommendations were wholly on a voluntary basis; and Flemingism in practice 'may be either a method of making the schools concerned more democratic or a device for enabling them to steal the abler pupils from other schools and convert them into little gentlemen in the interests of the existing social order'.[36] With Labour more or less quiescent, the strongest political reaction came from the TUC, stating unequivocally that it had 'no wish merely to transfer [educational] privilege from one group in the community to another group: they wish to abolish it'.

Butler himself was unimpressed. 'They are of course too late,' he scribbled in September 1944 on a briefing note ahead of a meeting with the trade unionists. 'The Public Schools are saved & must now be made to do their bit. All this is whining.' Yet as for 'their bit', he observed at about the same time to a sympathetic correspondent that 'the big Public Schools are so full' – their numbers having recovered significantly from the nadir of 1940–41 – that 'most of them feel that they could not take 25 per cent for very many years to come'.[37] Perhaps he also sensed that the larger wartime moment had passed? 'I overhear very little discussion of the wider issues of the war,' Orwell told his American readers later that autumn. 'Everyone wants, above all things, a rest.'[38] And when in early 1945 a national poll asked about education, less than half of those questioned had heard about the recent Education Act, while only 13 per cent were aware of its promise to remove fees from grammar schools; the issue of public schools was not even deemed worthy of being asked about.[39]

In the event, predictably enough, 'Flemingism' – the report itself and its aftermath – amounted over the rest of the 1940s to not much more than the proverbial hill of beans. Whether on the part of the public schools themselves (as fee-paying demand further picked up after the war) or the Ministry of Education (resistant to state bursaries) or the local education authorities (unwilling to see their brightest pupils creamed off) or working-class parents (reluctant to have their children removed to such an alien environment), the lack of enthusiasm was almost total – resulting in only minimal implementation of the scheme.[40] As for the left specifically, it was reluctant to accept a quarter of an inadequate loaf at a time when, following Labour's unexpected landslide victory in the July 1945 general election, the tantalising possibility seemed to exist of something altogether more ambitious: in short, full-scale integration of the private and the state systems, or even abolition of the private.

Such hopes reckoned without the prime minister, Clement Attlee, and his two successive education ministers, Ellen Wilkinson (to February 1947) and George Tomlinson. 'Attlee's only interests outside politics were cricket and his public school, Haileybury,' accurately recalled Denis Healey. 'He favoured anyone who came from Haileybury, such as Chris Mayhew and Geoffrey de Freitas …'[41] In June 1946 the PM visited the old place to offer personal reassurance. 'He saw no reason for thinking that the public schools would disappear,' ran the report of his speech. 'He thought that great traditions would carry on, and they might even be extended.'[42] That same month, Wilkinson – no longer the feisty Jarrow heroine of the 1930s – candidly told her party that the right approach to the public school question was 'to make the schools provided by the state so good and so varied' that it would seem 'quite absurd' to send children to the public schools.[43] Her successor, the proudly working-class Tomlinson, within months was visiting Eton and subsequently announcing that he had been much impressed by what he had seen.[44] Three years later, speaking to a gathering of prep school heads, he earned the weekend's 'most rousing applause' through his comforting words about Labour policy: 'There is no suggestion that your schools, or, I might add, the independent public schools, should be compulsorily absorbed into the state system or anything of that kind ... And personally I do not see the sense of getting rid of something that is doing a useful job of work, or making everything conform to a common pattern. I am all for variety, especially in the field of education.'[45]

Did it matter? Were not the public schools doomed anyway in the post-war New Jerusalem by now taking shape? Orwell continued to think so, describing in August 1948 a book about Eton as 'an apology for a form of education that is hardly likely to last much longer'.[46] The assumption that '1945' – already a date of powerful mythology – had marked a fundamental turning point in the British story was, of course, understandable. Back in the late July of that year, just after the results of the election had come through, a blazered, straw-hatted fourteen-year-old public school boy, John Rae, called out 'My man' as he stood with his trunk at Bishop's Stortford station. 'No,' came the porter's quiet but firm reply, 'that sort of thing is all over now.'[47] Perhaps post-1945 the hauteur did soften; but the underlying realities of privilege were destined to remain the same – and Rae himself would become the leading public school head of his generation.

1951–70: We May Say A Lot, But We'll Never *Do* Anything

'We now have a Conservative government [Harold Macmillan's] in which Old Etonians are prominent,' noted Vivian Ogilvie in 1957 at the end of his history of the English public school. And he went on:

The climate of opinion is kindly disposed to traditional institutions, even if their antiquity goes no further back than the reign of Queen Victoria ... It is arguable that at the moment the class structure of England is accepted with more equanimity than for many a long day. Full employment and good wages, together with the forms of security provided by the Welfare State, seem to have removed the desire for equality ... The spectacle of wealth and privilege – even the expensive

tomfoolery of high society, as reported in the popular press –
does not excite the resentment it once did ... The only proviso
about wealth and privilege is that they should at least appear to
be attainable. A little tact on the part of those who possess them,
a very small demonstration of democratic good-fellowship –
a handshake for the foreman – will suffice to keep everyone
happy ...[48]

In fact, after a lengthy pause, issues of wealth and privilege were just
starting to return to the table, as the relative social placidity of the
'high' 1950s gave way to the rather different, more critical mood of
the late 1950s and early 1960s. *Look Back in Anger, Room at the Top,
Beyond the Fringe, That Was The Week That Was* – the direction of
travel of these almost instant cultural icons was all one way: away
from privilege and towards a greater opening up of society.

Britain's private education system could hardly have hoped to be
exempt from the emerging temper of the times. 'Effectively an open
sesame to Oxford and Cambridge' was how in 1958 the economist
John Vaizey (rapidly turning himself into an expert on the
economics of education) described the 'privilege' enjoyed by public
school boys; soon afterwards, opposing a gradualist approach to the
problem, he claimed that 'the entry of the establishment children
into the state system would be followed very shortly by a dramatic
improvement of the state schools'.[49] Or take a trio of further
interventions. In 1960 the future playwright Dennis Potter declared
that 'all proposals for reforming our public education are pointless
in the aim of breaking down privilege and class-consciousness if
nothing is to be done about the private schools, the great "public
schools" of England'; next year, economic journalist Michael
Shanks in his best-selling treatise on how *The Stagnant Society* was
responsible for Britain's economic ills devoted a chapter to 'The
Social Barrier' dividing the two sides of industry; and in 1962, in
his pioneering, equally best-selling *Anatomy of Britain*, journalist
Anthony Sampson laid out for general inspection the striking
extent to which the top reaches of British life were dominated by
the privately educated. But his powerful sociological analysis came

with a warning: 'The complicated grafting of public schools on to [Oxbridge] colleges, of prep schools on to public schools, has produced over the decades a tangled thicket of roots, branches and trunks which daunts all but the most ardent reformers.'[50]

Gradually the issue began to gain greater traction in the Labour Party than it ever had before. By 1958 the policy document on education, *Learning to Live*, yielded nothing in its ferocious denunciation – 'damages national efficiency and offends the sense of justice ... all who desire equality of opportunity and social justice will agree that the existence of this privileged sector of education is undesirable' – while insisting that the nub was the question of priorities. Accordingly, 'smaller classes, better-qualified teachers, better equipment and a higher proportion of sixth-formers in our own [state] schools will open the door of opportunity and steadily reduce the influence of the privileged fee-paying schools in public life'. That neatly sought to get the best of both worlds, and the document was adamant that 'no scheme for "taking over" or "democratising" the public schools shows sufficient merits to justify the large diversion of public money that would be involved'.[51] But in 1961 a new policy statement, *Signposts for the Sixties*, reflected a significant shift, advocating 'integration' of the two systems and declaring that 'the nation should now take the decision to end the social inequalities and educational anomalies arising from the existence of the highly influential and privileged private sector of education, outside the State system'. That position broadly held for the next three years, when Labour's election-winning manifesto included a commitment about 'integrating the public schools into the state system'.[52] The new prime minister from October 1964 was Harold Wilson, explicitly modernising and, completely unlike his five post-war predecessors, very much not a public school product. That autumn, one of the authors began at public school and was soon aware of the prevailing nervousness.

Almost certainly Labour would not have reached that policy position without the influential writings of one man. 'We shall not have equality of opportunity so long as we maintain a system of superior private schools, open to the wealthier classes, but out of reach of poorer children however talented and deserving,' Anthony Crosland asserted in 1956 in his highly influential *The Future of Socialism*. 'This is much the most flagrant inequality of opportunity, as it is cause of class inequality generally, in our educational system.' And he went on in a famous, much-quoted statement: 'I have never been able to understand why socialists have been so obsessed with the question of the grammar schools, and so indifferent to the much more glaring injustice of the independent schools.'[53] Six years later, in *The Conservative Enemy*, the rhetoric of this rapidly up-and-coming Labour politician was stronger still:

> The public schools offend not only against the 'weak', let alone the 'strong', ideal of equal opportunity; they offend even more against any ideal of social cohesion or democracy. This privileged stratum of education, the exclusive preserve of the wealthier classes, socially and physically segregated from the state educational system, is the greatest single cause of stratification and class-consciousness in Britain ... It is no accident that Britain, the only advanced country with a national private elite system of education, should also be the most class-ridden country ...
>
> We must then grasp the nettle of the public schools, bearing in mind our basic objectives. These are threefold: first, to assimilate them into the state sector, so that they play a full and co-operative part in the national educational effort; secondly, to democratize their entry and so destroy their present socially exclusive character; thirdly, to create a more genuine equality of opportunity by limiting the power of the rich to buy social privilege through buying a privileged education.

'You must,' declared Crosland in ringingly absolutist tones, 'either have a radical reform or none at all'.[54]

What might that mean in practice? Crosland became secretary of state for education in January 1965, and within a fortnight or so was reporting to his wife Susan that he had been accosted by Vaizey and others about what he was going to do. 'If truth be known,' he told her, 'I'm not frightfully interested in the public schools at this moment.' In her diary, she gave a threefold explanation for this seemingly perverse reaction: '1. He has an extravagant mode of speech, 2. his powers of concentration are extreme (and can be exclusive), 3. in fact he does think only teacher supply and the comprehensive issue deserve priority at this moment.'[55] It was probably soon afterwards that Crosland invited to dinner a cluster of private school heads. 'Now,' drawled the minister at the end as he leaned back in his chair, 'what *are* we going to do about these damned Public Schools? I suppose we must have a Royal Commission, something like that.'[56] So it was, as late in the year – and with unmistakable echoes of 1942 – Crosland announced there would be a Public Schools Commission (PSC).

Subsequently, he was challenged at least twice about this decision, the first time by a journalist at around the time of the announcement. 'One had thought one's writing was fairly clear,' responded Crosland with what his wife described as 'patent weariness':

A. Arguments against abolishing fee-paying schools. (1) A democracy cannot forbid people to found schools and charge for going to them. (2) In any case, outright abolition unenforceable: heads and teachers would devise a way to get round the law. (3) Further waste of resources: many teachers at, say, Eton and Winchester, would emigrate.

B. Since they exist, how does one utilise public schools? (1) Make their resources available to a wider public, perhaps 25 per cent of places available to fee-paying children, 75 per cent distributed in a manner to be advised upon by the Commission that I am setting up for that purpose. The Commission will take a couple of years to complete its findings, but that's OK as there's no money currently available at Education to reform the public schools. (2) The state sector must be strengthened so that it can match all but the very best fee-paying schools. Hence teacher supply is one of my priorities.[57]

A second challenge to Crosland came five years later. 'When you set up the Commission did you really think it was going to come up with anything? Or did you regard it as a political move?' asked Maurice Kogan in 1970, eliciting a reply which was a long way from Crosland's earlier uncompromising cry of 'radical reform or none at all':

It was a political move in the perfectly proper sense that we were committed to it by our manifesto. There was also a good deal of pressure from the Parliamentary Labour Party. But of course it was more than that. I was convinced that we had to discover once and for all whether any compromise solution was practicable. By a 'compromise' solution I mean one that avoids the two extremes, one extreme being to 'abolish' the schools, whatever that means, the other being in effect to do nothing – just let in a handful of state pupils and fiddle around a bit with the tax concessions. I was convinced that we did not know what on earth a compromise scheme might look like, because nobody had ever looked in detail at the number of schools, their precise type and size, whether they could fit into a comprehensive system, what different kinds of entry might be possible, and so on. We were not competent to do this work in the Department because there was too much other work going on. The sensible thing was to set up a Commission to do it.[58]

Given how little the Commission achieved, Crosland alive or dead would over the years often be accused of having sold the pass and opted for the Butler-style long grass. One of his biographers, Kevin Jefferys, notes in defence Crosland's own belief that the Cabinet was only 'lukewarm' about tackling the private school question.[59] That was probably accurate. 'I am not sure we need to do anything in a public sense just now,' Wilson observed to Crosland in May 1965 about the issue, while two months later Crosland himself chided the Cabinet for its lack of enthusiasm over the question and its willingness 'to sacrifice basic socialist principles'.[60] Yet as one of his advisers, the Oxford sociologist A. H. Halsey, would recall, there was something else – more fundamental – also at work:

> Tony's love of freedom was fetishist, driven, immoderate. Alcohol, cigars, women, even opera, were avidly consumed … He wanted to see himself as the proponent of libertarian socialism and me as a stern egalitarian. I didn't see it like that: I saw us both as both. But the English sin in education, I thought, was inequality while his great fear was that we might impose unfreedom on those who wanted to send their children to schools in the private sector.

'I never wanted the Public Schools Commission,' added Halsey. 'He thought a full enquiry was politically obligatory.'[61]

The Commission itself was charged with two key tasks:

> To collect and assess information about the public schools and about the need and existing provision for boarding education; forms of collaboration between the schools (in the first instance the boarding schools) and the maintained system.
>
>   To recommend a national plan for integrating the schools with the maintained sector of education.[62]

Its chairman – after five people had turned down the job, including the historian Alan Bullock – was Sir John Newsom, a veteran educationalist but with little particular interest in the private school question; while its other fifteen members were described by a future *Guardian* editor, Peter Preston, as on balance 'carefully but firmly weighted in favour of change'. Undeniably it was a distinguished line-up, drawn from a range of backgrounds; but as Nicholas Hillman notes in his authoritative account of the Commission, 'the diverse members did not gel'.[63] Its eventual report (July 1968) revealed that the nearest it came to a truly radical recommendation was when it carefully examined the possibility of local education authorities taking over and running all private, fee-paying schools – a solution that 'most of us' would not view 'as being in principle wholly wrong, either morally or educationally'. However, the report went on, that solution had been rejected for four reasons:

1. Public opinion may not be ready to support this course.
2. The immediate cost to the Exchequer would amount to £60 million a year; this is 'considerable' and might lead to the postponement of other desirable reforms.
3. Local authorities which gave evidence (with one exception) showed no disposition to take over independent schools.
4. There was no evidence that pupils with boarding needs could fill all the places that would become available.[64]

Accordingly, the report recommended instead a form of super-Flemingism: in this case, a group of private schools that over the next seven years would assign at least half their places to state pupils with boarding needs, their fees to be publicly subsidised. Altogether, this would amount to 47,000 assisted boarding places, to be organised along national rather than local authority lines and with the annual net cost estimated at some £12 million.[65] Three of the PSC's members (the former headmistress of a girls' public school, the headmaster of a boys' public school and the director-general of the CBI) entered a 'note of dissent', claiming that the proposed approach was 'too static' and that their colleagues were 'in danger of trying to achieve the best at the cost of the good'; while among the five others expressing reservations was John Vaizey, whose expertise gave him particular clout and who argued in the *Sunday Times* just before the report was published that he was now converted to what he called 'the traditional Labour course' – namely, 'to spend whatever money is available on improving the maintained schools, and the public schools problem will tend to wither away'.[66] After his death, another prominent left-to-right public intellectual, Hugh Thomas, would recall how Vaizey after his appointment to the Commission had visited Eton and been 'very much impressed', to the extent that 'he began to argue that it was a serious error even to think of abolition of the private sector of schooling'.[67]

If reaction had been mixed to the wartime Fleming report, that was certainly not the case in the closing days of July 1968. (Was it coincidence that both reports appeared at the onset of the close season of the political calendar?) 'They certainly produced a detailed scheme,' Crosland recalled about Newsom and his colleagues, 'but unfortunately no one much liked it!'[68] Or as the *Times Educational Supplement* legitimately asked at the time, 'Has any educational report ever been so unanimously damned or derided?'[69] At least it put the Headmasters' Conference (HMC) and National Union of Teachers (NUT) on the same side. 'We see no reason why the public schools should abandon the values which they have defended in the past, and of which they are not ashamed, in favour of something undefined by the Commission but supposed to represent the values of a "social mix",' declared the former; while the latter called the Commission's recommendation to spend millions of pounds on broadening the intake of the public schools 'disastrous' at a time when 'money is not available to remedy the conditions in sub-standard primary school buildings or to deal satisfactorily with the deprived areas', adding that 'it appears that to the privileged help is to be given whilst to the under-privileged help is ignored'.[70]

Among the right-of-centre press, which for the most part overegged the Commission's radicalism, the *Daily Telegraph* was typical enough, deeming the report 'a gramophone record of the Government's social prejudices' and going on: 'Its recurring theme is that these schools are middle-class institutions, and this is why they must go ... For those depraved enough to want to defend their middle-class standards, Newsom has a most sombre message.' From left of centre, the *Guardian* was also disapproving. 'Impractical, expensive, and harmful to children' was how it condemned the central recommendation, summarised as being 'to use mainly backward, deprived, or maladjusted children to cure the public schools of their social divisiveness'; and, more generally, it took the line that 'no Minister can bring himself to legislate to prevent people spending their own money as they wish – nor should he'. Over the next few days, the paper's letters page was full of the public school question, with opinion about evenly divided.

'The "freedom to spend one's own money" argument is patently disingenuous,' claimed Michael Grosvenor Myer of Cambridge in one of the more memorable contributions. 'There is plenty of legislation to prevent the spending of money for purposes regarded as anti-social: on bribing a juror, for instance; or on a thug to beat up one's rival; or on a pound of pot ...' Likewise, he concluded, 'the coldblooded purchasing of privilege for one's own children at the expense of everyone else's, in order to exploit the deplorable class snobbery which exists in our society, is every bit as anti-social

Guardian letters page, 25 July 1968.

as corruption, or gangsterism, or dope-pushing, and should be similarly legislated against'. But the most telling item in these *Guardian* pages was Abu's cartoon which showed an elderly, cross-looking man scribbling a letter – 'Sir, with reference to your leader on the public school system's divisive influence on our society ...' – and above him a calendar. The date was 25 July 2068.[71]

Back in July 1968, the Labour Cabinet had already discussed the report four days before the world at large saw it. 'None of us have a good word for it,' recorded Barbara Castle about a brief discussion (and not encouraged by Harold Wilson to be otherwise), 'so we decide that it should be published on 22 July without any government announcement or not at all. It is pretty clear that in the end we shall decide not to proceed with it.' By this time, Crosland's seat at Education was filled by Edward Short, who called the report 'somewhat unhelpful'; while in the eyes of Tony Benn, it was 'a terrible report ... a ghastly document'.[72] That autumn, the party conference saw Labour debating the issue, but again on a fairly cursory basis. One MP, Christopher Price (who had been Crosland's PPS at Education), argued robustly that the government should take action to bring the public schools 'to heel', including abolition of charitable status (as recommended by Newsom); but the decisive speech came from Alice Bacon, who, speaking on behalf of the party's executive committee and to applause ('loud' according to *The Times*, 'mild' according to the *Telegraph*), urged conference to reject the report, which it duly did.[73] Hillman in his account of the aftermath of the PSC's report describes her speech as 'disingenuous', in that 'she implied that the government might take more drastic action against the schools when the truth was that the Commission found little favour in government'. That may be true; but, equally, there was an internal consistency on her part, in that during the 1950s as well as 1960s she had always argued that it was fundamentally a matter of educational priorities – and that 'despite her dislike for private schools' (in the words of her biographer Rachel Reeves), 'government for Alice was about delivery for working-class families'.[74]

In any case, the issue was now effectively dead. 'The divisive public schools will be dealt with – and dealt with, I hope, before very long,' Short would tell a Conservative MP in July 1969, though at no stage before or after did he act as if that divisiveness was a remotely urgent matter; and then in June 1970 his party unexpectedly lost the general election, meaning that all bets – including what had become an exceedingly long-shot bet – were off.[75]

It just might have been a different story if Newsom had not been saddled by Crosland with the requirement that his inquiry seek to solve by means of a 'boarding' strategy the broader and more fundamental problem of what to do about elite public schools. 'What has been missing all along,' justifiably pointed out the educational journalist Stuart Maclure in early 1968, 'is some really good argument why the educational question of boarding need should be linked with the social and political question of the public schools at all'; and he argued that Crosland had alighted on using boarding need – greatly exaggerated in any case – as 'a kind of *deus ex machina*' in order to find a solution to the bigger but seemingly intractable question.[76] Part of that intractability, from the point of view of a democratic politician, stubbornly lay in the state of public opinion. Back in 1957, a Labour Party study group had received the findings of a survey which had revealed 'the general feeling' to be that 'if parents wanted to send children to private schools there was no reason why they should not do so', in effect a shrug of the shoulders about an issue that for most people seldom if ever directly impinged on their daily lives; Crosland himself would often point out to Halsey how all polls showed education to be low among popular political priorities; and in 1968 itself, a poll that spring published by the *Sunday Times* demonstrated a clear majority – 67 per cent of voters – in favour of leaving the public schools as they were, with even a majority of Labour supporters taking that view.[77]

Of course, it is easy enough to point a finger, if one is so inclined, at the Labour politicians – whether at those of the right (like Crosland) unwilling to look harder at the issue of freedom of choice, or those of the left who, in Crosland's words, 'thought the scheme still left the schools in a fundamentally elitist position' – and who also, as Westminster School's John Rae would put it, 'have no wish to see the schools escape execution by donning egalitarian colours'.[78] Whether of left or right, the uncomfortable fact was that in 1967, as Newsom and his colleagues began to draft their report, almost half (42 per cent) of the Labour Cabinet was privately educated.[79] Perhaps that mattered in terms of political will, perhaps it did not. One of the party's leading politicians, spanning the Attlee and Wilson eras, was Douglas Jay, who had not only been to Winchester, but had sent his sons there. 'Don't worry,' he was heard to remark at Old Wykehamist parliamentary dinners. 'We may say a lot, but we'll never *do* anything.'[80]

It is tempting to end here this phase of the story – tempting, but arguably unfair to Crosland et al. In April 1970, just before the Labour government fell, the left-leaning philosopher Mary Warnock (at the time head of Oxford High School for Girls, a direct grant grammar) sought to explain why Labour had ultimately been unable to lay a glove on the major public schools:

> They [the schools] have sizeable endowments, great prestige, and, of course, influence. They command a kind of loyalty which is largely irrational. Some of them are very good academically. It might be both difficult and unpopular simply to legislate them out of existence; and who knows by what ingenious dodges they might even so manage to survive? Anyway, is one really prepared to take what may look like the grossly illiberal, crudely dictatorial position of saying that parents with money to spend *may* not, legally, spend it on buying education for their children?

As for a compromise, a Fleming-type solution 'of making these important schools really open to a less purse-selected range of pupils', she believed (but without supporting figures) this would be 'unavoidably extremely expensive', and therefore distinctly unattractive to taxpayers. 'Thus, about those schools,' reckoned Warnock, 'it is easy to come to the conclusion that, socially objectionable though they may be, nothing much can be done.'[81]

1970–79: The Wrong Target

Warnock's article, appearing in *New Society* under the title 'The wrong target', had a specific context. In 1968, after producing its much-maligned report, the PSC had reconvened under David Donnison's chairmanship in order to examine the question of direct grant grammar schools. Traditionally those schools had occupied since the inter-war period a somewhat anomalous position, being situated uneasily somewhere between the outright fee-paying private sector and the outright non-fee-paying state sector; and in March 1970, a few weeks before Warnock's analysis, the Donnison report had argued for abolition, on the grounds of the 'impossibility' (in the *Guardian*'s summarising words) 'of fruitful co-existence between a state system of comprehensive schools and a rash of state-subsidised, rigorously selective direct grant schools'.[82] Warnock's anxiety was that, from Labour's point of view, this policy would be attractively attainable low-hanging fruit ('an easier target to hit'), compared with the seemingly out-of-reach major public schools. 'It may not be at all as difficult to deal with them,' she predicted about the direct grants. 'Quite a lot of them will not be particularly well-known at all, and will have at most a certain local prestige, and could vanish without any noticeable fuss being made. It is easy to *make* them vanish: it is a matter of withdrawing their funds.'[83]

Nothing happened over the next four years of Conservative rule, but Labour's return to power in 1974 meant that their days were numbered. Two years later, legislation gave the direct grant schools a simple choice: go fully comprehensive or fully private – and in practice, some two-thirds (118 out of 171) opted for the latter route, thereby significantly strengthening the private sector and fulfilling the law of unintended consequences.[84] Historians and others remain divided about whether or not the enforced ending of the direct grants was the right thing to do; but what can be said with certainty is that they were assuredly not the target that really mattered.

By the mid-1970s, moreover, the 'Hattersley moment' had come and gone. 'A better social mix in no way makes the private schools more acceptable,' Labour's shadow education secretary Roy Hattersley, no Flemingite, told prep school heads in September 1973. 'It merely gives them a spurious political respectability.' And he went on: 'I must leave you with no doubts about our serious intention initially to reduce and eventually to abolish private education in this country.'[85] The outcry was immediate, loud and hostile, co-ordinated by the recently launched Independent Schools Information Service (ISIS) and epitomised by Frank Fisher, Master of Wellington College as well as chairman of the HMC, accusing Labour of proposing 'an act of educational vandalism unparalleled in the history of the free world'.[86] In the run-up to a probable election year, Hattersley's leader rowed the party back. He agreed in principle, Wilson explained on BBC's *Panorama*, about discouraging private education, but it was 'not a high priority'; off the record, he complained that Hattersley had 'got religion'.[87] Unsurprisingly, when Wilson made his ministerial dispositions in March 1974, he gave the Education post not to Hattersley but to the altogether more emollient Reg Prentice, greeted by the *Daily Telegraph*'s education editor as 'not violently anti-public school'.[88]

In effect, and especially given the economic crisis of the time and Labour's bare majority at best, the major threat was over. 'I think there will be an independent sector for a long time to come, whether we like it or not,' Prentice told *The Times* the following year. 'We couldn't afford to take it over ...'[89] Instead, at an altogether lower order of threat level – but still assiduously opposed by the recently formed Independent Schools Joint Committee, forerunner of the present-day Independent Schools Council (ISC) – the Labour government looked to attack the financial exemptions and reliefs enjoyed by the public schools as a result of their charitable status. They did not get very far, with ministers having to concede by 1977 that their lawyers had been unable to redefine charitable activities in such a way as to ensure that organisations like Oxfam and Save the Children did not also lose out. 'A weakening of resolve' is one historian's retrospective verdict on the politicians at this point, and that is probably correct.[90]

More generally, the 1970s were no different from previous decades in the way that a mixture of division, confusion and complacency characterised Labour's approach to the private school problem. John Rae's invaluable diaries give a couple of revealing glimpses. In 1973 he discussed the issue with Shirley Williams (who later in the decade would preside over the end of the direct grants). 'Says she is in favour of a state system that educates all children with no independent schools outside,' he noted; 'but,' he added, 'she is opposed to abolishing public schools until choice is a reality in the state system'. Then in early 1976, Rae was approached by Wilson's 'extra limb', Lady Falkender (the former Marcia Williams), about getting her two sons into Rae's school. Rae apparently obliged, because a few weeks later he was at No. 10 being given a thank-you drink by the PM. The matter was not discussed, but both men knew the score.[91] Jim Callaghan, who succeeded Wilson soon afterwards, was similarly unfired-up about the issue, while his two ministers who now led Labour's left, Michael Foot and Tony Benn, had seemingly virtually nothing to say about the issue. Benn's *Arguments for Socialism* – published in 1979, the year that Labour lost power – was entirely silent, apart from a passage about the need to change 'the balance of power in society' that included a fairly oblique reference to how 'the education system, in one respect, is producing people to meet the needs of society based upon a certain pattern of ownership'.[92] In practice, reflects his daughter Melissa on the basis of many discussions, he was 'always against the abolition of private schools, on the grounds that you can't take away the legal right of people to spend their money as they wish'; and, especially in the context of the ongoing comprehensivisation of state secondary education (often under serious media attack), 'to get bogged down in that legal/rights argument would be a distraction'.[93]

Taking the Labour government as a whole, Gathorne-Hardy's assessment in 1977 (the end-point of his history of public schools) was that its policy had been to reckon that a combination of high inflation and shrinking middle-class incomes would 'allow the public schools to wither away, hoping that eventually just a very few schools would alone remain, the preserve of a few hundred rich boys and some Arabs'.[94] Two years later, the party's election manifesto did include the statement that 'independent schools [as the public schools had increasingly managed to brand themselves] still represent a major obstacle to equality of opportunity' and that 'Labour's aim is to end, as soon as possible, fee-paying in such schools'; but of course, after eleven years in government since the heady days of 1964, the political tomorrows for such an aspiration to come to fruition were about to disappear for a very long time.[95]

1979–2017: Off the Table

Margaret Thatcher's victory in 1979 presaged not only eighteen years in power for the Tories, but a rightwards shift of the political centre of gravity that would last for at least a third of a century. That shift included what was in effect a freezing out of almost any sort of meaningful debate about the moral validity or otherwise of private education. During those long years of silence – above all the 1990s and 2000s, but far from confined to those decades – it was as if the past had become not just a foreign country, but another universe altogether.

The Tories, of course, had always broadly upheld the public schools, going back to Butler and earlier, though with the occasional somewhat critical voice. 'The Conservative Party makes do with an attitude of embarrassed acceptance,' complained Rae in 1973. ' "You have a right to exist," they say to the schools, "but you must not expect active support from us." '[96] Indeed, back in the early 1960s the education minister Sir David Eccles had committed himself to seeking, as 'wise and just in our generation', to 'bring the two educational systems closer together', including strongly urging that all children from five to eleven be sent to state schools; while in 1976 a classic one-nation Conservative, Christopher Chataway, publicly reflected that it was 'a most unfortunate legacy of British history that leaves us, alone among the great democracies of Western Europe and North America, with a system which ensures that the 5 per cent or 6 per cent with the most money educate their children almost exclusively in the company of others of similar means'.[97] But for Thatcher herself, it was seemingly a black-and-white issue. 'Please never apologise for independence,' she instructed pupils at Bloxham in 1971 (when she was education secretary). 'It is worth stimulating and nurturing for its own sake. You do not have to justify it. It is those who wish to finish it who have to justify their case.'[98]

A decade later, it was Thatcher's government that set up the Assisted Places Scheme (APS), providing over its lifetime some 75,000 government-subsidised places at private schools, even as it cut spending on the state sector, left demoralised as well as underfunded.[99] Her government also gave the private sector unswerving political support, with Mark Carlisle, a former education secretary, even declaring in 1982 that 'parents who can afford the fees have "a right and a duty" to send their children to independent schools'; and during the 1980s, with rising income inequality augmented by a fiscal policy that lowered the tax bills of the rich, it became possible for the private sector to make its great leap forward in the provision of facilities.[100] The Thatcher era (as opposed to Thatcherism) ended on the most piquant of notes. 'At the Albert Hall in November 1990, at a special Songs concert to commemorate the fiftieth anniversary of Churchill's first visit in 1940, Harrow appeared in the heart of London *en fête* to celebrate the modern [public] school cult,' records Christopher Tyerman in his history of that school (where Thatcher had sent her son Mark in the 1960s):

The building was packed with the school, masters, OHs, and the great and good … That same day Mrs Thatcher, who was to have been a guest, had announced her resignation. In a moment of symbolism no less telling than the event itself, when the Chairman of the governors, the Cabinet Secretary, F.E.R. Butler, in a remarkable address, ventured to send the assembly's best wishes to the former Prime Minister, there erupted an extraordinary roar of approval the like of which few present had ever experienced.

'It was,' notes Tyerman, 'the cry of a tribe that had lost its totem.'[101]

For the next twenty years, Conservative politicians barely uttered a word about private schools, as that sector took advantage of a virtual political vacuum and for most of the time flourished exceedingly. But in 2010, two years after the financial crash had set off a chain reaction of disenchantment about politicians and the political system, the new Conservative PM was not only privately educated (unlike Heath, Thatcher and Major) but an Old Etonian to boot, often the single thing that most people knew about him. 'It's not where you've come from that counts, it's where you're going,' David Cameron would regularly insist, adding if pressed that he was 'not embarrassed' to have gone to 'a fantastic school'.[102] Even so, by mid-way through his first term, and for all his vigorous rhetoric about the need to increase social mobility, it became a regular trope – including from within his party – to criticise as excessive the dominance of the privately educated in public life, not least in the Cabinet and senior staff at No. 10. 'Truly shocking' was Major's phrase in November 2013; four months later the education secretary, Michael Gove, described as 'preposterous' and 'ridiculous' the concentration of Old Etonians in Cameron's top team; in July 2014 another minister, Justine Greening, said that she would like to see 'more people from a state-school background at the Cabinet table'; and soon afterwards a recent minister, Baroness Warsi, characterised those around Cameron as 'public schoolboys'.[103]

Gove by this time was speaking regularly about ending the 'Berlin Wall' in British education, as well as publicly conceding that 'the wonderfully liberating education offered by our great public schools is overwhelmingly the preserve of the wealthy'.[104] Yet in practice, Gove and his party went into the May 2015 election – the Tory manifesto written by six people, five of whom were Old Etonians – without any serious policy to tackle the deep social divide in Britain's education.[105] Then, a year after Cameron had won his unexpected majority, the Hancock/ Waldegrave episode painfully exposed the underlying political realities for any Tory would-be radical reformer. Matt Hancock, the Cabinet Office minister in charge of social mobility policy, proposed that leading employers should be required to check the 'socio-economic' background (including their schooling) of those applying for jobs, with a view to identifying 'potential, not polish'; Lord Waldegrave, a former Conservative minister and by now Provost of Eton College, threatened to resign the party whip; the *Spectator* ran an indignant cover story about 'Purge of the posh'; and within days Hancock had backtracked, insisting that the privately educated would not be discriminated against. 'I'm a product of, and proud supporter of, Britain's independent schools,' he declared. 'Meritocracy can only be promoted by eschewing quotas and sticking rigorously to appointment on merit.'[106]

That was in early June 2016, shortly before the referendum vote for Brexit that terminated Cameron's premiership. Two candidates emerged to succeed him. 'If you're at a state school, you're less likely to reach the top professions than if you're educated privately,' announced Theresa May at her campaign launch, setting out her 'vision of a country that works not for the privileged few but for everyone, regardless of who they are and regardless of where they're from'.[107] 'There could be an advantage in having people who have gone through the state system,' asserted Andrea Leadsom about future Conservative leaders. 'People feel more comfortable with somebody who knew what it was like in their playground or in a class that's too big.'[108] The position went to May, who as she prepared to enter No. 10 made a strong anti-privilege speech – repeating her line about the disadvantaged state-educated – that seemed to strike quite a chord with many people, a favourable impression further strengthened when she announced a pointedly meritocratic Cabinet, with less than one-quarter privately educated.[109]

Then two months later, in September 2016, she gave a much-publicised set-piece speech on 'Britain, the great meritocracy' in which she accused 'the major public schools' of having become 'more and more divorced from normal life' and demanded that they take significantly more substantive action – upping their sponsorship of state academies and/or funding more means-tested places – if they wanted to retain their charitable status.[110] The reaction from the schools was even more outraged than after Hancock's rash suggestion:

I think it's a bit cheap. *(Peter Green, Rugby)*

There is a mythology about the nature of independent schools and who attends them. We in the independent sector recognise our responsibilities as we cannot abide the waste of human potential. *(Patrick Derham, Westminster)*

It's a shame if the language is binary and divisive. Independent schools shouldn't be treated as figures from nightmare. *(Andrew Halls, King's College School, Wimbledon)*[111]

Briefly absent from the Tory front bench, Michael Gove further upped the ante in early 2017. Writing in *The Times*, first he revealed how, as education secretary, 'I lost my temper with ministerial colleagues who defended subsidies to private schools when I wanted to give more money to state schools'; then he gave chapter and verse about those subsidies and the hugely privileged private sector, urging the chancellor, Philip Hammond, to use his forthcoming budget to 'end the tax advantages enjoyed by private schools' – an appeal that fell on deaf ears.[112] Not long afterwards, May called a snap election, with the accompanying Tory manifesto devoting one whole sentence to the private school question: 'We will work with the Independent Schools Council to ensure that at least 100 leading independent schools become involved in academy sponsorships or the founding of free schools in the state system, keeping open the option of changing the tax status of independent schools if progress is not made.'[113] Polling day in June saw the Conservatives lose their overall majority. If the pledge was never likely to turn into a life-threatening event, there was perhaps nevertheless a certain sigh of relief, even of *Schadenfreude*, from the aggrieved schools.

Traditionally, of course, the main political critics of the sector had been on the Labour side. Back in the immediate wake of its 1979 election defeat, the party had swung sharply leftwards, including in the force of its opposition to private schools – a mood that culminated in the 1980 party conference, when an overwhelming majority endorsed the plans of the shadow education secretary, Neil Kinnock, to deploy a range of punitive measures in order to eliminate private schools over a ten-year period. 'It will be Armageddon,' he predicted to journalists. 'I think the public school system is the last redoubt of the establishment. It is the citadel to which the middle classes would cling most defiantly.'[114] Three years later, when Labour fought the general election under Michael Foot's leadership, its manifesto spelled out its approach:

> Private schools are a major obstacle to a free and fair education system, able to serve the needs of the whole community …
>
> We shall withdraw charitable status from private schools and all their other public subsidies and tax privileges. We will also charge VAT on the fees paid to such schools; phase out fee charging; and integrate private schools within the local authority sector where necessary.[115]

It would have been difficult for the party to claim that its approach chimed with public opinion. British Social Attitudes Surveys from 1983 through 1987 consistently showed that only around one in five adults held the view that there should be fewer or no private schools, albeit only one in ten being in favour of *more* private schools. In effect, most were not concerned enough – either way – to want to see change.[116]

By then, following the crushing defeat by Thatcher in the 1983 election, the party was starting to make its long journey back towards the political centre ground. At the 1987 election, the commitment was only to end public subsidy, albeit with abolition still an eventual target; in 1991 the shadow education secretary, Jack Straw, affirmed the legitimacy of parental choice; at the following year's general election, the threat of removing charitable status was taken off the table; and from 1994 came New Labour.[117] 'Politically and personally – ex-Durham Cathedral School, Fettes, St John's College, Oxford – he was not minded to put himself seriously at odds with the private schools,' Andrew Adonis would write about Tony Blair as prime minister from 1997, and that was true about him in opposition too.[118] Ahead of the 1997 election, his shadow education secretary, David Blunkett, wanted the party to commit to taking away charitable status, but Blair refused to go any further than the promise to end the APS.[119] 'Constructive collaboration and partnership is the way forward in education,' Blunkett himself would tell the private schools soon after New Labour's landslide victory. 'We know that there is much that we can learn from the private sector and much that the private sector can share. We want to put aside the divisions of the past and build a new partnership which recognises that private schools can make a real contribution to the communities in which they are situated.'[120]

During New Labour's thirteen years in government, and to the despair of long-standing critics of private schools like the Socialist Education Association, the concordat held remarkably firm. Even so, there occurred a trio of hiccups to disturb an otherwise notably harmonious relationship. First, in 2000, came Gordon Brown's unfortunate Laura Spence moment, when after a high-grades student from a Tyneside comprehensive had failed to gain a place at Oxford he fiercely criticised the university's admissions system ('the old-boy network and the old-school tie'), which in turn brought such press ordure on his head that thereafter he stayed entirely clear of the private school issue; then in 2002/3 a briefish stand-off saw the sector (backed by the right-wing press) accusing ministers of seeking unduly to influence top universities to broaden their admissions criteria in order to make the outcomes more socially inclusive; and finally, not long afterwards, Labour initiated an attempt, via the Charities Act of 2006, to make charitable status conditional on meeting a public benefit test – an attempt watered down in 2011 when the courts ruled against the Charity Commission's definition of public benefit.[121]

The politics of that third 'hiccup' were instructive. In May 2004 the Labour government published a draft Charities Bill, making private schools – traditionally accorded fiscally beneficial charitable status – not only accountable to the Charity Commission, but required to demonstrate that they worked for the public benefit. What would that mean in practice? Fiona Mactaggart, charities minister and Cheltenham Ladies' College alumna, sent reassuring signals: 'I do not believe that charging means you do not automatically provide a public benefit.' Even so, the stakes seemed later that year to be raised significantly, as a joint committee of the Commons and Lords, chaired by Labour's Alan Milburn, recommended that private schools be stripped of charitable status altogether (a potential threat to their governing boards' ability to retain control of their historically accumulated assets) and only given tax breaks if they could prove sufficient quantified public benefit. 'For a split second,' the educational campaigner Fiona Millar would recall, 'it appeared that change might actually be on the way.' Not so. First came the delay of the May 2005 election (Blair re-elected); then, after a new bill (not featuring the Milburn recommendation) had been published, the Labour whips that autumn ensured the defeat in the Lords of a crucial amendment by the Liberal Democrat peer Lord Phillips of Sudbury which sought to ensure that the Charity Commission, when consulting about its guidance on public benefit, 'consider the effect on public benefit on the charging policy of any charity'; in June 2006, during the second reading stage, the Cabinet Office minister Hilary Armstrong resisted proposals to strengthen the public benefit clause; and so, too, as he steered the bill through to Royal Assent later in 2006, did the new minister for the third sector, Ed Miliband. 'A classic piece of woolly New Labour triangulation, probably designed to keep the *Daily Mail* happy' is Fiona Millar's caustic verdict. 'Schools would have to prove public benefit, but the government wouldn't legislate for what that meant in practice.' Or, as two charity experts (Alice Faure Walker and Stephen Lloyd) noted at the time, especially about the

failure of a last-ditch amendment similar to the Phillips one even
to reach a vote in the Commons, 'the common belief' was that 'all
this stemmed from a Prime Ministerial veto on anything that could
be considered an attack on public schools'.[122]

Otherwise, apart from this trio of fairly mild blips, there existed
between 1997 and 2010 an almost wholly hands-off relationship
that in essence saw Labour giving the schools the operational and
indeed political freedom that they wanted. 'As we've got to know
the independent sector more we've been more honest and open
about what we can learn from it,' the schools minister Estelle
Morris told private school heads in 2000. 'We would always respect
the parents' wish to choose an independent school for their son or
daughter. New Labour, no matter how many terms we have, will
never go back on that.'[123] Indeed, there were moments when the
relationship almost had the feel of a love-in, especially when from
the mid-2000s Lord Adonis as schools minister pushed through
the idea and early implementation of state academies – a vision of a
new form of state education governance that took inspiration from
the private schools.[124] His strongest supporter was Blair, who in
his memoirs would include a striking passage asserting that private
schools were of high quality not solely because of resources and the
socio-economic background of the pupils: 'They are independent.
They have an acute sense of ethos and identity. They have strong
leadership, and are allowed to lead. They are more flexible. They
innovate because no one tells them they can't. They pursue
excellence. And – here is a major factor – they assume excellence is
attainable. In other words, they believe failure is not inevitable ...'[125]

What neither Blair nor Brown did in their respective
autobiographies was to consider whether the lack of significant
action about private schools had compromised their oft-stated
commitment to equality of opportunity. Indeed, it was arguably
that commitment that lay somewhere near the very heart of the
New Labour offer. 'Labour conveyed a strength of communitarian
values that would make the New Labour government very different
to the Conservatives, with a belief in equality of opportunity in
contrast to Thatcherism's narrow individualism,' proudly recalled

Peter Mandelson in 2017 about what in his view had underpinned the whole project.[126] Yet in real time, as New Labour vacated power in 2010, the elephant in the room was still waiting for serious attention.

Over the next four years, under Ed Miliband's leadership, nothing changed. Stephen Twigg, shadow education secretary, raised in 2012 the possibility of private schools ('a major barrier to achieving a more just society and greater social mobility') losing their charitable status if they failed to serve the community, but that was about it.[127] Eventually, in November 2014, his successor Tristram Hunt did come up with a firm policy, possibly in response to the *New Statesman*'s campaign earlier in the year about what it called 'The 7% Problem'. If Labour won the May 2015 election, he announced, private schools would over the following five years lose £700 million, through measures to prevent them as charities accessing business rate relief – unless they played a much fuller role in helping to improve the quality of education and university access in state schools. 'Step up and play your part,' he warned. 'Earn your keep. Because the time you could expect something for nothing is over.'[128] Hunt found his proposals attacked from almost all sides – 'deeply depressing' according to the head of Hampstead's University College School, his alma mater; 'class envy' according to the *Daily Telegraph*; 'lamentably feeble' according to the novelist Margaret Drabble – and she was clearly right, given that the schools would have lost less than 2 per cent of their fee income, easily recouped in one annual fee increase.[129] In the election itself the proposals barely surfaced.

Then, from left field after Labour's defeat, came Jeremy Corbyn, elected Labour leader in September 2015. The general expectation was of the party adopting more left-wing policies than at any time since 1983 (and possibly earlier); but, in relation to private education, Corbyn had little or nothing to say during his first eighteen months as leader.[130] When a policy did at last emerge, in April 2017 just days before May called her snap election, it was to put VAT on private school fees in order to fund free meals for all primary school children. 'I'm not suggesting that we should abolish all private schools, but I don't see why the taxpayers and the state should subsidise them,' declared the shadow education secretary, Angela Rayner, on the day of Corbyn's announcement.[131] A few weeks later that proposal was included in Labour's *For The Many Not The Few* election manifesto, which otherwise was entirely silent on the broader issue. 'Why is Corbyn so unambitious on education reform?' asked journalist Robert Verkaik in *The i*, and his not implausible explanation was the understandable reluctance not to be exposed to charges of hypocrisy: Corbyn himself had been to a prep school; his two closest aides, Seamus Milne and James Schneider, had both gone to Winchester; and two of the key members of his shadow Cabinet, Diane Abbott and Shami Chakrabarti, had controversially sent their children to private schools.[132] More fundamentally, the absence of any drive to do the necessary thinking and to prioritise the reform of private education remained all too familiar. It seemed a feeble state of affairs.

History Lessons

More broadly, looking at the whole story across the last century and a half, but above all the last eighty years or so, one is left with an unmistakable sense of *la même chose*. It is not too difficult to identify (in no particular order) several key continuities: a lack of intellectual will, even among progressives, to prioritise the issue; a lack of political will to take on major, long-established institutions; the personal 'embeddedness' of the schools in those in power or positions of influence, because of their own schooling and/or their parental choices; an enduring attachment to libertarianism at the expense of equality of opportunity; and, similarly enduring, the fallacious belief – in effect wishful thinking – that the schools will somehow 'wither' away. All five continuities remain highly relevant today. If serious action is ever to be taken (before 2068?) about Britain's deeply damaging private school problem, they will have to be surmounted, not ignored.

3

The Making of a Service Industry

It is time to turn to the schools themselves: in the next chapter a close-up look at what they are like in the early twenty-first century, but in this a broad historical survey of their development between the late fourteenth century and the end of the twentieth. What did they offer – academically and otherwise – in return for the fees they charged? Who went to these old schools with their proud and unmistakable aura of tradition? What were the values and ethos that their pupils took with them into later life? And above all, how did they evolve to become the exclusive and luxurious institutions they are today? This cannot be a comprehensive account of private schools over some six centuries, but those are the key questions.

1382–1860: Poor and Needy Scholars?

We start with a bald fact which the most venerable and prestigious private schools still find understandably difficult to accept, let alone publicise: namely, that a major part of their original core purpose – the purpose that conferred charitable status upon them – was to educate not the affluent, but the poor. 'There are and will be, it is believed, hereafter many poor scholars intent on school studies suffering from want of money and poverty,' affirmed Winchester College's foundation deed in 1382; and thus, unambiguously went on the founder William of Wykeham, 'for such poor and needy scholars, clerks, present and to come, in order that they may be able to stay or be busy at school, and by the grace of God become more aptly and freely proficient in the faculty and science of grammar, and become as is desirable more fit for the sciences or liberal arts, to increase the roll of all the sciences, faculties and liberal arts, and expand as far as in us lies the number of those studying and profiting in them, we propose from the means and goods bestowed on us by God, with the aid of the clemency of God, to hold out helping hands and give the assistance of charity'. So too in 1440 with Eton College, where the founder, Henry VI, insisted in his charter that the majority of boys going there came from poor backgrounds; while at Westminster School, refounded by Elizabeth I in 1560, at least one-third of the intake were to be scholars chosen on the grounds not only of their 'teachableness', 'goodness of disposition', 'learning' and 'good behaviour', but also their 'poverty'.[1]

Nor, among the historic private schools pre-dating Victoria's reign, are these three schools just the embarrassing exceptions. When John Colet refounded St Paul's in 1509, the pupils comprised 153 non-fee-paying scholars; half a century later at Merchant Taylors', also in the City of London, the livery companies' founding charter conceived the majority of the intake being the offspring of 'poor men'; and at nearby Charterhouse in 1611, another mercantile creation, the founding statute explicitly stated that the school was being established 'for poor people, men and children'. There was often also a specifically *local* dimension, very different from the national, supra-local institutions that the great private schools would become. Shrewsbury, Rugby, Harrow: all three schools were established in the second half of the sixteenth century – and all three were intended to service the local community, for free.[2] Clearly, to coin a phrase, charity began at home.

What then happened over the next few centuries was the rise and rise of the fee-payers (as opposed to foundationers), often coming from far afield and sought by the schools themselves for obvious if somewhat ignoble social-cum-economic reasons. Headmasters naturally wanted to increase the prestige of their school as well as their own emoluments; impecunious assistant masters had, with the accompanying rise of boarding, the opportunity to become reasonably well-rewarded housemasters; and the memory of founders' visions gradually faded.[3] The most detailed school history we have – Christopher Tyerman's superb history of Harrow – charts the process by which that school 'was able to ride the tide that was flowing in favour of socially as well as professionally elite classical education and the consequent growing popularity of fee-paying boarding', so that by the late seventeenth century Harrow had become 'a recognised competitor for the education of the gentry'.[4] Of course, there was still the odd lowly exception – Ben Jonson at Westminster was a bricklayer's son, Thomas Gray at Eton a scrivener's son – but the larger tide was indeed flowing one way. T. W. Bamford's analysis of the intake of the historic 'public' boarding schools during the first half of the nineteenth century confirms the high degree of social exclusivity: 'The boys came from aristocratic, gentry or near-gentry homes, with minor additions from the clergy, and even less from the armed forces and other professional groups.'[5] By 1861, of the 2,283 boys attending Eton, Winchester, Westminster, Harrow, Rugby, Shrewsbury and Charterhouse, all but 342 were fee-payers.[6]

Who were those minority foundationers? Inevitably there was a certain amount of wishful thinking. The Provost of Eton, Dr Goodford, defended soon afterwards the selection as King's Scholars of clergymen's sons and naval officers' sons as being 'as near as may be, the class of persons whom our Founder meant to benefit'.[7] But about the same time, a former teacher at Charterhouse, Augustus Saunders, was clearer eyed as he explained that foundationers there were no longer chosen on the basis of the limited means of parents: 'The boys are to a boy almost connexions – Lord G's grandson and Lord H's nephews and to the end of time it will be so. The fact is that the first men in the land might be well pleased to have his sons there.'[8] Since the early nineteenth century, the term 'public school' had been in use, with the implication (to quote the historian of Shrewsbury School) that 'such schools were accessible to the general public, typically because their endowments had been

provided for the general public benefit'.⁹ But already the concept of
'public' was at best a debatable one.

Similarly problematic at this stage – but ultimately far more
remediable – was the quality of education on offer. Take this chorus
of complaint from four men who flourished in later life despite
rather than because of the teaching they had received as boys:

> Seven or eight years merely in scraping together so much
> miserable Latin and Greek, as might be learned otherwise easily
> and delightfully in one year. (*John Milton, St Paul's, 1615–25*).

> I arrived at Oxford with a stock of erudition that might have
> puzzled a doctor, and a degree of ignorance of which a schoolboy
> would have been ashamed. (*Edward Gibbon, Westminster,
> 1748–50*)

> Nothing could have been worse for the development of my
> mind than Dr Butler's school, as it was strictly classical, nothing
> else being taught, except a little ancient geography and history.
> The school as a means of education to me was simply a blank ...
> (*Charles Darwin, Shrewsbury, 1818–25*)

> During the whole of those twelve years no attempt had been
> made to teach me anything but Latin and Greek, and very
> little attempt to teach me those languages. I do not remember
> any lessons either in writing or arithmetic. French or German
> I certainly was not taught. (*Anthony Trollope, Harrow, 1823–5,
> Winchester, 1827–30, Harrow, 1830–4*)¹⁰

The problem was also large class sizes (prompted by headmasters'
mercenary considerations), but by the early nineteenth century
it was the narrowness of the curriculum that was increasingly
under attack. 'Boys are taught nothing of the age or country in
which they live nor of science,' declared the *Westminster Review*
in 1824, while six years later the *Edinburgh Review* simply stated
the truth in its assessment of the academic lacunae of a pupil
studying at Eton: 'Utterly ignorant of mathematical or physical
science, and even of arithmetic ... the very names of logical, moral,

or political science, are unknown to him ... modern history and modern languages are, of course, out of the question.'[11] The schools themselves remained for many years almost entirely unrepentant. Asked in the early 1860s to assess the relative values of the classics and modern languages, Eton's head responded crisply: 'Fifteen to one.'[12]

Equally striking was the pervasive brutality. 'Fags and their Masters', 'Liquor and Violence', 'The Unspared Rod' – such are some of the chapter titles in John Chandos's comprehensive survey (*Boys Together*) of the largely unreformed, pre-1860s public school world. That brutality was not new – Pitt the Elder in the mid-eighteenth century reckoned that he had 'hardly known a boy whose spirit had not been broken at Eton' – but seems to have reached its apogee in the first half of the nineteenth century.[13] 'Abuse, neglect and vice' was how Sydney Smith in 1810 characterised the schools, finding in them a 'premature debauchery that only prevents men from being corrupted by the world by corrupting them before they enter the world'; during the 1820s the son of the Earl of Suffolk died from injuries sustained at Charterhouse – having been the actual football in the school's distinctive version of the game; and in 1844 a fourteen-year-old boy, the future prime minister Lord Salisbury, wrote home forlornly from Eton: 'I have been kicked most unmercifully since I saw you last for refusing to do a fellow's theme for him ... He kicked me and pulled my hair and punched me, and hit me as hard as ever he could for twenty minutes and now I am aching in every joint and hardly able to write this.'[14] The archetypal figure is Flashman, the bully's bully. Originally depicted in Thomas Hughes's celebrated 1857 novel *Tom Brown's School Days*, set in the Rugby of the 1830s, he would live on in George MacDonald Fraser's latter-day series; and although Hughes in the original has him eventually expelled for drunkenness as well as bullying, the real-life Flashmans remained firmly in situ.

Yet in practice it was all part of the training for the country's future rulers. 'Throwing boys headlong into those great public schools always puts me in mind of the Scythian mothers, who threw their new-born infants into a river,' reflected the religious writer

Hannah More in around 1812. 'The greater part perished, but the few who possessed great natural strength came out with additional vigour from the experiment.'[15] Half a century later, with typical realism, Trollope looked back on his time at Winchester: 'There we became men; and we became men after such a fashion that we are feared or loved, as may be, but always respected – even though it is in spite of our ignorance.'[16] Perhaps the classic affirmation of the value of the toughening-up process came from the *Saturday Review* in 1860. 'Boys, like nations, can only attain to the genuine self-reliance which is true manliness by battling for themselves against their difficulties and forming their own characters by the light of their own blunders and their own troubles,' it asserted in unashamedly survival-of-the-fittest mode. 'The object of the public school is to introduce a boy early to the world, that he may be trained in due time for the struggle that lies before him.'[17] As the British Empire approached its zenith, and leadership qualities and resilience became ever more in demand, few doubted the value of that training, even if they sometimes regretted the harsh asperities associated with it.

1860–1945: The Certainties of Privilege

The closing decades of the Victorian Age saw the sector taking recognisably modern shape. Not only did the Clarendon Commission of the 1860s strongly affirm the unique value of the historic public schools – 'their capacity to govern others and control themselves, their aptitude for combining freedom with order, their public spirit, their vigour and manliness of character, their strong but not slavish respect for public opinion, their love of healthy sports and exercise' – but it led to significant improvements in their internal governance.[18] The continuing national dominance of the historic schools would now be a permanent fact of life. 'Eton, Harrow, Winchester, and a half dozen more public schools are really the nidus [i.e. nest] out of which is bred our present aristocratic conservatism in Church and State,' declared the radical reformer Frederic Harrison in 1882. 'The entire prelacy [archbishops and bishops], civil and military service, governments, army and navy, and even literary potentates issue out of these seminaries, which are the true keystone of British society.'[19]

Just as importantly, the sector by this time was expanding rapidly. Many of the new potential rivals to the historic schools had in fact already been established – Marlborough College in 1843, for example, or Wellington College in 1859 – but it was during the late nineteenth century that they truly established themselves as permanent features of the educational and social landscape; while at the same time, preparatory (prep) schools mushroomed, with numbers up from around a dozen in 1870 to some 400 by the end of the century.[20] What for all these new schools was the target market? 'Somehow or other we must get possession of the Middle Classes, and how can we so well do this as through Public Schools,' declared in 1871 the strongly religious Nathaniel Woodard, whose 'Woodard schools' included over the years Lancing, Hurstpierpoint, Ardingly, Bloxham, Denstone, Ellesmere and Worksop; while from a more secular perspective, the Liberal politician James Bryce noted in 1868 that 'when a Lancashire merchant or manufacturer sends his sons away from home, he desires as often as not to send them a long way off, partly that they may lose their northern tongue, partly that they may form new acquaintances, and be quite away from home influences'.[21] Moreover, though often looked down upon by male eyes, there were already some equivalent schools for girls: the pioneer North London Collegiate had been founded by Frances Mary Buss as early as 1850; Cheltenham Ladies' College flourished from 1858 under Dorothea Beale, a prominent suffragist educator; later schools included Camden School for Girls (1871, Miss Buss again), Roedean (1883) and Wycombe Abbey (1896); while, by the turn of the century, the less socially exclusive (but still fee-paying) schools belonging to the Girls' Public Day School Company (later the GPDST) numbered thirty-three.[22] One way and another, across the sector as a whole, a very considerable vested interest had been born.

The conventional historical wisdom identifies the famous Dr Thomas Arnold (real-life headmaster at Rugby during Tom Brown's school days) as the presiding spirit of the Victorian public school. 'ist, religious and moral principles: 2nd, gentlemanly conduct; 3rd, intellectual ability': such he sought to instil in his charges, and over the next century and more few heads would have dared to gainsay the Arnoldian legacy.[23] Yet in truth, it was by the late nineteenth century a tarnished legacy, as instead a very distinct, non-Arnoldian type of gentleman began to emerge from the system. 'Boys learnt religion in the public schools as a social habit; at its core was unswerving devotion to house and school,' observes the historian Anthony Fletcher, adding that 'it was in the period from the 1880s to the 1920s that caning of boys by boys became rife, schools developing their own particular sadistic rituals', tacitly endorsed by the adults.[24] Nor was that all in terms of a tarnished legacy; for as another historian, David Newsome, reflects, 'the doctrine of the stiff-upper-lip', which 'came in with the manliness cult of the 1870s and 80s', was 'no part of the public-school code of the Arnoldian period'.[25] The price was not only a stifling conformity, but a profound emotional shortfall. 'It is not that the Englishman can't feel – it is that he is afraid to feel,' wrote E. M. Forster (who had been bullied at Tonbridge) in the 1920s. 'He has been taught at his public school that feeling is bad form. He must not express great joy or sorrow, or even open his mouth too wide when he talks – his pipe might fall out if he did. He must bottle up his emotions, or let them out only on a very special occasion.'[26] Further testimony emerged in the 1930s in a collection of largely reminiscent essays, *The Old School*. Harold Nicolson described how at Wellington circa 1900 'my whole conscious energy was concentrated upon the necessity of seeming manly, of giving no offence'; L. P. Hartley recalled of Harrow circa 1910 how 'the necessity of disguising what one felt, of keeping the famous stiff upper lip when cursed by a Sixth-former, or wounded by a friend, or hit by a cricket ball, sometimes found its logical outcome: after many repetitions one felt nothing at all'.

Did things loosen up between the wars? Nicolson thought so, visiting his old school in the early 1930s and finding that 'a boy who possessed a taste for water-colours was allowed to smear his washes to his heart's content', that 'a boy who was interested in iambics was allowed without let or question to revel in his eccentricity', and that in general 'the old pine-laden heartiness had lost its cruel tang'. Yet the most striking – and persuasive – piece in the collection came from Derek Verschoyle, who had been at Malvern in the 1920s and was now literary editor of the *Spectator*. Arguing that 'the Public Schoolboy abandons or suppresses the normal impulses and energies of childhood', he let himself go as he described that 'standardised commodity' which was the public school 'product':

At his best a practical man, a little limited in his views but tolerant towards those of different opinion, well-mannered and polite, neat in his appearance and punctual in his ways, a shade superficial perhaps but perfectly adapted to climb gradually to the top of any of the professions for which he has been produced, a smoothly turning cog in the machine; at his worst a complacent philistine, unable to think for himself and leaning on a code for moral conviction, lacking in imagination and in vision, eager for popularity, emotionally dwarfed and blandly adolescent in sexual matters, insensitive to beauty and confused towards truth …

That worst sort of public school product was also, added Verschoyle in his extensive charge sheet, 'a creature lost to progress in his obsequiousness towards convention, his inability for innovation, his class-consciousness and smug confidence in his own superiority, his faith in his own powers at a crisis, his narrowness and prejudice …'[27]

The single greatest driver, determining the character of the public schools between the 1870s and the 1930s, was undoubtedly the British Empire. The historian J. A. Mangan has brilliantly described how, in what he calls 'the new imperialism' of late Victorian Britain (an imperialism that in its essence continued into the inter-war period), three sets of values became enmeshed, each of which was relentlessly nourished and propagated by the schools themselves: first, 'imperial Darwinism – the God-granted right of the white man to rule, civilise and baptise the inferior coloured races'; second, 'institutional Darwinism – the cultivation of physical and psychological stamina at school in preparation for the rigours of imperial duty'; and third, 'the gentleman's education – the nurture of leadership qualities for military conquest abroad and political dominance at home'.[28] 'Grit,' declared J. G. C. Minchin at the time in *Our Public Schools* (1901), 'has built up for Great Britain her united Empire', adding that 'long before the British Public at large had been fired with a faith in the British Empire, one and indivisible, that was the faith in which every English public-school boy was reared'. The classic expression of that faith was 'Vitaï lampada', the celebrated poem of the 1890s by an Old Cliftonian, Henry Newbolt, which summoned up what believers in 'the public school spirit' conceived as its very essence and purpose. The first verse evoked the tense finish to a school cricket match, the second a desperate military situation in the far-away desert, the third the crucial importance through life of never forgetting the school ethos – and each of the three verses ended with the deathless line encapsulating that ethos, 'Play up! play up! and play the game!'[29] The slaughter of the Great War was, of course, just round the corner. Yet although – perhaps because – a huge number of public-schoolboys-turned-officers were slaughtered, the military-cum-imperial ethos remained almost as strong after the war as before; and even in 1964, when one of the authors went to Wellington, he was solemnly informed in his first week that one in ten OWs had been killed in action since the school's foundation.[30]

Newbolt's cricketing first verse was no accident. The cult of athleticism, the rise of organised games, the assumption of their character-building qualities: all this became integral to the schools during the late nineteenth century. The infrastructural as well as social and ethical implications were profound. 'There are 50 fives courts where before there was one; 20 games or thereabouts of cricket as against three; compulsory football for every house four or five times a week; to say nothing of beagles and athletic sports in the Easter Term, and rowing and bathing daily through the summer,' itemised one Eton insider in 1898 about the revolution of the previous few decades. 'There are house colours for football and school colours for football, cricket, rowing, racquets; there are challenge cups, senior and junior ...' So it was too, he noted, at 'the other great public schools': 'The comprehensive net of athletics has closed around them all, sweeping in our boys by shoals, and few are the puny minnows that swim through its meshes.'[31] Increasingly, and inevitably, it was 'the hearties' who now called the shots. 'Boys were bullied, coerced and tortured for their diversion,' recalled the artist C. R. W. Nevinson about Uppingham around 1905. 'In the popular pastime known as the "flying kick", the cricket eleven wore their white shoes and any junior who was captured was bent over for their sport. They took running kicks at our posteriors, their white shoes marking the score and a certain place counting as a bull.'[32] It was the same time that a future Indian prime minister, Jawaharlal Nehru, arrived hopefully at Harrow – only to find 'how dull most of the English boys were as they could talk about nothing but their games'.[33]

It is hard not to feel that the cult, the obsession, had some sort of infantilising, retarding effect, or at the very least helped to turn individuals into uncritical conformists. 'In the football eleven each will wear a cap, shirt, shorts, stockings of precisely the same pattern' was a regretful observation in 1912 about the typical team photo. 'They stand and sit so that the line of the peaks of their caps, of their folded arms, of their bare knees is mathematically level. And even their faces! You can hardly tell one from another ...'[34] In his history of the English prep school, Donald Leinster-Mackay cites the Reverend E. L. Browne, headmaster of St Andrew's, Eastbourne, from 1890 to 1933, as the very epitome of what was often called 'muscular Christianity'. Browne's analogy in his sermons when it came to explaining the Trinity? Obviously, 'three stumps, one wicket'.[35]

This was not, by and large, an environment that encouraged sustained intellectual and academic effort. '*Cleverness* – what an aim!' expostulated in 1883 a Fettes master, C. C. Cotterill, in his *Suggested Reforms in the Public Schools*. 'Good God, what an aim! Cleverness neither makes nor keeps man or nation. Let it not be

thought that it ever can. For a while it may succeed, but only for
a while. But self-sacrifice, – that is what makes and preserves men
and nations, yes, and fills them with joy – only this.'[36] Some four
decades later, the young Samuel Beckett tried his hand as a teacher
before soon giving notice. 'But, Mr Beckett, don't you realise you're
teaching the cream of Ulster?' asked Campbell College's baffled
headmaster. 'Yes,' replied Beckett, 'rich and thick.'[37] In reality,
academic ability varied greatly – but for many, many years, at almost
every public school, there was invariably a significant slow-witted
minority. Nor did it help the educational cause that the schools
themselves were so resistant – despite the urgings of Clarendon and
others – to broadening their curriculum in a meaningful sense and
moving away from the time-honoured dominance of the classics
(a dominance closely linked to all the scholarships at Oxbridge).
In particular, as an official inquiry reported in 1919, 'there has in
the public schools as a whole been no general recognition of the
principle that science should form an essential part of secondary
education'; while on what the inquiry called the 'modern side',
including modern languages, 'the general educational conditions
are in many ways unfavourable'.[38] So it went on: Eton in the mid-
1930s had thirty-nine classics masters, exactly three times as many
as science and history together.[39]

What was so special about the classics? David Ward has
convincingly argued, in an analysis of the damagingly semi-detached
relationship between the schools and industry, that 'their very
uselessness in the vocational sense seems to have been an asset', in
other words to social standing; and that, indeed, 'their relationship
to the traditional education of the gentry and aristocracy made
them necessary for the education of the aspiring gentry as well', as
that aspirational class sought to make fully fledged gentlemen of
their children.[40] Moreover, whatever the subject taught, the overall
quality of the teaching was almost certainly patchy. 'No effort
was spared to make them [the classics] as uninteresting and as
unprofitable as possible,' remembered Lord Berners about the Eton
of the 1890s; while as for the inter-war years, in the absence of firm
quantitative evidence, Jonathan Gathorne-Hardy's characterisation

of teachers who 'knew they would only be sacked if they were grossly incompetent or grossly immoral', and who inhabited an 'uncompetitive' world of 'huge holidays' as well as 'pleasant houses and gardens', has the ring of truth to it.[41] Anything harder edged or more thrusting would not, after all, have been setting a gentlemanly example.

What about social composition? 'It is a rich man's Bill,' complained the *Harrow Gazette* in 1867 as the legislation prepared to go through for what would become the Public Schools Act of 1868, effectively eliminating over the next few decades long-established local foundation rights for poor boys living near the schools, which now became entirely national not local in their identity.[42] Similarly enhancing social exclusiveness was the system of apparently open competitive scholarships which replaced those rights. As we have seen, the idea sounded progressive on paper in the 1860s, but in practice was anything but. 'Does the system at present in existence exclude any class of the community, in your opinion, from the benefits of those scholarships, i.e. entrance scholarships, to what are called the large public schools?' a parliamentary inquiry in the 1890s asked a knowledgeable witness. 'It virtually excludes any parent,' he answered, 'who cannot for three years pay £100 a year [well above the average income] for his son at one of the regular preparatory schools.'[43] That indeed was the truth: expensive preparation was virtually indispensable for such an exam. As for intake more broadly, the classics continued to perform their role as a social excluder, while the character of the leading schools perceptibly changed. Analysing Harrow's intake between 1885 and 1910, Tyerman discerns 'a significant and growing shift towards money rather than land as the basis of Harrovian wealth', with it 'ceasing to be an aristocratic school' and instead becoming 'a cradle of plutocracy', with, of course, appropriately high fees.[44] Appreciably more mixed by social background (although seldom penetrating the working class) were, during the inter-war period, the day schools known as direct grants – schools such as Manchester Grammar for Boys or South Hampstead for Girls (part of the GPDST group). There, in return for grant-aided support from the state though not at the expense of loss of self-government, up to 25 per cent of places were free to holders of local authority scholarships; and for a long time those schools occupied a nebulous position, not quite in either the private or state sector.[45]

Yet the larger story of social apartheid is clear enough. 'The darker and harder sides of life are excluded,' noted Harrow's headmaster, Cyril Norwood, in the 1920s about the typical public school boy. 'Cities and their industries, the factory, the mill, and the mine, and all the problems which they carry with them, are beyond the horizon … With the affairs of House and School to occupy all his thoughts in term, and the Swiss holiday, the new car, the first gun or the first rod to fill his thoughts in vacation, it is easy for him to grow to manhood with but slight sense of social obligation …'[46] The schools themselves went to considerable lengths to enforce the everyday gulf, with public transport, pubs, cafés, fish and chip shops, cinemas, garages and much else tending to be off-limits for those boarders who comprised Britain's cloistered elite.[47] Or as W. H. Auden (who had taught at prep schools as well as been to Gresham's) put it in the 1930s: 'The fact remains that the public school boy's attitude to the working-class and to the not-quite-quite has altered very little since the war. He is taught to be fairly kind and polite, provided of course they return the compliment, but their lives and needs remain as remote to him as those of another species.'[48]

In his litany of the faults of what he saw as the worst sort of public school product, Derek Verschoyle ended by identifying 'above all his absurd Loyalty'.[49] Sometimes that loyalty took financial form – Tyerman, examining Harrow's finances across the twentieth century, has observed that 'the impact of Old Harrovian donations cannot be underestimated' – but more often an essentially tribal expression. Membership of old boys' associations (flourishing by the late nineteenth century), faithful attendance at major sporting fixtures (quintessentially, Eton v Harrow at Lord's) and regular reunions, doing one's best to help out or facilitate a fellow old boy (the famous/infamous 'old boy network') or even just a fellow public school man: in all these ways, and a host of others, the loyalty was total and unquestioning.[50]

'There's a blessed equity in the English social system that insures the public-school man against starvation,' reflects Captain Grimes, the rackety, amoral prep school master in Evelyn Waugh's *Decline and Fall* (1928). 'One goes through four or five years of perfect hell at an age when life is bound to be hell, anyway, and after that the social system never lets one down.' During the Great War, when he is about to be tried for desertion, Grimes has his bacon saved by a major from another battalion who comes to try his case. ' "God bless my soul," he said, "if it isn't Grimes of Podger's!",' relates our anti-hero years later. ' "What's all this nonsense about a court-martial?" So I told him. "Hm," he said, "pretty bad. Still, it's out of the question to shoot an old Harrovian. I'll see what I can do about it." And next day I was sent to Ireland on a pretty cushy job connected with postal service. That saw me out as far as the war was concerned.'[51]

A shared experience or type of experience, a shared way of looking at the world, a shared social code and cluster of institutional memories (the historian Arthur Bryant once described a great public school's ritual as 'as intricate and finely woven as a Beethoven sonata'), even a shared imaginative experience through generation after generation of school stories from *Tom Brown's School Days* onwards – it was hardly surprising that the instinctive tendency was to close ranks.[52] And when Arnold Lunn in 1913 had the impudence to write a novel (*The Harrovians*) about his old school that declined to buy into all the character-building myths, but instead accurately described the prevailing conformism, such was the anger this treachery provoked that he was compelled to resign from his five London clubs.[53]

Whether through academic achievement, or networking, or social polish, or just being a good chap, this peculiarly British form of education provided the high road to the top. A cluster of statistics from the 1930s – well over half a century after the Education Act of 1870 had seen the state and local government start to get seriously involved in the provision of education – sufficiently make the point. In 1939, for instance, the public schools were responsible for 76 per cent of bishops, deans, judges and stipendiary magistrates, senior civil servants, Indian civil servants, dominion governors, and directors of banks and railways; of that 76 per cent, almost two-thirds had been to the twelve schools (Clarendon and a few others) generally acknowledged as the leaders of the pack; and in Neville Chamberlain's Cabinet of 1937, all but two had been to public school.[54] As in the nineteenth century, it remained a sector with considerable variety within it, ranging from the great and historic boarding schools to the many small and obscure private or 'proprietary' establishments often educating just a few children. Yet taken as a whole on the eve of the Second World War, that private sector (including the 'public' schools) still educated only some 7 per cent of pupils in Britain.[55] To them went the glittering prizes; to the others the crumbs from the table.

1945–79: Challenges

The rise of highly academic and motivated state grammar schools, the broader rise of 'meritocracy', the coming by the 1960s of the 'modernity' zeitgeist together with social liberalism shading into a mood of anti-deference and anti-authority – one way and another, it was a challenging context in which the private schools operated during the quarter-century after 1945. Nor did it help them that the middle class was – or anyway felt itself to be – increasingly under the fiscal squeeze, especially in terms of higher taxation. 'My days are disagreeably full of school governors' meetings,' reported George Lyttelton, a retired Eton housemaster who was governor of many schools, to a friend in 1956. 'The knell of the independent schools seems to have struck – literally – six times as many parents are talking of last straws and camels' backs than ever before ...'[56] In the event, at no point were there mass closures, but the unmistakable trend over the next decade and a half was one of steady decline: in 1963 some 8 per cent of all pupils in England were in private schools; by 1970 the proportion was barely 6 per cent.[57]

Irrespective of politics, and even before the economic shocks of the ensuing decade, these were not easy years.

How did the schools respond? Did they, for instance, broaden their social composition and become less socially exclusive? 'All society, from the duke's son to the shopkeeper's boy, is found there,' boldly claimed George Snow in his 1959 apologia, *The Public School in the New Age*. 'Only the wage earner is normally excluded, because he cannot pay the fees …'[58] And indeed, perhaps even the odd wage earner's offspring made the cut, given that by the 1960s, as a continuing result of the wartime Fleming Scheme (seeking to open up 25 per cent of places to non-fee-payers), some 15 per cent of public school boarders were receiving a degree of assistance from central or local government.[59] Even so, taking the sector as a whole, the evidence points overwhelmingly the other way: towards continuing social homogeneity and exclusivity. The schools themselves had what the historian of Fleming has called a 'waning interest' in making the Scheme a genuine game-changer; as for fee reductions more generally, the schools by the mid-1960s were devoting to them less than 5 per cent of all income; while at about the same time, a comprehensive survey of their intake established that 84 per cent of public school boys (and 92 per cent of boarders) had fathers in the Registrar General's social classes I and II, the 'top' two classes – which across society as a whole accounted for less than one-fifth of the male population.[60]

Certainly there was social homogeneity at Harrow in the 1950s, to judge by Daphne Rae's recollections of speech day there: 'Parents started to arrive at about ten o'clock, driving up in a magnificent array of cars, polished to a high showroom gloss, and ranging from shooting-brakes (some carrying an occasional black retriever) to a mauve Mercedes, a gold-plated, star-spangled Daimler, and one or two privately-owned London taxis.'[61] Or take Winchester, where a 1956 survey found that less than 1 per cent of the school had fathers who were skilled manual workers or clerks or shopkeepers or salesmen; whereas over 90 per cent were sons of military officers, business executives, scientists, teachers, civil servants and other professionals. 'Today the exclusiveness of the public schools is well known,' commented T. J. H. Bishop and Rupert Wilkinson in their 1967 study, *Winchester and the Public School Elite*. 'Over the past century the fees charged by major boarding schools have been beyond the means of 95 per cent of Britain's population. Quite simply: the public schools are for the rich.'[62] The apartheid was almost total. Staff at public schools, noted John Wilson (Second Master of King's, Canterbury) in 1962, 'refer, on the whole, rather slightingly to the state schools, and display a somewhat proud ignorance of national institutions like the 11+ exam and the precise meaning of "secondary modern"'; six years later the Public Schools Commission observed that 'public schools play games chiefly against other public schools', that 'they rarely exchange pupils or fraternise with maintained schools in their area', and that in general 'they belong, in a remarkable degree, to a world of their own'.[63]

All schools, of course, had to cope with 'The Sixties', and David Turner's plausible judgement (in his historical survey, *The Old Boys*) is that overall those in authority in the private sector coped intelligently enough, 'giving in over practices that had become so divorced from wider society that they could no longer be defended, including compulsory CCF [Combined Cadet Force] and daily chapel, and by adopting a flexible approach to youthful experimentation while drawing a clear line beyond which pupils could not go'.[64] Corporal punishment more or less disappeared, and the general aura of brutality gradually lessened, but for boarders day-to-day living conditions remained distinctly spartan. There was also during these post-war years, picking up pace in the 1960s but already under way in the 1950s, a significant shift of underlying ethos and orientation: in essence, away from sport (with its accompanying reign of 'the Bloods') and towards the academic. A levels began in 1951 and were initially taken quite lightly; but from the late 1950s that attitude changed – partly because of increasing competition from the direct grants and the grammars for university places, partly because of pressure from parents aware of the more competitive and less nepotistic jobs market, and by the mid-1960s partly because of largely unwelcome media attention on the academic performance of the public schools.[65]

Undoubtedly, that shift took place more in the boys' than the girls' schools, where Mallory Wober in the late 1960s conducted a detailed survey of twenty-three of them across the UK. 'While depending on fee-paying, some took only very able girls, others chiefly the less able ones,' she reported. 'Schools for the latter seemed to serve a middle-class sector of society who feel that their daughters would not "hold their own" in local schools. They would be socialized with manners, attitudes and tastes that are not middle-class. Therefore they are sent to schools which may not aspire to high academic results, but which concentrate on cultural training.'[66] And the ultimate purpose of that 'cultural training'? An early marriage, of course, to the right sort of man, as Ysenda Maxtone Graham makes clear in *Terms & Conditions*, her intensely evocative oral history of life in girls' boarding schools between 1939 and 1979.[67]

What about social obligation? In a 1955 essay on 'Character Training', the head of Christ's Hospital, H. L. O. Flecker, expressed the traditional uplifting orthodoxy from on high: 'Most boys leave their public school with some idea of the duties which life in a civilized community demands of them, some idea of justice and fair play, some desire to make a corner of the world better and happier than it was before.'[68] But John Wilson in the early 1960s, in a refreshingly cant-free passage, was perhaps closer to the truth:

> Public school pupils are often lectured about the responsibility which goes with their privilege, and about their being the leaders of the future; but such talk cuts no ice with most of them, since they regard their privilege (in so far as they ever think about it) as the natural and proper prerogative of the class to which their parents belong. They feel responsible towards their parents and towards their school: but they, like those parents and that school, are part of a class system in which one class does not feel responsible for any other.[69]

So what instead did they take into the world? 'Typical public school products – by which I do not mean Etonian individualists or Wykehamist intellectuals – have many excellent qualities: they are basically secure, at least on a superficial level, generally honest, reliable and responsible,' reflected Wilson. 'But they are not critical, and one could hardly say that they are filled with love of reform … By and large they think things are all right.'[70]

The shift may have been towards the academic, but for quite a long time the quality of teachers in the sector remained decidedly patchy. 'Our teachers were the usual collection of eccentrics, drunks and no-hopers,' Jeremy Paxman has recalled about his prep school of the early 1960s. 'Latin masters whose threadbare jackets rattled with matchboxes filled with pinched-out fag-ends, their cigarette fingers stained the colour of mahogany, and the occasional young teacher whose enthusiasm carried him through it all regardless. One retired colonel who taught French was fired in front of the school over breakfast for failing to pass the marmalade to the headmaster's wife.'[71] Likewise, somewhat subjectively, the authors remember the teachers at their public schools later in the decade as varying from talented and inspiring on the one hand to more or less useless on the other.

Results could also vary wildly. At Westminster, for example, a consistently superb Oxbridge entrance and scholarship record was combined with an A-level failure rate in the mid-1960s of around 25 per cent.[72] 'In general there is little doubt that the public schools are fairly efficient academically,' claimed Wilson in 1962.[73] Others found a definitive judgement at the time almost impossible and, later, Wilson's optimistic assessment was not supported by one of the first scientific studies of private schools' effects, comparing boys at HMC (Headmasters' and Headmistresses' Conference) public schools with those at other types of school in this period. Using a large 1972 survey, A. H. Halsey and his colleagues analysed the academic achievements of the generation of boys at school in the post-Butler generation in the 1950s and 1960s, and found that 'boys of the *same* social background at HMC, Direct Grant, or grammar types of school had very similar O-level records', all three types doing signally better than children at other schools.[74] For those who stayed on till eighteen, the same equivalence between HMC, grammars and direct grants was largely true of A levels. What that study could not do was make full allowance for pupils' earlier achievements (at Marlborough in 1961, around one-third of the pupils had failed their eleven-plus, which, of course, was not the case at the grammars). Those at minor private schools had more academic success than those at secondary modern schools. 'For the affluent parents of less able children,' Halsey et al. concluded, 'the choice [private/state] was probably much more significant.' Nevertheless, by the 1960s class sizes were falling in the state sector, and its pupil–teacher ratio was starting to converge down towards what the private schools were offering: roughly one teacher for every thirteen pupils (see Figure 4).

Increasingly, the crux was how the public schools compared with the grammar schools. Whereas in 1959 the public schools were responsible for 55 per cent of the Oxbridge intake, by 1967 they were down to 38 per cent, with the majority of places going instead

FIGURE 4 The pupil–teacher ratio in England

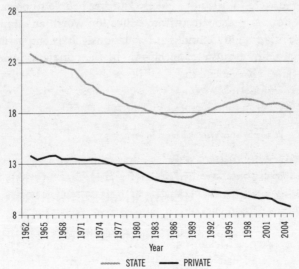

Source: Green, F., S. Machin, R. Murphy and Y. Zhu (2011), 'The Changing Economic Advantage from Private Schools', *Economica*, 79, 658–79.

to the grammars and direct grants.[75] 'The trickle of grammar-school boys to Oxbridge has turned into a flood,' observed Anthony Sampson in 1971, adding that 'both in intelligence and ambition they compete strongly with the public-school boys'.[76] A rival academic elite, in short, was threatening.

All of which raised the question, in the 1970s even more than in the 1960s, of whether the sector could justify its increasingly high fees. Ultimately, this depended on whether the schools could continue to deliver on their implicit promise of pupils going on to prestigious, well-paid careers. The contemporary evidence was reassuring enough. By 1970, for instance, 83 per cent of ambassadors, 80 per cent of the judiciary (high court judges and above), and 80 per cent of directors of clearing banks had been privately educated (see Figure 5); while in 1979, so too had 85 per cent of Church of England bishops, 86 per cent of top army officers (major-general and above), and 80 per cent of directors of financial institutions.[77] In terms of earning power, 1971 General Household Survey figures revealed that the privately educated were four times as likely as other people to be earning over £3,000 a year, with private education worth an additional £800 a year, a tidy sum then.[78] Obviously it is impossible to prove a definite causal connection, but the correlation was still striking.

FIGURE 5 Percentage privately educated in 1970

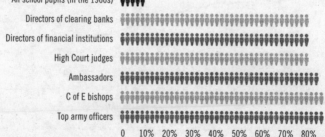

Even so, in the context of the steadily increasing importance of academic qualifications, would that school background go on being the golden ticket? Perhaps it would. For accessing the Oxbridge route, John Wilson noted 'a strong pull in favour of the public schools', and he cited the case (one among 'plenty of the same kind') of the boy who got a place at Oxford with only four O levels to show for him; while to read John Rae's diaries from the 1970s, when he was headmaster at Westminster, is to be struck by the almost shameless string-pulling ('one or two telephone calls are still necessary to find places for the borderlines').[79] Moreover, it was still far from necessary for the privately educated to go to Oxbridge, or even to university, in order to do well. Sampson, in his original *Anatomy of Britain* (1962), wrote illuminatingly about what he called 'the public school proletariat', who may have lacked a degree, perhaps even decent A-level grades, but instead had the old school tie, a face that fitted and were capable of flourishing in a club-like environment like the City, where whom you knew still mattered far more than what you knew.[80] Although ultimately their days were numbered, during the 1970s there were still plenty of them about.

'Are the public schools still going strong?' P. G. Wodehouse, living on Long Island, asked a British acquaintance shortly before his death in 1975.[81] It was a reasonable inquiry, given that the sector by the mid-1970s was under considerable financial pressure against a wider background of high inflation, substantial tax increases and a badly faltering economy. 'What are the economic chances of survival for the public schools?' wondered Gathorne-Hardy in 1977. 'Inflation has attacked them even more viciously than it has attacked everything else. This is because it is attacked from both ends. As the costs to the schools continue soaring, their fees become astronomical … Soon many schools will cost £2,000 a year.'[82] By 1978 the total of privately educated (prep school and public school) children in England and Wales was down to a post-war low of 403,000, representing some 4.5 per cent of the school population.[83] The pattern, though, was decline rather than collapse. Would it have been different if the second half of the 1970s had not also seen the conclusive ending of the great majority of state grammars and the decision by most of the direct grants, with the pending removal of their state funding, to move wholly into the private sector rather than become non-selective state schools? That is the great imponderable – and soon afterwards, one head, Shrewsbury's Eric Anderson, speculated that '60 per cent of the public schools would have gone under if the grammar schools had remained'.[84]

Even in adversity, or perhaps because of that adversity, the pace had been quickening of what John Rae would call 'the Public School Revolution'. In his 1981 book with that title, covering 1964–79 but majoring on the 1970s, he claimed that 'the admission of girls to boys' schools, the elevation of academic and cultural excellence above athleticism and philistinism, the aggressive and professional financial management, were all to a greater or lesser degree revolutionary, propelling the schools forward into a future that might in other circumstances have been delayed for a long time'.[85] While not denying that significant progress was made, subsequent assessments of those years have been more cautious, not only noting that it was not exactly the dark ages beforehand, but also pointing to the plentiful evidence of continuing academic patchiness. Take a trio of fairly typical recollections: a common room still inhabited by some 'veterans of the second world war, probably shell-shocked, or with some sort of hang-up, who led groups of boys to exam failure year in year out without ever being challenged'; of a science teacher, 'I don't recall one experiment ever working'; and, from landed families, boys at Eton who 'read only the *Sporting Life*, and that with difficulty'.[86] A leading sceptic of the Rae thesis is Mark Peel, who in his book *The New Meritocracy* (2015) argues – in our view convincingly, whatever our doubts about the title – that the *real* take-off in the private sector was after rather than before 1979. 'The truth was that the ancient regime wasn't yet history,' Peel contends. 'The atmosphere in schools may have relaxed, but facilities often remained Dickensian, the governance was amateurish and the common room still resembled a rarefied gentleman's club somewhat detached from the real world.'[87]

During the 1970s – a time when the middle class probably felt more threatened than in any other decade of the century – the deal on offer became increasingly explicit. Well aware that in 1978 a survey of fee-paying parents had found an average income of almost £13,000 a year, well over double the average family income, Rae the following year publicly described as 'privileged' his own school, Westminster, and went on: 'Parents are hardly likely to pay large sums out of taxed income so that their children can enjoy the benefits of disadvantage. The small classes, the good teaching, the beautiful, historic surroundings are there for all to see.'[88] Later studies which drew on the National Child Development Study – a cohort of children who had been born in 1958 and were at secondary school mainly in the 1970s – would bear out Rae's perception that, even when compared with children from similar backgrounds, the children at private schools were starting to perform distinctly better in public exams (as well as continuing to earn more in later life).[89] Rae himself was too committed a believer in the intrinsic (as opposed to instrumental) virtues of a high-quality, rounded education to wish to draw out the implication that the ultimate benefit that those parents really wanted was a significant increase in their children's life chances, above all in terms of getting good, well-paid jobs. That, though, was the reality. 'If they cannot accumulate or pass on money, the only way parents can benefit their children is by giving them a good education,' reflected Gathorne-Hardy in 1977 in the context of the Labour government's fiscal and other policies. 'Indeed, giving them a good academic education, or rather exam-passing education, is the only way to transmit wealth; a good education leads to a good job which leads to enough money to give your children a good education which …'[90] The ellipses were the author's, and he hardly needed to go on.

The pupils themselves by this time knew the score. 'Now more Wykehamists than in 1970 are thinking how best to achieve a reasonable income level when they are 25, and fewer are moved by the Great Causes – the Third World, Conservation, Pacifism,' regretfully concluded John Thorn, headmaster of Winchester, in 1978. 'Their aims are more familiar, and more comfortable. They are the bourgeois values of "getting on" …'[91] The political weather had not yet decisively changed, but the ground was already becoming fertile.

1979–2000: A Machine is Built

In the early 1980s the sociologist Irene Fox interviewed 190 sets of parents who for the academic year 1979–80 – the first full year of the Thatcher era – had sent their sons to various of 'the 122 traditionally independent public schools'. Strikingly, three-quarters of those parents had 'no first-hand knowledge of the provisions at the secondary level which they have rejected', while 45 per cent of the parents belonged to 'a social network where private education is the predominant mode of educating the children'. Why *exactly*, she asked, had they made their particular choice? The most frequent reason given was 'better academic results', but there were also strong showings for 'character and discipline training', 'children treated as individuals', 'get on better in life', and 'mix with a better type of child'. Fox then asked the parents *how* they reckoned that private schools would provide academic success for their children. Here the three main categories of answer were 'the nature of the teachers', 'the facilities at their disposal' and 'the other children in the school'. Altogether, she concluded, 'the overriding concern of the parents is to secure their sons' positions in the world of work'.[92]

Fox's findings undoubtedly chimed with what was now emerging as the unmistakable temper of the times. The 1980s – and their legacy – can be fairly characterised as being about explicitly encouraging and giving moral licence to people to 'get on' in a turbo-charged, individualistic, guilt-free way. What did 'get on' mean? Partly it was indeed about jobs, money and all that; but it was also about social status – and that, for some, meant private school for their children. Nor was it just a prevailing zeitgeist that now so dramatically favoured those private schools. 'For a long time in the 1980s, real spending on state schools stagnated, while the disposable incomes of the wealthy rose, as did spending in the private sector, and pupil–teacher ratios [in private schools] improved,' noted the political philosopher Harry Brighouse. And, writing in 2000, he added wholly justifiably that 'this has played no small part in the flourishing of the sector'.[93]

That was not all in the complicated balance (or imbalance) between the two sectors. 'In the competition for good jobs, it is the actual level of your qualifications that counts for most,' pointed out the sociologist Anthony Heath in 1981. 'Family background counts for less than it used to among the unqualified.' Put another way, the power of the old school tie was already in decline and would continue to be so, especially as recruitment methods for professional and managerial jobs were modernised. But Heath then added the crucial rider: 'The public schools may find it easier to win the competition for exam results against the new ranks of inexperienced comprehensive schools than they did in the heyday of the grammar school.'[94] So it proved: partly no doubt because of academic failings in the badly under-resourced state sector, but also because of very substantial academic improvement over the ensuing decades in the increasingly super-resourced private sector, during which time the gap between the private and state sectors in the pupil–teacher ratio was widening (as can be seen in Figure 4 above; see p. 85) – unlike in the difficult times of the 1960s when the gap was palpably becoming narrower. Importantly, the private schools were also not afraid, in response to changing pressures in the jobs market, to adjust their academic offering, including devoting significant resources to computers as well as non-traditional subjects like business studies.[95]

Then in 1991 came the first authoritative publication (in the *Daily Telegraph*) of league tables, almost instantly sending into overdrive the school-cum-parental focus on exam results.[96] Increasingly competitive between themselves, the private schools now left the state sector trailing. By 2000, the chasm was stark indeed. For GCSEs that year, over 51 per cent of private school entries attained grades A or A*, compared with the national rate of less than 16 per cent; for A levels, 36 per cent of private school entries achieved grade A, just over double the national percentage.[97] Back in 1991, only fourteen private schools had managed a 70 per cent A-level pass rate at A and B; by 2002 this was true of ninety-one private schools.[98] Again, the scientific studies that allow for the prior attainment and the social background of the pupils subsequently bore out the academic prowess that private schools had now achieved.[99] In what most parents probably *did* want most of all, the schools and their increasingly well-qualified, well-paid, non-maverick teachers were bringing home the bacon.

Academic success was supported and complemented – in terms of the overall offer to parents, if not necessarily in terms of educational value – by the so-called 'arms race' from the 1980s in infrastructure. 'You should always have a building on the go, like your knitting,' Heather Brigstocke, high mistress of St Paul's Girls, urged her bursar, as across the sector sports halls, theatres, new technology centres and much else sprang up, epitomised in 1988 by Harrow's gleaming, lavishly equipped CDT (computer and design technology) centre.[100] Boarding facilities began to be transformed, while at Tonbridge by the 1990s the sporting facilities were such as to make not only a casual visitor from the neighbourhood but any old boy from a previous generation rub their eyes in astonishment:

> We had [recalled the England cricketer Ed Smith] twelve rugby pitches, each tended to perfection and cut in geometric stripes. We had two hockey Astroturfs that doubled up as twenty-one tennis courts. We had a rackets court. We had seven fives courts. We had four squash courts. We had an Olympic-standard running track. We had more cricket nets – ten artificial ones, and ten grass ones – than any professional team I ever played for.

'Astonishing' is Smith's word for the quality of the 1st XI cricket pitch and playing area. 'Lord's, the most famous ground in the world, has the smoothest outfield I ever fielded on. The *second* best is my school ground.'[101] All the time the amount of money flowing into these schools continued its relentless upwards trajectory. 'These are the highest levels of investment in the fabric and facilities of schools ever recorded,' reported the sector's annual census in 2000 about the schools spending on building almost £800 per pupil (up 28 per cent), 'reflecting expenditure on information and communications technology, updated boarding accommodation and new facilities as schools expand their age ranges or become co-educational. They also follow other substantial rises in previous years.'[102] At a time when the state sector was taking stock of the implications of two decades of serious under-investment, J. K. Galbraith's famous contrast between 'private affluence' and 'public squalor' could hardly have been writ any larger.

'It is a business nowadays,' observed Jeremy Paxman in 1990 after a field trip to Rugby. 'A quarter of the pupils are the sons of old boys, but it is a declining proportion, and marketing is the name of the game ... The school has a press officer and employs a firm of public relations consultants. The prospectus is impressive – facilities for art and sculpture, biology and physics, music and languages as well as the inevitable range of sports ...' In short: 'What the successful public schools offer now is a service industry.'[103] Or as David Hare (Lancing) would succinctly put it, 'Private schools have changed from being places where you're flogged to places you flog.'[104] The sector as a whole was indeed now becoming a business, a service industry, in almost every sense except the obvious profit-making one. Looking back in 2015 on the makings of 'A very British business', *The Economist*'s 'Schumpeter' identified the 1980s as the decade when the private schools first 'spotted a big business opportunity, as the market for secondary education globalised along with everything else'. To attract the children of what would soon become identified as the super-wealthy global elite, British private schools had, added 'Schumpeter', two distinct advantages: not only teaching 'in the world's de facto business language', but also with many being situated 'within striking distance of London, one of the world's great global cities'.[105] Crucially, and underpinning its offer to the affluent (whether from abroad or not), the 1980s and perhaps above all the 1990s were the decades when the sector went through a notable governance revolution: this involved (among other things) much greater accountability to parents, the schools being inspected by a government-approved agency, regular staff appraisals, and boards of governors comprising fewer bishops and more businessmen.[106]

Overall, the 1980s and 1990s can be viewed as the period in which the private sector took a major gamble – increasing fees at a rate far above inflation – and, through a mixture of its own efforts and a largely benign environment, came up smelling of roses. Numbers increased significantly in the course of the 1980s and, after a significant blip caused by the economic downturn of the early 1990s, recovered strongly towards the end of the century; by 2000 there were 561,000 children, 6.7 per cent of all school children, at private schools in England.[107] A distinct contributor to the sector's fortunes, funnelling government money to the schools, was the Assisted Places Scheme (APS), introduced by the Tories in 1980 and abolished after New Labour came to power in 1997. At the time it ended, some 40,000 pupils were APS beneficiaries.[108] Who were they? In theory, according to the avowed intentions of the APS's founders, they were bright and high-potential working-class children; but in practice, over the course of the APS's life, the beneficiaries were almost entirely middle-class, as creative accountants made mincemeat of means-testing based on income not assets.[109] For the schools themselves, it was, without being unduly cynical, a triple win: subsidy from the state; no loss of independence; and minimal dilution of social exclusiveness – that crucial if seldom explicitly articulated selling point.

What about the impact of scholarships and bursaries on their intake? The two most detailed analyses – by Clive Griggs in the mid-1980s and Ted Tapper in the mid-1990s – both reached essentially the same conclusion. 'The widely held belief that scholarships are available on a lavish scale is completely unfounded,' asserted Griggs. Moreover, most of those scholarships that were available 'help to reduce the fees of those already well able to afford them'.[110] As for bursaries, Tapper noted that 'an interesting feature of many bursary schemes is not so much that they are designed to aid those with financial needs, but that assistance is often directed at very specific occupational groups', such as clergy and officers in the armed services, not to mention former pupils, with relatively few from those earmarked groups falling into the category of the 'especially needy'.[111] 'The trouble is that the competition for these awards keeps the academic standard of the scholarship exam very high,' reflected Winchester's James Sabben-Clare about the situation there in the late 1980s. 'The best preparation for it is to be found at a good private school, and that cannot but limit the field from which the scholars are drawn. Untutored genius is very hard to measure against skilfully coached competence.' No change, then, from a century earlier following the Clarendon Commission; while more broadly, he declared – with undoubted sincerity – that 'it would be in accordance with the wishes of the founder and of all present members of the staff to see a Winchester education made available to any who would like it and could profit from it'. However, went on Sabben-Clare, 'this would be impossible without sacrificing the independence that makes the place what it is'.[112]

That was a debate for another day. In the meantime, the private schools of the late twentieth century had a demanding, high-maintenance, high-expectations service to deliver. What, though, was that service's ultimate purpose? Harrow's headmaster, Ian Beer, was clear enough in 1989 about what he envisaged as his own institution's purpose: that it was 'to be seen to be producing from the School pupils who will become men of integrity to manage our own country and its institutions, and also pupils who are motivated by the power of the spirit to go out into the world to work to the service of others'.[113] Yet in reality the prevailing ethos by this time was very different. Geoffrey Walford's well-researched and admirably objective *Life in Public Schools* (1986) included evidence all pointing in the same direction: the careers master who summed up the main concern of the pupils as, 'How do I get on in this rat race, and how do I make money, and how do I get a good job?'; the headmaster coming under sustained pressure from parents of sixth-form pupils not to waste their offspring's time on general studies instead of taking an extra A level; the shift from team games to individually competitive sports; and the questionnaire revealing that fewer than a quarter of the pupils 'felt that the school promoted service to the community', with instead 'most convinced that the school's main purpose should be to ensure that they got the required examination results'.[114] In 1987, not long after stepping down from Westminster, John Rae wrote strikingly in *The Times* about 'Tom Brown's Porsche days', arguing that the schools, whatever their misgivings, now endorsed 'the priorities of the age: every man for himself in the competition for good A levels, a good university, a well-paid job and a red Porsche to roar up the school drive, scattering your former teachers like nature's rejects in the race of life'.[115] Such was seemingly the case at Rugby itself a century and a half after Thomas Arnold. 'By comparison with the vision of nineteenth-century idealists, there was a frankly selfish streak to their view of the world,' Paxman found at the end of the 1980s after interrogating some of the boys. 'The question "Does the idea of service mean anything to you?" drew only bewilderment.' He also quoted a bishop who was a frequent visitor to several major private schools: 'The idea of Vocation has almost disappeared. It's quite frightening how selfish the pupils have become. They are overwhelmingly out for themselves.' All of which left Paxman to conclude that 'the idea that duty is owed in return for privilege is deeply unfashionable'.[116] No doubt it is possible to exaggerate; no doubt there were exceptions. But in the end a service industry, putting its services up for sale at ever more expensive prices, lives and dies by the priorities of its customers.

Six centuries on from William of Wykeham, and looking across that lengthy span, a trio of conclusions might have suggested themselves by the end of the twentieth century: that never since almost the earliest days had – whatever the intentions of the founders – a private school education been other than highly socially exclusive; that it was only very late on that the overall quality of education at private schools reached a genuinely high level; and that any reformer of the structure of British education would have to start by acknowledging that these are deeply entrenched institutions with no tradition of openness to the rest of society. All that, though, is now history, if far from irrelevant history. What about the schools in the new millennium?

4

Learning and Luxury: Private Schools in the Twenty-First Century

After many years of super-investment, modernisation and development, private schools might seem unfamiliar places to those who knew them in the 1970s and before. For the great majority of the population who have never set foot inside a private school, they are an alien world. Yet schools are schools, there for educating children. What does it feel like to be educated at a *private* school in twenty-first-century Britain? What is it about these schools that delivers a good-quality education? Do they have something that could be harnessed to society at large to give a fairer and more effective national system of education? And why have they become so astonishingly expensive?

It might seem self-evident that, with all their improvements and riches, these schools should be happy places in which to learn and grow up. 'The many opportunities offered to children at private school shower a feeling of well-being and prestige on all pupils,' observed one contributor to a Mumsnet conversation in 2012.[1] Yet to judge from some headteachers' fears, an increasingly competitive, individualistic society has spawned pressurised hothouses, with overly driven children egged on by parents and teachers alike to excel both in their academic work and in their cultural and sporting pursuits. Older generations of privately educated boarders might well rue, looking back, the spartan conditions they once endured; but those complaints have been replaced by modern anxieties – exam pressures, body image and anorexia. Andrew Halls, head of King's College School, Wimbledon, has voiced his concern about teenagers' obsessions with physical perfection, and called for help to equip children with 'emotional resilience'.[2] Chris Jeffrey, head of Cheshire's Grange School and chair of the HMC's wellbeing committee, has agreed that 'young people in the schools we represent need more help in coping with much of what life throws at, and demands of, them'.[3] Many private schools – in addition to absorbing the lessons of historic scandals relating to physical and sexual abuse – have been learning to cope with children misusing social media, including cyber bullying. Since 2006 Wellington College has pioneered wellbeing lessons in the curriculum. By 2015 nearly half the HMC schools had increased their provision of counselling; and to address the more serious mental health issues, some of the wealthier schools deploy the services of in-house clinical psychologists or psychiatrists.

Welfare activities like this give the false impression, however, that children are more especially at risk in *private* schools. Young people in *all* types of school have twenty-first-century pressures to face up to as they approach adulthood. Notwithstanding the mental health worries – and despite the clutch of sexual abuse revelations surrounding some boarding schools – the reality is that private schools have the resources to address the concerns facing young people, even if they cannot always be resolved. Many parents temper their ambitions for their children's success with a desire that their children should also enjoy school, as one in-depth study of girls' lives at top private schools has found.[4] And on the whole, the evidence tells us, private school children tend to be more content with their lives than state school children. Among the Millennium Cohort Study's representative sample of children born in 2000–1, those being privately educated at the age of fourteen were more likely to be happy with their school work and the way they looked, and generally more likely to be satisfied with themselves. The children at the richer private schools were even happier. On the downside of mental health, we get the same picture: 23 per cent of the privately educated – as opposed to 32 per cent of those in state schools – said that it was 'true'/'sometimes true' that they 'didn't enjoy anything at all'. And children self-harming – an inordinately distressing phenomenon – is no more common for private school pupils than it is for state school children.[5] The image of an especially stressed and unhappy *private* school child is illusory.

A Question of Resources

The key to private school children's higher wellbeing – greater resources – applies across the board to all the schools' activities. Most ordinary members of the public would be frankly astonished were they ever to stroll inside one of the more affluent private schools and just look around. Let us dwell, for a moment, on the riches of Eton, alma mater of so many of Britain's political leaders over the years. Inside the gates we find a cornucopia. There are twenty-four well-equipped and staffed science laboratories, an amazing set of libraries, resource centres (backed up by a study centre in Florence), a research centre to improve children's learning outcomes, societies covering anything from astronomy to entrepreneurship, multiple orchestras, bands and choirs, and music lessons in most instruments. The visitor would observe a large number of academic staff and small class sizes: the school boasts a ratio of one full-time teacher for fewer than eight children, together with a multitude of support staff. For nascent artists there are stimulating exhibition trips, an 'artist in residence', and facilities – including 3D studios – for printmaking, drawing, painting, sculpture, ceramics, computer graphics and photography. For hopeful actors and dramatists there are three well-equipped theatres, and other convertible drama spaces. There is a budget for extensive field trips and foreign exchanges, concerts and mountaineering expeditions. There is a sports programme of rugby, hockey, football, cricket, rowing, athletics, squash and any number of minor pursuits from badminton and beagling to water polo and windsurfing. From the Olympics-spec rowing lake to the famous 'playing fields', every sport is extremely well equipped.

The Combined Cadet Force (CCF) has its own purpose-built 'orderly room', and a set of staff trained in the military. There are also extensive organised opportunities for community activities. As for their living conditions, the children have their own study-bedrooms, while their health and wellbeing are supported by three school doctors, five nurses, a consultant psychiatrist and a multi-faith pastoral support team.

Of course, not all private schools have such luxury, and there are many less well-known, less affluent schools which do not figure in *Tatler*'s annual schools review. Even these, however, can boast impressive resources, not least in their high number of teachers. Class sizes have been coming down ever since the start of the Thatcher era as private schools took on more and more teachers. By 2016 the pupil–teacher ratio had reached just 8.6:1; meanwhile, despite better financing following New Labour's renewed emphasis on education, the pupil–teacher ratio in state schools still stood at more than 17:1.

Thus, remarkably, each state school teacher instructs roughly twice the number of pupils faced by teachers in private schools. It is sometimes also claimed that teachers' skills are greater in the private than in the state sector, but this comparison is complex. It is not easy to identify effective teaching from afar, as any head will testify, so one should not be at all confident about generalisations concerning teacher quality. Moreover, teaching in the two sectors may sometimes require notably different skill sets. While teachers in the private sector are less likely to have a teaching qualification, proportionately more private school teachers have obtained degrees from high-ranking universities and earned good grades; more also have a post-graduate qualification, and more are specialists in maths and sciences, typically the subjects where teachers are in short supply.[6] Private school heads are also increasingly successful at attracting experienced teachers from state schools; this matters because teachers' skills develop considerably over the first few years in the classroom. In 2017–18 the net annual transfer of full-time experienced teachers from the state to the private sector numbered over 1,800: this had become the single largest source of new teachers, twice the total recruited from Initial Teacher Training courses and other university degrees.[7] In London and the South-east – where teacher-intensive private schools are concentrated and where, as a result, one in four teachers is working at a private school – private schools' poaching of state-trained teachers accentuates the teacher shortages often faced by state schools, especially those in the scarce specialisms of science and technology. From the science teachers' perspective, part of the private sector's attraction is the more abundant opportunities to teach their own specialist subject at A level.

The private/state gap in other resources is even larger than the teaching gap; indeed, the most expensive schools spend (proportionately) more of their budgets on facilities and non-teaching staff, as well as the little things that make life bearable.[8] At St Paul's Girls' School, for instance, a typical menu includes such sophisticated dishes as Spanish smoky samfaina (a Catalan-Valencian dish) with eggs and rocket; slow-baked Moroccan lamb with broad beans, prunes and preserved lemon; and Malaysian snapper curry with okra and tomato.[9] Or take boarding infrastructure. 'Chic interiors, designer lighting, ocean views and a rave review in *Tatler*'[10] is how the *Daily Telegraph* describes the new accommodation at Roedean, thought by its head to be good for business, attracting rich girls to apply. According to one architect working to equip private schools, en suite bathrooms are included in all projects. 'Gone are the days of big dorms – it's got to be more of a home away from home. Parents want carpets, sinks in bedrooms, nice cupboards and space. You don't want a child having to do their homework sitting on their bed.' The parents of one recent applicant to Rugby School inquired after 'a duplex with *en suite*' for their child.[11] And a *Sunday Times* investigation in 2017 found that private schools in London have fifty-nine theatres – many of them state-of-the-art – compared with the West End's often dilapidated forty-two. Its findings 'highlight the extraordinary facilities on offer at many of Britain's private schools, unlike some in the state sector that do not have much beyond a small playground'.[12] Likewise, private schools' lavish music facilities, when set against the decline

FIGURE 5 Resources for State School Pupils and Private School Fees in 2016
(£ per annum)

State Schools in England Resources per pupil		Private School Fees (UK)		
			Day	Boarding
Pre-school	1,700	Nursery	3,001	n/a
Primary	4,800	Prep	12,234	22,716
Secondary (up to age 16)	6,200	Senior (below 6th form)	14,466	30,651
6th Form	5,000	6th Form	15,333	32,208
FE College	5,600			
All boarding	10,500			

Source: various.[15]

of music teaching in state schools, are ensuring that musical
education is becoming even more confined to the elite.[13] With so
many remarkable sporting facilities thrown in, journalist Ben Chu's
jokey epithet for Britain's private schools – 'luxury country clubs
with quite a nice school attached' – is strikingly close to the mark.[14]

Just how large the per capita resources gap between private
and state schools actually is cannot be found in any published
source; but piecing together the jigsaw from several places reveals
a pattern of gross disparity. The main story comes from fees, by far
the largest source of private schools' income. For private primary
and lower-secondary day pupils, the fees in 2016 were about two
and a half times times the annual resources devoted to educating
each pupil in state primary schools – see Figure 5, above. In sixth
forms the ratio was more like three times, though a little less for
students in Further Education colleges. Indeed, given that many
state-educated pupils are not in school or college beyond sixteen,
the state's education spending per head of the 16–18 population
was, at £3,500, *less than a quarter* of the £15,333 that the families of
private school sixth-formers were spending on school fees. Even
more striking is the private–state gap for boarders, for whom the
annual fees were £32,208. This boarding fee income delivers the
luxurious living conditions; yet much more is involved, including

numerous educational and developmental opportunities which would normally not be available to pupils at home. In the relatively small number of state boarding schools, resources for each child were just £10,500 a year.

Schools' fee income is eaten into by about 10 per cent because income is foregone when fee reduction assistance is provided through scholarship, bursaries and other discounts. Yet private schools also benefit from other sources of income. A few have notable commercial interests, such as those schools that have opened foreign branches in China, selling their English brand of education to China's elites. Dulwich is a leader, with four branches in China and one each in Myanmar, Singapore and South Korea. Another source is charitable donations and legacies, normally from school alumni or their families – satisfied and grateful customers. Needless to say, charitable donations to schools in the state sector are minute; but for the private schools, donations build up over the long term to make a sizeable contribution to their facilities. Over the two years 2014 and 2015, Wycliffe School (an all-through private school in Gloucestershire) struck lucky – receiving donations of £347,000, some 1.3 per cent of its income. In other schools, donations of rather less than 1 per cent of income are more common.[16] For example, Rugby received in that period only 0.6 per cent on top of its fee income; while Barnard Castle School, an all-through private school in Durham of far lower means and relatively low fees, benefited only £72,000, less than half a per cent of its income. At The Purcell School, a specialist music school in outer London, donations ran to the tune of 0.7 per cent.

Even if they do not amount to a great deal each year, in time donations make a real difference when invested in private schools' infrastructures. Previous years' gifts become capitalised into the schools' assets, physical and financial; present-day private school governors are, then, custodians of the generosity of philanthropists long gone. The effect is to add considerably to the resources available for current students to use, especially in the case of the older schools.

A school's present endowments stem from all such former donations together with other investments. Taking the country as a whole, private schools' capital spending in 2013 was increasing following a pause in the wake of the financial crash of 2008, reaching £1,500 per pupil;[17] after that no figures have been reported. Assuming that the increase continued after 2013, along with rises in fees, the capital spending for each child would have been approximately double the amount spent in English state schools in 2016 (just £860). With such a gap in investment, the cumulative effects on wealth are potentially huge. The schools' endowed facilities must therefore also be reckoned with, if we are fully to grasp the differences between children's access to resources in the two sectors. 'Tangible assets' – their buildings and facilities – are normally by far the largest part of schools' wealth, and the divergence between the private and state sectors is there to be seen by the naked eye as one walks through the school gates.

Some of this wealth is tallied in schools' published accounts, public access to which is thankfully assured for all those among schools that are registered as charities (see Figure 6). Thus, Wycliffe had net assets valued in 2015 at roughly £23 million, nearly twice its annual income, amounting to some £30,700 per pupil. Barnard Castle's assets were a great deal lower, at just £8,500 per pupil. In contrast, Purcell's net assets were £68,700 per pupil, while Rugby and Eton had accumulated as much as £141,400 and £281,600 respectively for each pupil. At the primary level, St Christopher's (Hampstead) had assets worth £52,500 per pupil. Compare these amounts with some typical state schools: Skipton Academy, a secondary school in Yorkshire and part of a multi-academy trust, had net assets of £7,400 per pupil; Chadwell Heath Academy, a more affluent state secondary school in the London Borough of Redbridge, had £14,300 assets per pupil. At Latchmere School, a state primary in affluent Kingston upon Thames, there was £13,400 per pupil; while St Bunyan Academy Primary School in Penzance came in with just £6,800 per pupil.

Taken together – the fees, the donations, the resources flowing from endowed capital – all this means that the size of the private/

FIGURE 6 Examples of school wealth as assessed by net assets per pupil

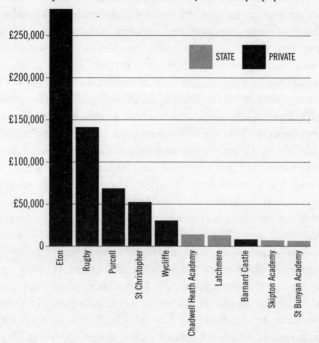

state resources chasm looks to be a ratio of roughly three to one (though it may be somewhat larger than this at certain ages, somewhat smaller at others). Three to one: in anybody's arithmetic, the fundamental unfairness is a huge and unconscionable scar on the face of our children's future.

The Resources Gap and the Gilded Path

So what are the implications for life chances? The evidence of Chapter 1 is unequivocal: when compared with children from similar backgrounds who go to state schools, the children at private schools generally perform better in exams, have easier access to high-status universities and in turn enjoy better fortunes in their later work lives. The privately schooled then exercise a huge and disproportionate influence on British society. When we see how well they perform in so many cultural and sporting fields, who can doubt that these successes stem in large part from an education that is steeped in these same sporting and cultural activities, using the very best facilities available? Or that the head start in access to high-ranking universities and then to well-paid and influential jobs is greatly aided by all the schools' wealth of ancillary resources?

Part of the superior resources is devoted explicitly to working the system, securing 'positional' advantages for their pupils. An analysis by BBC Radio 4's *Today* programme finds that the schools first gain a small but significant edge in exams by securing additional time for disproportionately more students. They can do this, according to one insider, because they can devote more resources than state schools to identifying potentially entitled students by virtue of their special needs.[18] Private schools also spend liberally on exam mark challenges – which often pay off – while state schools must closely watch their exam budget purse, and can more rarely appeal their students' given grades. The imbalance, notes one private head (Richard Russell of Colfe's in Lee), is 'inherently unfair'.[19] In Scotland, figures from the Scottish Qualifications Authority in 2017 show that private schools are almost three times more likely to challenge the marks their pupils receive in national exams.[20]

Perhaps most striking is the deployment of expertise in order to secure places at high-ranking universities, through the recruitment of teachers with experience of these universities and a cadre of specialist advisers. Top private schools have copious staff and consultants on hand to assist pupils and parents, not only with British university entrance, but also with access to universities in the United States or continental Europe. As journalist Paul Mason observes, there is a 'massive asymmetry of information in the post-16 education system ... Kids at private school can rely on schools that have continual informal contact with elite universities', resulting in 'an inbuilt advantage based on informal knowledge'.[21] Thus private schools have been particularly adept at persuading their pupils to apply on an informed basis, steering them to less popular subjects where their chances of acceptance are maximised, making advantageously optimistic A-level grade predictions, and coaxing universities – especially the elite Russell Group universities – into accepting them.[22]

For all these reasons, private school children have enjoyed a significantly greater chance of admission into one of these top universities, when compared with state school children who have the same A-level scores and social class background. The unequal balance of resources in the two school sectors has thus supported an unfair system of university access. Meanwhile, well-staffed alumni offices are able to marshal the social networks of 'old boys' and 'old girls' to assist with inspirational career talks and employment links.

It is less *immediately* obvious, however, that private schools' superior resources contribute to their pupils' good academic performance in tests and national exams. Parents believe that small class sizes help, but for many years some educational economists have been sceptical whether class size and resources overall matter so much. Hundreds of studies have been conducted around the world to try to find out how much difference it makes to have fewer pupils in the classroom. It has been a tricky issue to untangle, because one cannot get at the answer simply by comparing the results of how children in small and large classes perform. The differences are affected by the fact that children may be in smaller classes because they need additional attention, for reasons that could affect how well they perform; so the differences do not reflect the *causal* impact of being in a smaller class. The ideal would be a randomised control trial (RCT) to test the question experimentally – just as is done when health scientists want to know the effect of a medical treatment – by allocating pupils at random to smaller classes for a period of time and then logging their results. A rare example of an RCT among educational economists is Project STAR, which took place at seventy-nine schools in the US state of Tennessee during the 1990s. This study found that a reduction of seven pupils per class led to a substantial increase in students' test outcomes, and also to positive long-term educational outcomes.[23] Nevertheless, there were difficulties with the study, including drop-outs from the experiment; sometimes the pupils, it turned out, were not genuinely assigned at random to the smaller classes, and as a result there is no consensus about the strength of the findings. And in most circumstances an RCT is impossible for practical or ethical reasons.

Instead, in later studies social scientists have examined the effects of coincidental variations in class size that sometimes arise from idiosyncratic educational policies. This requires some ingenuity. One notable example is from Sweden where, during much of the 1960s to 1980s, the law stipulated a class-size cap of thirty.[24] When school enrolment randomly rose above a multiple of thirty a new class had to be generated, which lowered class size substantially. Accordingly, the children in the smaller classes were there by chance, not because they were selected to be there. This study found that a large reduction in class size, between the ages of eleven and thirteen, led to substantial long-term improvements in performance – both later on in their education and beyond in the workplace. A similar inventive trick has been used in a 2016 United States study to untangle the impact of total funding. Court-mandated reforms have varied the level of funding from state to state, district to district, and over time. Using these externally driven changes, it has been shown that more resources in total can and do substantially improve educational attainment in the long run – especially for lower-income pupils – and add to pupils' later chances in the labour market.[25] Other studies, however, have found smaller effects; and some have held that only modest gains would derive from lowering class size in state schools by the small amounts that would be feasible with constrained budgets, relative to what could be achieved with an improvement in the quality of teachers.[26]

Nevertheless, with the teacher–pupil ratio difference between private and state schools in Britain so large, so very far from marginal, the only credible conclusion is that the private schools' much greater resources do make a substantial difference to educational performance, even if this is far from all there is to it. So, with the state-of-the-art evidence, it seems that, if parents believe that the private schools' *much* smaller class sizes – and very superior educational resources – will benefit their children, they are almost certainly right.

Private School Peers

If these parents also think that the other children at school affect the learning and development of their own offspring, they are again wise. Each child is influenced by the environment created by friends and other pupils in the classroom and across the school. It might be competition with smart fellow pupils that leads a child on, or the 'shining light' of a few model hard-working students. Conversely, it might be the disruptive behaviour of a few 'bad apples' that distracts the teacher, or the absorption of an anti-intellectual culture that holds a child back.

We know from studies around the world's classrooms that peers make a difference.[27] Just as before, to assess the impact of peers requires some ingenuity, and one of the most convincing studies took advantage of a natural freak event. Hurricane Katrina, when it struck the New Orleans area in 2005, causing thousands of casualties and enormous damage, also had a big educational impact. Schools had to close, families were rehoused, and large numbers of evacuee children were reallocated to schools elsewhere in Louisiana or in neighbouring Texas. Salvaging knowledge from disaster, education economists found, by studying the effects on the children whose classes they joined, that high-achieving students benefited when they were joined by high-achieving evacuees. Other studies show peer effects not only on children's academic achievements, but also on social outcomes as diverse as sexual experimentation, healthy eating and swimming speeds. The importance of all these effects varies: for example, a study in the Netherlands finds that children's English and Dutch language grades, but not their maths marks, are positively affected by their friends' grades.[28] Just occasionally the effects are seen to work in the opposite direction: through loss of self-esteem, some children in the presence of high-ability peers reduce their effort.[29] On the whole, however, peer effects from industrious children on other children are positive. In English state schools, both girls and boys do appreciably better if there is a low proportion of classroom peers having very poor prior attainment; while girls of all abilities, but not boys, appear to benefit from the presence of especially smart peers.[30]

Whether stemming from the private school children's home environment – largely affluent, mainly with university-educated parents from the professional and managerial classes, carrying high hopes for their children – or from the schools' scholarship programmes, or from their freedom to refuse entry to or expel difficult children, there is a concentration of pupils in the private sector with higher than average aspirations and prior attainments, and fewer than average behavioural or psychological challenges. Among the children of the Millennium Cohort Study, we can compare those who were at private and state secondary schools at the age of fourteen, ranking their verbal skills at a time (aged eleven) before they arrived at their secondary school from 100 down to 1. The verbal skills of the middling private school child stood at the 68th rung, well above the 50th rung for the general population. If we rank children's psychological problems (again, at eleven) on a standard scale from 1 to 100, the middling private school child comes in at thirty-five, that is, down in the bottom half of the spectrum. The scale sums up emotional symptoms, conduct problems, hyperactivity and difficulties with relationships – all factors that affect *other* children's learning.[31]

Thus, even though it will vary from school to school, on the whole private schools benefit from a peer-resource advantage on top of their advantage in financial and material resources. The disproportionate concentrations of children with high self-esteem and self-confidence from affluent, high-social-class families are part of what lies behind the famed private school 'polish and push'. The cultivation of upper-class values and attitudes, the stimulation of high aspirations in the children, the generation of a sense of entitlement – all these are likely to come as much through peer influence as from any conscious school policies.

And a new substantive peer group has significantly penetrated private schools in the twenty-first century: the children of foreign nationals, paying to gain the advantages of a high-quality education and an immersion in English language speaking and British upper-class culture. The number of foreign pupils from all continents has climbed steadily, and by 2018 there are almost 30,000 studying in Britain's private schools while their parents continue to live abroad. The largest group is from mainland China and Hong Kong, and there are also substantial contingents from Russia, Nigeria, Germany and elsewhere in Europe. These pupils bring the high-social-class attitudes and aspirations of a foreign culture. Yet according to one in-depth study of girls in four private schools, the presence of foreign pupils far from guarantees that pupils will adopt more cosmopolitan attitudes.[32] For the schools, moreover, the influx is mainly about money, even if, to minimise the risk of alienating British consumers, it is presented as part of the schools' ethos. The export of the English public school goes hand in hand with internationalisation in many areas of economic and social life, notwithstanding the cultural retreats that may come to surround Britain's exit from the European Union. One symptom is the broader spectrum of destination universities now being advanced by private schools' advisers, with the United States a favoured place for those with sufficient resources: between 2014 and 2016 the number of British private school pupils heading to American universities rose by a fifth, with New York University the most favoured choice, at a cost of £136,000 for a four-year undergraduate degree.[33] Globalism is also manifested in private schools' many international tours and exchanges.

Independent governance: another factor, producing better management?

The huge gaps in teaching and physical resources complemented by the peer-resource gap are thus the main features of Britain's private schools that enable them to promote their pupils' path to prosperity and influence. Are there also other factors contributing to these schools' advantage? Sometimes it is airily maintained that private schools do better, especially in exams, *simply because* they are private and independent of government. According to one confident private school insider and protagonist, 'The freedom of the independent sector to use resources as it thinks best, employ additional staff, teach a broader curriculum, impose its own disciplinary code, meet particular needs and promote independent thinking have all been central to its success.'[34] Andrew Adonis – New Labour's schools minister from 2005 to 2008 – later appeared to take a similar view when he urged that state academies should be sponsored by successful private schools, whose 'DNA' incorporated 'independence, excellence, innovation, social mission'.[35]

Is there any substance behind these claims? Autonomy, when backed by good professional training for teachers and strong regulatory bodies such as England's Ofsted or Wales' Estyn, or the private schools' Independent Schools Inspectorate, has been shown across the world to have beneficial effects on schools and their pupils.[36] Yet the reality in Britain is that any private/state differences in the freedom to use resources are minor, compared with the huge divergence in the magnitude of those resources; and the presumption that private schools are somehow better managed than state schools is, from the available evidence, simply not correct.

The main way in which state school and private school freedoms and independence are very different concerns pupil recruitment: state school admissions must generally conform to government-imposed codes. In about half of schools, admissions decisions are approved by Local Authorities; academic record is only a minor factor in state schools, the exception being areas with grammar schools. Private schools, by contrast, often look to a child's assessed academic record or feeder school recommendation; residence in a particular area is rarely relevant. There is also a difference, of course, in how the size of the budget is determined: the state school must accept the per-student funding set by government, whereas the private school can, within market realities, decide on the fees it will charge, as well as managing its reserves with fewer constraints.

Beyond these, the differences in this area between private and state schools can easily be overstated. On the whole, Britain's schools have, by international standards, a high general level of autonomy from the state.[37] For example, it is *not* the case – as it is in some countries – that state school teachers are centrally employed, formally allocated to schools, and especially hard to dismiss for poor performance. Deciding how budgets are to be spent is an important dimension of autonomy, and this is a key area where the evidence confirms a beneficial effect.[38] In virtually all state schools (96 per cent), headteachers have considerable responsibility for this allocation. Almost all state school leaders (with their governing boards) can, like private school heads, select their teachers, though a few do so in combination with their Local Authorities; most can also establish disciplinary policies (94 per cent).[39] There are no large private/state differences in the extent to which the teachers or headteachers believe they can determine course content. All teachers, whatever their idiosyncrasies, are ultimately constrained in what they teach by Britain's centralised examination systems. Where they diverge is that the resources of private schools enable them to offer a broader curriculum with more optional subjects, including, for example, more opportunities to study languages of one's choice, ancient and modern.

Differences in autonomy between the two sectors have become smaller as a result of the conversion since 2010 of many thousands of state schools, primary and secondary, into 'academies'. The freedom to manage independently is considerable for the leaders of stand-alone academy schools that are not part of academy chains, and also for the trustees and executives of academy chains, though less so for the heads of schools within multi-academy trusts.[40] But unlike the first wave of 'sponsored academies', which brought some improvements during the 2000s to low-performing schools through a rejuvenation of their leadership, the main wave of post-2010 'converter academies' has seen no discernible overall impact on their pupils' academic performance at either primary or secondary level, though there is variation between different academy chains.[41]

Competition is also held by some to be good for school performance, though since school choice has become integral to state education policy there is now moderate competition among both private and state schools. A more plausible possibility is that direct parental pressure on teachers and on management might contribute to the different outcomes for private and state-educated children. Despite the formal presence of parents on state school governing bodies, parental pressure is stronger in private schools. Teachers complain, notes Mary Bousted, president of the Association of Teachers and Lecturers, about parents' 'sense of entitlement' when they assert 'we are paying all this money for our children to be educated, therefore we expect you to get them through exams with very good grades and go to a top university'.[42] Because parents are typically in managerial or professional positions in which they are used to exercising authority, they often have the cultural and material resources to intervene in schools. The City banker's child, when things are not going well at school, is likely to find her father calling up her private school headteacher. Some argue that overzealous interventions at all hours have served only to stress both teachers and heads. In truth, while ex-Fettes history teacher Mark Peel concludes plausibly that 'despite the tension caused, accountability to parents has undoubtedly forced schools to raise their standards', nobody knows quite how much difference such parental pressure makes.[43]

Notwithstanding the private/state parental-pressure divergence, and any small differences in the autonomy of school leaders, Britain's private schools are in general no better managed than state schools. Pondering the stop-start record of the government's private-public sponsorship strategy, *Guardian* journalist John Harris asks whether 'beyond smaller class sizes and the comparative ease of teaching students who know that their schooling is costing a fortune and are therefore minded to behave, what exactly are the secrets that private schools can pass on?' A fair question. Smaller private schools, in particular those not associated with the Independent Schools Council (ISC), have been found wanting, slated with 'fundamental weaknesses in expertise' by Ofsted inspectors, with many heads having no educational training.[44] According to a 2017 study from the National Institute for Economic and Social Research, state schools remain ahead of private schools in the use of recognised good management practices – such as professional development – which encourage staff commitment.[45] Another authoritative study, looking at a wide set of management practices (including operational, monitoring, target-setting and people-management) which are known to be associated with raised student performance, found that in Britain good practices are used just as frequently in the state as in the private sector; this contrasts with some other countries, for example Brazil, where private schools and autonomous government schools are better managed than centrally controlled state schools.[46]

In short, the suggestion that children from Britain's private schools are sent on their privileged ways just by virtue of the fact that their schools are private holds no water when confronted with the evidence. If policy-makers still think that being private per se is the key to success, one can only wonder where this wisdom came from.

Learning and luxury: an ungainly coupling

We are left with the conclusion that it is the resources, backed up by peer groups, which are the key to understanding private schools' advantages. Yet one further serious question remains, if we want to understand the incredibly high fees. Why has the resources gap come to be so huge? Why for each pound devoted to educating a state school child is something in the region of three being spent on a private school child?

It seems that learning and luxury have become conjoined in an ungainly coupling. The additional resources devoted to private school children, over and above those spent on state school children, serve three main functions for the schools – call them the educational, the positional and the luxury functions.

The educational part of what the private schools spend their money on is the extra per capita amount that the state would ideally need to find, if it were to provide a high-quality education for all – that is, enough funds to have smaller class sizes, build more and better teaching facilities, offer a more extended curriculum, raise the status and rewards of teachers, and compensate at school for difficult home environments. Thus, a signal contribution of modern private education in Britain, backed by its extra resources, has been unwittingly to validate a concept held by educational optimists the world over: namely that it is perfectly possible with enough resources to develop a generally high-quality education system that brings out and develops the best in young people.[47]

The 'positional' function of the additional resources devoted to private school children is to deliver that edge – moving private school children up the ladder in life after school. Some expenditure is specifically aimed at positional advantage, as, for example, where a private school employs staff who devote their time to ensuring as many of their students as possible gain entrance to top universities. From the schools' and parents' perspective, this money targeted at working the system is money well spent. With the rise over the last thirty years of mass higher education, competition for places at the top end of Britain's hierarchical university system has intensified; and accordingly, the positional element of the private school offer has become increasingly important.

Some expenditure contributes simultaneously towards both the educational and the positional. This is the case where the new skills, knowledge and attitudes acquired through the educational function of private schools' additional resources are used as filters for advancement to scarce university places or good jobs – *unless*, the big qualifier, those universities or jobs were somehow to take account of applicants' school background in their admissions and recruitment policies.

The 'luxury' function of the huge resources gap can be thought of as providing what modern private school parents expect (unlike the less engaged and less affluent parents of past generations), enhancing the children's enjoyment of being at school, but not particularly adding to their learning and development. For some old boys and old girls, modern-day luxury is nothing less than exasperating. 'The truly annoying aspect of this is that there is absolutely no need for private school fees to be so astronomically expensive', writes Stephen Robinson in the *Spectator*, under the headline 'Private Grief'. Of course, it is always going to be difficult to decide exactly where the needs of learning end and those of luxury begin. Moreover, this luxury aspect also serves a positional purpose. Imagine being raised and taught in the sumptuous surroundings of one of the top private schools, and one can begin to appreciate how the schools develop in students the sensibilities of a privileged class, the feeling of being special. The facility to move with ease in affluent and august settings, together with the aspirations and sense of confidence they inspire, prepare children for a privileged future. Making luxury an integral part of the modern private school experience adds, by virtue of the higher fees, to the exclusion of ordinary families from sharing in the benefits of the high-quality learning environment. There is also the social capital – the shared networks and perspectives which have positional benefits for private school children in their lives after school, gains which are socially exclusive and produce no benefits for society as a whole. Thus, coupling learning with luxury purloins and concentrates in one sector the best advantages of great learning facilities, peer effects and social capital.

In a reformed – more egalitarian – setting for Britain's school system, only the educational purpose of the additional resources would have to be maintained if we wanted to have high-quality education and learning for all children. Thus, crucially, a radical integrating reform would not require raising state education spending to anywhere near the current spending in private schools. The aim should be to celebrate and enhance children's learning and development, while shunning the extravagance, social class segregation and all those efforts at working the system which have become intrinsic to it. This way of thinking provides no magic bullet or formula for saying just how much additional resources should be devoted to education; but it *does* imply that the state need not foot the bill for an unnecessarily luxurious lifestyle.

As it is, to the dismay of would-be customers, the fees have inexorably climbed to among the highest in the world in order to fuel Britain's engines of privilege. According to a *Sunday Times* headline report in 2014, fee-paying schools by then had become so expensive that some had become 'little more than "finishing schools for the children of oligarchs"'; while the following year *The Times* led one day with an editorial 'Educating Nikita', accusing Britain's best private schools of 'pricing themselves out of the market they have served for centuries'.

But the high fees have not suddenly emerged – they are a product of creeping increments over several decades; there have been few occasions when fees have not been lifted faster than the rate of inflation. Only in the years immediately following the financial crash of 2008, when many rich wealth-holders endured losses, have we seen any substantial restraint. A continuing source of concern among commentators, worried that the schools are indeed pricing themselves out of the market, the price rises have been branded a misjudgement, sure to end in tears – bankruptcies, forced mergers and closures, or conversion into state schools; or construed as an 'arms race', each school endlessly trying to outdo its competitors' facilities.[48] Yet even after all the hand-wringing, fees in 2018 are still leaping ahead of general prices. For a while, a price-fixing ring by major public schools was fingered as a reason for the high fees: between March 2001 and June 2003, some fifty leading schools exchanged information about future price-setting through a confidential survey organised by the bursar of Sevenoaks School, and were subsequently fined £10,000 each for their infringement of competition law – a 'slap on the wrist' is how one journalist described it – when the ring was exposed by the Office of Fair Trading (OFT).[49]

None of these explanations seems satisfactory, however. That schools should overreach themselves in their charging policy is conceivable in individual years, but that this should continue virtually every year stretches credulity. Competition-infringing behaviour might in theory account for a one-off rise, but not a persistent pattern of increase; besides, the behaviour ceased with the OFT's investigation, and an authoritative study later found that the schools' cartel had had, in practice, no discernible effect on fees.[50] The 'arms race' metaphor, though perhaps appealing at first sight, is shallow. In a real arms race, both sides to a conflict arm themselves to the teeth, but neither benefits through feeling more secure. In the case of private schools' price hikes, it would be hard to argue that the schools are not immensely better off than they were back in the 1980s.

The fees have risen, first, because a major focus on improving school quality does not come cheap. Falling class sizes and investments in improved learning facilities have contributed to the rise in fees since at least the 1980s. As with any sector that has been investing in buildings, land and facilities, private schools will have been affected by rising building prices. But these substantive additional costs of a high-quality learning environment cannot possibly account on their own for the exorbitant fees.

Rather, the increasing private school need for positional advantage, and for an immersion in the symbolic power (and in many cases the historical aura) of an imposing, opulent physical environment, also account in good part for sky-high fees. To deliver this positional advantage requires a sustained level of social exclusion, while affluent surroundings and living conditions give the sense of confidence, entitlement and exalted expectation. Not *everyone* of limited means has to be excluded in this new, post-1980 model, but the logic demands that the benefits have to be largely available to those who can pay handsomely. The concentration of the social composition enables private schools to sustain their peer-resource advantages, needed to maintain their level of academic and other successes. By coupling high-quality learning with luxury and the associated expense – something that became achievable in the modern era with rising income inequality since the end of the 1970s – the required social composition is sustained.

Thus for the last four decades, the competition for teachers and facilities has preoccupied headteachers. Annual price hikes have been enabled by the rising wealth and incomes of the very rich, their customers; only a relatively small proportion of these have been from Russia and China, and it seems odd to blame them. Few heads can afford to cool things down, and instead offer a decent education for less money and fewer luxuries. For the core of their customers, it has been important that the fees are high enough to maintain the exclusive social composition of the pupil population. The implication of all this is that Britain's very high fees are likely to be here to stay. They are not the result of some mistaken pricing policy; nor can the finger be reasonably pointed abroad; and nor, in all likelihood, will there be – without external political intervention – any going back to the relatively more modest fees of yesteryear.

Under threat?

When private school leaders gathered in November 2017 for a national conference, talk was of the calm before a potential storm. 'In many ways, everything is quite peaceful,' said the ISC chair, while the chair of the HMC declared that 'the political scene is as good as it possibly could be'.[51] Leaders were thankful for the political doldrums engendered by preoccupation with Brexit, though concerned about a potential change of government. Outside commentators, meanwhile, have highlighted rocketing fees as a major source of instability, and schools are accused of short-sightedness for taking an easy route to financial security. The 2015 closure of St Bees, an old and traditional school on the coast in Cumbria, seemed to some to epitomise a crisis which, according to one alarmist headline, could even signal 'the end for private schools'.[52] The dependence on foreign oligarchs, whose wealth is sometimes credited for sustaining the 'monster high fees', is also thought to be risky – they might at any time withdraw, particularly with Brexit politics potentially limiting Britain's attractiveness. 'The rate at which super-rich people are arriving in London is slowing,' warns John Arlidge in *Tatler*. With little understanding of actual financial crises, commentators liken fee rises to a financial bubble about to burst. Improved state education is also feared; in appearing to justify claims made by deniers of private school quality, the performance of the top selective state schools highlighted in *The Good Schools Guide* raises what may be the private schools' worst nightmare, that families will desert the fee-paying sector in large numbers if they can get the same quality for free. And, despite efforts to provide a 'public benefit' as charity law requires, private schools, according to *Spectator* journalist Ross Clark, 'have invited an attack on their charitable status owing to their shameless march upmarket'.

Yet, almost certainly, such fears are vastly overplayed. High prices cannot be laid solely, or even mainly, at the door of foreign oligarchs or short-sighted private school leaders, even if an export market of 10 per cent of the business has become important to the sector in the modern era. The fact is that at the most expensive, most socially exclusive schools, parents rush to register their children at the earliest opportunity after a child's birth, sometimes even before. In the event of a future financial crisis, most schools would be resilient, as in 2009, and able to protect themselves against a fall-off in demand through prudent cost management – it is not as if they have no luxuries to trim. Decades of stability provide testimony to this resilience. True, there has been some regional divergence, with London schools becoming more numerous, while the North-west and South-west of England have seen a disproportionate number of private school closures since 2010.[53] Yet, over time, not that many schools have folded or merged, and the total number has remained relatively steady since the 1980s, with no visible blip even during the financial crash.

It is also unlikely that the academic performance of private schools, relative to state schools, will be undermined during a period when there is an expanding cohort of children and when fiscal austerity still largely holds sway, with declining state spending on each child's education. There are many fine state schools around the country whose pupils receive an excellent education; and there are some schools where, because of a concentrated intake of high-achievers, the pupils rival the top private school children in their academic performances. Accordingly, those who deny the *relative* high quality of private schools may appear to be vindicated in individual cases; but on the whole, they are not supported by the best scientific studies of how *similar* children turn out on average. As long as they can stay clear of the political centre stage, Britain's private schools are not going to wither away, or slide seamlessly into a fairer national system. In the absence of radical reform, those interested in maintaining the status quo for private schools do not have all that much to worry about.

This picture could change, of course, if there developed a whole new attitude to the level of education which we should provide for all our young people in this country, including a move towards substantially narrowing the resource gap between the sectors. Yet anyone interested in addressing the problem of Britain's private school system would be well advised *not* to repeat the mistakes of the past – when politicians chose at crucial moments to concentrate their hopes for better life chances on the state sector improving. It should *not* be assumed that the problem will somehow resolve itself through a market-driven evolution of the private school service industry. Neither the state of the industry itself (healthy), nor the socio-economic environment of early twenty-first-century Britain (glaringly unequal, with a flourishing wealthy class), can reasonably justify any more such wishful thinking.

5

Who Chooses Private School and Why?

Britain's 'public schools', and the prep schools that feed into them, seem to embody the essence of what it means to be 'posh'. And it will be self-evident to anyone familiar with British culture that these schools are predominantly populated by the children of the rich – even if the degree of this concentration is sometimes not realised. Families planning for private school fees may be looking at six-figure sums just for secondary day schools, and the overall bill can easily beat the half million pounds mark where multiple children, boarding and prep school are involved. Unlike in many other countries, where private schools are mainly providers of religious or alternative education but not so much better resourced than the state's schools, in Britain they are especially closely linked with social class and money.

Yet it would be wrong to assume that *all* the children of affluent families are sent to private school. Often the decision follows a long and agonising process, and many parents who could easily afford the fees choose a local state school. Moreover, some private schools have been making decent efforts for years to open their doors to children from working- and middle-class families with modest means. Christ's Hospital, near Horsham in Sussex, is the leader in this pack: with its large endowments, it has to an exceptional degree honoured its founders' wishes back in the sixteenth century that it should seek to provide a boarding-school education for children from poorer families. It still helps three-quarters of its pupils with means-tested bursaries ranging from 100 per cent to 5 per cent of fee remission. Eton allocates bursaries or scholarships for a quarter of its pupils and, like other wealthy schools, finds room for some pupils who pay low or no fees. Most schools have some sort of bursary system, even if it is only the odd token, means-tested scholarship.

These facts pose two important questions for this chapter. First, are the schools becoming less socially exclusive? If there were such a trend, and it looked like continuing, it might be reasonable to hope that the problem of the private school system is on its way to a sort of solution without any need for radical change. And second, what are parents' underlying reasons for choosing to pay for private education? This question is important because, among their sometimes complex motives, some of what underpins them – especially the instinctive desire and enthusiasm of parents for a good education for their children – will need to be respected and co-opted in a more socially inclusive education system for Britain.

'Choosing' was not such a thought-through, conscious process for earlier generations of the well-off, for whom going to a private school was just something you naturally did if you came from a family that was educated privately. When the Public Schools Commission investigated in the 1960s why parents sent their children to private school, they found that family tradition and loyalty to particular schools were among the chief reasons that parents gave.[1] But from the time of Margaret Thatcher onwards, school choice has become a preoccupation of most parents at some point in their children's lives, in parallel with a market-based orientation in many other areas of life. Encouraged to choose, many of those with enough income or wealth have found themselves contemplating paying for a private school, especially if they feel dissatisfied (rationally or otherwise) with local state schools.

Affordability

Still, unless you can afford it, or you somehow obtain help, you simply cannot choose private schooling; and the fees explosion has greatly reduced its affordability. By 2018, the average annual day fee had reached £14,562, with £33,684 for boarding, in real terms three times the rates for 1980.[2] Extras are piled on top, with expensive school uniforms and globe-trotting school trips. For some, there are also the costs of advice on schools and admissions procedures from consultants.

For a family on the middle rung of the income ladder, the fees rose between 1980 and 2015 from 20 to 50 per cent of their income, while even for highly affluent families on the 95th rung the fees doubled from 10 to 20 per cent of their incomes.[3] *The Good Schools Guide* has bewailed how the continuing increases are driving middle-class families in London out of private schools, leaving only the super-yacht-owning super-rich and a few low-income families with bursaries.[4] The bare facts of declining 'affordability', then, suggest if anything that Britain's private schools can hardly be opening up to a wider clientele, no matter how much parents are moved to take school choice seriously.

But there are some ameliorating factors, with reduced fees or, occasionally, free places at private schools. The Assisted Places Scheme of the Thatcher/Major years was the largest single source of help: at its height, some 8 per cent of all private school pupils were included. The children who went to private school through the scheme, now in their adulthood, have reported mixed but generally positive experiences.[5] The main problem, however, was that the scheme was colonised from the start by the middle classes and controlled by the private schools. The scheme never commanded popular support outside the private school sector, and its potential impact on the schools' social exclusivity was diminished, even if it was a considerable boon for the schools themselves. It was contested by the Labour Party in opposition, and quickly abolished after the 1997 election.

Yet the schools had by then already been expanding their discounts, scholarships and bursaries to mitigate the growth in fees, and this continued in more earnest after the millennium. Means-tested bursaries, in particular, have become the vehicle for the schools to be able to claim that they are contributing to upward social mobility. A prize-winning garden exhibit by Wellington at the 2017 Chelsea Flower Show, entitled 'Breaking Ground', depicted receding barriers to social mobility and promoted a bursary for poorer children. In some cases, undoubtedly, the bursaries on offer are essentially a response to pressures from the Charity Commission to provide a 'public benefit'; but other schools, probably the majority, genuinely regard their bursary or scholarship provision as enlightened self-interest, attracting children who enhance the school's academic or sporting reputation, and improving the diversity of its population.

Bursaries are commonly based not just on a family's circumstances, but also on how well children perform in entrance tests; they can be additional to fixed-sum scholarships where families cannot otherwise afford the remaining fee. Places are not always easy to fill, and some schools try hard through advertising and other means to attract candidates from low-income families. These and other forms of fee assistance typically help the school as well as the parents. Discounts, for example, are a well-known revenue-increasing device widely practised by retail sellers, so it is unsurprising to find some schools offering small fee reductions to certain groups of buyers such as their own staff. Parents in unexpected financial difficulties are often allowed leeway with their fees when their children are already well established in the school. And more exotic forms of marketing are not ruled out in the future: according to a former head of Eton, schools should also consider offering parents 'customised experiences', such as free air travel, to engender customer loyalty.[6]

How extensive is the amount of fees reduction on offer? The short answer is: not very. Since 2000, one in three children in private schools has received some sort of assistance, an oft-quoted statistic which makes it seem that a great deal of financial relief is being provided. Yet for the most part the amount of assistance is small, and the largest category of assistance is for 'eligible families' (including clergy, HM Forces and staff or sibling discounts). With scholarships, it is often the prestige of the award, as much as the fee reduction, that is promoted.

Despite the schools' professed best efforts, the monetary volume of help through bursaries has remained proportionately the same for many years. Overall, among all the schools belonging to the Independent Schools Council (ISC), only 4 per cent of the annual fee income is devoted to means-tested bursaries, which are spread over just 8 per cent of their pupils. Every year, no more than 1 per cent of pupils at private schools are educated entirely free.[7]

The help with fees does not all go to low-income families. At Godolphin & Latymer School, for example, bursaries are offered to families with incomes as high as £140,000;[8] and scholarships may go to any child, no matter what their family income is. While 16 per cent of private school children from families in the bottom half of the income ladder received, over 2004–8, a bursary or a scholarship, so too did 14 per cent of those from the richest families on the top ten rungs of the ladder (see Figure 6, below). Since 2004–8 the availability of bursaries and scholarships has been aimed somewhat more at low-income families; moreover, the

FIGURE 6 Scholarships and Bursaries for Private Secondary School Pupils in Britain, 2004–15

Family income	% of private school pupils in receipt of a scholarship or a bursary		Average annual value of scholarships and bursaries per supported pupil (expressed in 2015 prices)	
	2004–8	2009–15	2004–8	2009–15
All	15	14	£4,600	£4,800
Position in the family income ladder:				
Richest (top 10%)	14	11	£3,800	£3,300
From the middle to the 90th rung	15	17	£4,600	£4,600
Below the middle	16	18	£6,300	£7,300

Source: Family Resource Survey; authors' analysis.

average value of each bursary or scholarship has increased at the
bottom – from £6,300 to £7,300 – and fallen at the top – from
£3,800 down to £3,300. In short, the schools have been devoting
a little more of their assistance to lower-income families. Overall,
the amount of bursary and scholarship relief per private secondary
school child has remained steady in real terms – at £680 since before
the financial crisis of 2008, even while the fees have, as always, kept
ahead of inflation. Of course, some of the wealthier schools are able
to afford significantly above the industry average. Yet on the whole,
bursaries and scholarships are, for the purposes of alleviating high
school fees, small beer.

Tax planning is another way that the costs can be reduced a
little, using tailored fee-payment methods.[9] For example, one
scheme suitable for the super-rich works through the payment
of fees in advance: the schools deploy their charitable status to
invest the money more advantageously than could parents who are
subject to higher-rate tax. The difference allows the schools to offer
a small but significant reduction in fees (for example, 3 per cent
in the case of Harrow). Other schemes might involve channelling
untaxed income to children, who then settle the fees. Such schemes
can involve grandparents or the tactical deployment of offshore
bonds, with the help of independent financial advisers who keep it
legal. Whether or not these forms of tax planning directly help the
schools or the families, the net effect is the same: lowering the cost
a little and relieving the government of tax revenue. The schemes
evolve through time as the rules are tightened and financial advisers
innovate. It is hard to gauge how prevalent this taxman's subsidy has
become. It is likely to be sizable only for especially affluent parents,
those higher-rate taxpayers who can pay their fees in advance and
afford an accountant's advice.

For everyone else, including the majority who receive nugatory
help, there is no option but to come up with the fees in full.
The ameliorating efforts of schools and tax advisers amount to
little, when confronted by the huge fee rises seen since the 1980s.
Advisers advocate advanced financial planning. There are ways
of economising – buying less private schooling – available to

some medium-wealthy families. Parents can choose differently at successive school stages. A third of private school children aged fourteen have previously been at a state primary school, saving perhaps half of the total cost of their education. A few pay just for the sixth-form years. More than a third of private school families with multiple children divide them between the state and private sector.[10] Some parents, writing on the social media forum Mumsnet, echo private school spokespersons when they relate how they have had to make sacrifices, forgoing foreign holidays and other luxuries for the sake of their children's education; while other Mumsnet commentators take issue, saying that for them it is not their unwillingness to make sacrifices – but, rather, as one puts it, 'I could live on beans and still never afford the 16K that our nearest independent school charges'.[11]

Yet still they keep on coming, even after all the years of price increases. There remains a cadre of families at the top who can afford it, whose incomes have risen far more than for the rest of the population; whose affluent older generation of grandparents can chip in when needed; or whose saved-up or inherited wealth is waiting to be used for this purpose. The skewed concentration of access to the schools in the twenty-first century – perhaps the single most important fact in this book – is portrayed by the figure on page 2.

And, crucially, there appears to be no meaningful trend towards access being opened up, in practice, to a wider spread of the population. The concentration of high-income families is as high as it was before the millennium.[12] The persistence of private school from one generation to another was just as strong over the years 2006–13 as it had earlier been between 1996 and 2005: in both periods, four out of ten privately educated parents sent their children also for private schooling.[13] Nor has the social exclusivity diminished during the twenty-first century so far. In 2004, when the English children in the Next Steps study were fourteen, just over three-quarters of private school attenders were drawn from families in the managerial and professional classes; a decade later in 2014, when the English children of the Millennium Cohort had reached the same age, the share of the managerial and professional classes occupying places in the private schools was unchanged.[14] It must be disappointing to anyone sincerely hoping that bursaries could open up the schools to a broader cross-section of the nation's talents: despite schools' efforts, some more determined than others, no significant inroads seem to have been made into unpicking their social exclusivity. But is that surprising, when in fact bursaries only amount to 4 per cent of turnover?

Inevitably, any remedy via bursaries for a lack of affordability is strictly limited by the very nature of the beast. Even though the majority of ISC schools are legally construed as charities, when parents shell out for school fees they do not see what they are paying for as charity. They do not want to pay much over the odds in order to help poorer children. Nor, according to the opinion of some heads, would parents sanction a substantial number of less affluent children changing the make-up of their own children's peer group.[15] Abroad, the same is true of foreign families, lured to the proliferating international campuses of some of Britain's select private schools; they too would probably hold back if the schools were to use those outposts as cash cows for a purely British-oriented bursaries programme. Instead, if philanthropic action is to make an appreciable difference, it would have to grow very much throughout the sector; it would also have to be earmarked for means-tested bursaries, rather than for the next Olympic-size swimming pool or state-of-the-art theatre (the rich giving to the rich). Last but not least, the bursaries would have to be broadened and made available to children across the ability range. Perhaps a handful of schools, the wealthiest and most prestigious, might be able to change their social composition; but in the round, all of this seems improbable – in the absence of radical changes to the policy environment.

Motives

Even among the affluent who can somehow afford it, only a minority of families actually choose private schooling for their children. Many privately schooled parents choose state schools for their own children. So why do some people choose private, and others not? What, if anything, can we learn from their motives?

Let us first deal with what may seem all too obvious. Most parents of private school teenagers are quite clear in their own minds that they are buying a better academic quality.[16] They believe in the value of very small class sizes and much better equipment, and in this they are generally supported by the evidence. A small minority of parents, approximately one in twelve, still choose private schools to suit their religious beliefs. Then there is another minority who either prefer or need to send their children to boarding school. Back in the 1960s, the Public Schools Commission occupied itself intensively with the need for boarding. Yet the numbers diminished in subsequent decades as the armed forces shrank, and as parents returned home from Britain's ex-colonies or preferred that their children grow up with them rather than in an institution. Boarding numbers have then held steady at a low level in the twenty-first century, bolstered by increases in foreign pupils: in 2018, only one in eight private school children is boarding. The proportion is greater away from London.

More striking, however, are the hidden motives, those not revealed in simple surveys and rarely acknowledged in public. An exception in 2014 was Sarah Vine, *Daily Mail* columnist and wife of then education secretary Michael Gove, who struck a chord when, after they had decided to send their child to a state school, she declared that the private sector's agenda was about selection and pupil potential, yes, but also 'about snobbery'. 'Of course,' she argued, 'the parents of private school children are paying for the best teachers and facilities. But let's be honest: they're also paying for their child to mix with the right kind of kids.'[17] She is almost certainly correct. The 'snobbery' of private school choice is a type of conspicuous consumption, a sign that a family has 'made it'.[18] The objective of lifting their children's aspirations and self-confidence in facing the world are also rarely mentioned in simple surveys of parents' motives, but private schools do not miss this trick in their marketing: they know that their pupils are among their chief assets, and that the aspirations of the many children from affluent families pervade the ethos of a school.

In-depth studies tell us that Vine was right. As we have seen, it had already been clear to Irene Fox, from her interviews in the early 1980s, that the other pupils in the school were important for parents. She found that 27 per cent had chosen private schooling because they wanted their children to 'mix with a better type of child'; another 18 per cent wanted teachers to 'polish' their children.[19] Even the parents who talked about their academic-sounding reasons for going private showed some anxiety about their children's peer groups, concerned that their own sons grew up with the appropriate social graces. For fear of being drawn down the social hierarchy, they wanted their children to associate 'with their own type'. One mother of a private school child confessed ruefully: 'The advantage of an independent education is to get him away from the local boys who speak badly. One disadvantage is that the local boys don't want to play with him now – he has no one to play with.'[20]

Later studies suggest that little has changed.[21] Anne West and her co-authors spoke with the parents of 231 children choosing schools in London in the mid-1990s. Their in-depth interviews reveal that state schools at the time were viewed by some affluent families as too risky, with fears of academic failure and of mixing with the wrong sort. 'Not the riff raff,' remarked one of the mothers, when proclaiming her three most essential reasons for choosing the private sector. She 'wanted a similar peer group, similar viewpoints, nice backgrounds', and wished it to be 'normal' for parents to help their children with their work at home. 'Big decider of private: deprived backgrounds,' she insisted.[22] Two decades on, and middle-class parents interviewed for a study of school choice in London and Paris sound remarkably similar. 'Obviously, the thing that is a big issue for parents in London is school . . . that is where it all starts to hit the fan in terms of social mix and politics and culture and everything,' declares one London mother living in a socially mixed neighbourhood.[23] Both the social and the ethnic mix of a school are still important concerns for those choosing private; researchers detected in London an especially strong aversion to their children having a socially mixed school peer group, more so than in Paris.

convinced from his own particular experience that the quality of private schools is nothing special. In the past, the financial return – as measured by the extra pay a privately educated person can expect to earn throughout a career – averaged very approximately around 13 per cent, though less for boarders for whom the costs were so much greater.[26] In other words: it was a pretty good investment for the *average* family who could afford the fees. But this is a retrospective calculation applied to those educated during the 1970s and 1980s.

What does the investment look like, when looking forward? With heightened pay inequality – and with education ever more important in the twenty-first century – one could expect the pay gap for the privately educated to be greater than before, even if expectations about the future are notoriously shaky. The benefits of marrying a richer spouse might also be included in a family's calculations.[27] We should also factor in the broader aspects of a private school education. As for the high-quality accommodation and other luxuries, though they may not be needed for a good education, at least today's private school children get the benefit of this largesse in their youth, unlike earlier generations who faced a much more spartan, toughen-them-up environment; an extravagance can be seen to be worth it, if you have enough money. And all those theatres, playing fields and support staff will also have some pay-off in the future, albeit obtained at a high cost: not only raising the chances of landing a successful and financially rewarding career in the worlds of pop music, the arts and elite sports, but also facilitating the development of a child's artistic, musical and general aesthetic sensibilities.

Nevertheless, with the fees three times higher in real terms than in 1980, the private school advantages have to be a lot larger if the net return is to match that of earlier generations – especially for those families who, by virtue of where they live, have little choice but to choose the boarding option if they want to access private schools. Private day schools are less abundant in Scotland, even scarcer in Wales, and in Northern Ireland there are very few available. Many parents, particularly those unsure about the educational gains their own children would achieve or about the future income this would deliver, unsurprisingly opt for alternative ways of spending their money, or at least economise by only going private for part of a child's time in education. Often, the affluent parents who shun the private sector are those who live near excellent state schools, of which there are many.

For others, the key is not so much whether private schooling is financially wise, as whether the offered academic education is good enough to balance out the negatives of being in a socially narrow environment. Thus the second main motive for families *not* choosing private schools, even when they can afford to, is the desire that their children grow up amidst a genuine cross-section of society. Author and broadcaster John O'Farrell has related thoughtfully why, through the broader social mix at the local state school, his children can gain 'an understanding of how society works that you could never get in an institution from which most of society is excluded', and why he values this broader wisdom more highly than 'an extra grade A GCSE here and there'.[28] Journalist Rachel Johnson has had the same concerns – before concluding that, for herself as a parent, the negatives of social segregation do not outweigh the academic advantages that a private education brings.[29]

The Politics of Hypocrisy

For some families there is a third motive for saying no to private schools, stemming from their political beliefs: the sense of unease, even guilt, if they were to pay for a private advantage over others while at the same time subscribing to the view that a high-quality education should be available for all children. The political theorist and philosopher Adam Swift has offered a beguiling guide for such families, aiming to interrogate the circumstances under which they could indeed be deemed hypocritical, were they to send their children to private school.[30] For him, the key is whether the available state schools are 'adequate'; if not, then the choice of a private school is morally defensible. Needless to say, this position is the cue for a long discussion of what it means to have an adequate school nearby.

Yet even a careful reading of Swift's argument may not resolve the question for potentially guilt-ridden parents. There is undoubtedly a minority of parents who choose state schooling because private advantage would make them feel morally unsettled.[31] Nor is Swift's philosophical resolution likely to be enough to neutralise the moral obloquy accorded by some to private school parents. A recent chairman of the HMC has bemoaned the way that private school parents are made to feel like 'social lepers';[32] while the ex-head of Cheltenham Ladies' College laments that a hostile environment for private schools 'leaves those who run them feeling "slightly immoral"'.[33] According to Lee Elliot Major, chief executive of the Sutton Trust, private school parents' latent guilt is inevitable, given the schools' close association with class.[34] Or take the *cri de coeur* of one London-based financial services professional: 'Ideologically I'm quite left-wing, I'd much prefer him to go to a state school than a private school, but in the end I can't put my political conscience ahead of his educational needs.'[35]

Knowing whether politicians and commentators were privately educated, and where they choose to educate their children, may be salient if we want to try to understand where they are coming from. Clement Attlee's unwillingness to challenge the position of private schools in the post-war re-organisation of Britain's education system was, as we have seen, directly related to his personal affection for his alma mater, Haileybury. We know how schooling can colour a person's world view, and how so many people (including politicians and policy-makers) erroneously base their prescriptions on their own, often narrow, experiences. Potential education reformers, moreover, have good reason to fear a hypocrisy charge from all sides, should they try to take the lead on private school reform, if they themselves have been using the private sector. It has taken an outsider – Joris Luyendijk, a Dutchman – to observe:

It is quite ironic that a nation that gave the world the term 'fair play' sees the fact that rich children receive a better education than poor ones as a perfectly natural thing. I remember asking around at the *Guardian*, where I had been hired to investigate the City of London, why this progressive newspaper did not put the school system centre stage. This is how the elites clone themselves, is it not? The answer: most of our management and prominent writers went to private school themselves and most are sending their children there, too, so that would invite the charge of hypocrisy.[36]

Among journalists, Rachel Johnson is a notable exception. 'Private education underpins almost all that is wrong with British society', this privately educated parent of three children at private school has declared. 'Although our public schools are some of the finest institutions, they entrench inequality and immobility and should be phased out.'[37]

Parents' motives for choosing – or not choosing – a private school need to be respected. Their decisions often stem from their own particular circumstances. And even if these motives and decisions are sometimes hard to pin down, often ambivalent and confused, they are what they are. We are not advancing a moral argument against parents' natural wishes to make the best decisions for their children. We are at one with an anonymous first-generation immigrant who wrote in 2012, intervening in a social media debate on private school choice, 'I just sense a lot of bitterness and pointless stone throwing.'[38] Our reticence about condemning also extends to parents who are in a position to influence educational policies. As long as politicians do not advocate that others should use the state sector while doing differently themselves – the very essence of hypocrisy – we distance ourselves from the common charge of double standards: an accusation made against those politicians who have both their own concerns as parents and their wider aspirations for a fair education system, and sometimes heed the former.

Blaming parents is an individualistic response to a social issue, and it will not work. Moral reprobation, even where it might be justified, is most unlikely to be sufficient to bring down an economically successful private school system, or to resolve its unfairness. Parents' instinctive desires to choose the best education they can for their own children will usually supersede what guilt may exist, and consciences are quite easily salved. Condemnation of parents leads nowhere, and the politics of hypocrisy are a dead end.

Using the best motives

We have seen in this chapter how access to Britain's private schools remains as socially exclusive as ever, despite the efforts of some schools and philanthropists to open them up to poorer households and move towards a meritocratic, means-tested admissions process. Incomes in Britain have risen enormously at the very top of the income spectrum, and it is this which has sustained the seemingly permanent fee rises and expansion of facilities since the 1980s. Yet the parents that do have the means to choose private have a complex mix of motives, and by no means all of the very wealthy families actually go for the private option.

Whichever way they do choose, a dominant motive of most parents is for their children to receive a good academic and well-rounded education. To us, this seems both unsurprising and optimistic. It is a reminder that any solution to the problem of private schooling should retain some features of what those parents legitimately want for their children: a good academic education; behaviour and ethos conducive to learning; and an education that, going beyond just the passing of exams, includes development of their children in broader fields of human endeavour. These are simple, valid and powerful motives, and, to the extent they have led some parents to choose a private education for their particular children, it does not serve the cause of progressive change to pursue a silo-reinforcing moral crusade against private school parents, let alone pupils. New solutions must be sought that can capture broad support and unite the desires of the vast majority of parents – in both sectors – to have their children well educated.

But it is *not* part of any solution that private schools should be coupled with luxury amenities, there to exclude all but the very well-off. Parents should not have to choose 'country clubs' in order to access a high-quality education. Moreover, solutions need not and should not aim to satisfy those desires (usually latent and undeclared) for social exclusiveness or for purely positional advantage. Where exclusiveness gives advantage – for example through the concentration of beneficial peer effects – it is only at the expense of others, and flouts the principle of a fair society. Where naked positional advantage is found, for instance when schools pull strings or deploy extensive resources on ensuring their pupils attain entry to high-status universities at the expense of other children equally or better qualified, their win is usually someone else's loss.

For many people, private schools are a foreign world, an isolated and hidden corner of the educational scenery; it is their social exclusiveness that has helped to keep the schools from intruding too much on the public. In five out of six families, neither parent nor any of the daughters and sons have ever been to a private school.[39] Unless they happen to work in one of them, it is hardly surprising if for most people the problems that are posed by the schools impinge rarely on the experiences of daily life. In opinion polls about private schools there are typically quite a few who sit among the 'Don't knows', or otherwise indicate that they have no strong views. Nevertheless, there are parts of the population, especially in London and the South-east, where passions run deep, with some people very favourably disposed to the schools, but others strongly against.

What do Britain's opinion-formers, our influential commentators and politicians, *think* about the issue? Just occasionally, despite a widespread nervousness about tackling the subject, simmering ideas do break out into a hesitant public conversation.

6

Bubbling Under

'When more Etonians make it to Oxbridge than boys and girls on benefit, then we know we are not making the most of all our nation's talents,' declared the education secretary, Michael Gove, in a May 2012 speech which detailed the extent to which the privately educated were 'increasingly dominating' British life.[1] It was a striking statement, perhaps especially coming from a prominent Conservative. Yet, over half a decade later, the issue is still significantly under-represented in public discourse. In this chapter we try to give some sense of what debate there has been during the six years between summer 2012 and summer 2018: those fleeting moments when the issue has acquired some temporary larger traction; the debate's silences and evasions; and what has so far been put on the table – in the nature of substantive proposals – by those relatively few who have seriously examined the question.

Moments

In May 2012 itself, Gove was quickly followed by the deputy prime minister, Nick Clegg, arguing that leading Oxbridge colleges should enhance social mobility by lowering their A-level entry grades for state school candidates; and later that month by Alan Milburn's Social Mobility Commission, highlighting how employers unfairly favoured the products of private schools.[2] More full frontal, and the culmination of this 'moment', was Matthew Parris in June in *The Times*. 'Schools that sell privilege can't be charities' was the title of his stirring piece, which saw the former Tory MP insisting that 'many parents' sent their children to private school for other than educational reasons – namely, 'to learn the relaxed and breezy confidence, the loose manner, the intangible sense of entitlement, that comes with a good private education in Britain':

> This is not education, but privilege; the social advantage of your child over other children. I am not persuaded that this is the 'public benefit' that our definition of a charity requires it to offer. And I dismiss out of hand the hoary old argument that private schools save taxpayers the cost of educating pupils in state schools. You might as well claim charitable status for your car on the ground that it saves local authorities the cost of subsidising your seat on the bus.[3]

Provoked by this mini onslaught, defenders and attackers responded in roughly equal numbers. One head, Taunton School's John Newton, attributed the success of private school pupils to 'the ambition of committed, hard-working parents who wish to give their children a better chance in life', adding that 'it is aspiration and sacrifice on the part of those parents that puts such high numbers of independent school pupils at the top of the tree, not privilege and elitism'; another head, Magdalen College School's Tim Hands, invoked those 'many parents' who were 'just ordinary people who value education over everything else, making big sacrifices'; among *Independent* letter writers, one blamed the comprehensive system ('has failed to equip its students with the means or desire to compete in the modern world') for the lack of social mobility, but another held responsible the parents of the 7 per cent ('to think that people who have paid very significant sums to secure advantage might be cajoled by a "fairness" argument to favour social mobility, is utter nonsense'); so did the former Conservative MP Tom Benyon ('another problem that faces public education is that the people with the sharpest elbows and who are prepared to fight for their children's education are not generally involved, for their children are being educated in the private sector'); while Bob Holman, one-time Easterhouse guru of Iain Duncan Smith, was adamant that 'no major political parties are sincere about promoting social mobility because they will not tackle the privileges and powers of Oxbridge and private schools'.[4]

2012 was, of course, the imperishable summer of Mo, Jessica and Bradley, all of them from a state school background; but it was also, across Team GB as a whole, the summer in which over a third of its Olympic medallists were privately educated – four years after more than half of British gold medallists in Beijing had likewise gone to private schools. 'Wholly unacceptable,' declared Lord Moynihan (chair of the British Olympic Association, former Tory minister, privately educated) about the latter statistic. 'There is so much talent out there in the [state-educated] 93 per cent that should be identified and developed.'[5] His comments went down poorly on the right. 'They seem to be freighted with the usual resentment of independent schools – as though Eton College should be stripped of its rowing lake, on which the Olympic regatta is taking place, and its alumni, such as Matthew Pinsent, forced to hand back their medals,' riposted the *Daily Telegraph*, blaming instead state school teachers for their reluctance to supervise after-school sport without financial reward; while a few weeks later, in the *Spectator*'s annual *Guide to Independent Schools* ('we want to applaud Britain's independent schools rather than snipe at them'), the head of Bedford School, John Moule, conceded that a child in the UK was nearly eight times more likely to win a gold medal if privately educated, but argued that 'we should be grateful to independent schools for setting an example', based on 'an ethos of success and competition' that 'flourishes in independent schools simply because it is allowed to do so'. Moule also reached for the bigger picture. 'Are we prepared,' he asked, 'to admit that the desire to promote the false gods of "equality" and "fairness" has dampened our ability to be the best, as we have eschewed competition and lowered our expectations?' Still, his conclusion was cheerful enough: 'We British love to win and we love our winners. As far as I can see, we don't really care where they went to school. So rather than succumbing to knee-jerk reactions of guilt, we should really be saying: thank heaven for independent schools.'[6]

A full year elapsed before the next eruption. 'Thin stuff' was what Ofsted's Sir Michael Wilshaw accused the private schools of offering to neighbouring state schools by way of partnerships, in the course of a trenchant address in October 2013 to the Headmasters' and Headmistresses' Conference's (HMC's) annual meeting – an address that by the end, especially after Wilshaw had reminded the assembled company that 'Harrow, Eton, Westminster, Charterhouse, Winchester and scores of others were endowed and established with the express purpose of providing an education for the poor', had the speaker being surrounded by incensed heads.[7] *The Times* next day sided unequivocally with the beaks: 'He has no business sending teachers on guilt trips for wanting to teach at top schools. Nor can he expect parents, many of whom have made huge sacrifices to acquire a better education for their own children, to subsidise underperforming state schools.' And after reflecting that it was 'hard to imagine such a speech being made in a country whose state schools were good and where private schools were unnecessary', the paper concluded that 'our best independent schools should be championed as world leaders'.[8]

Then, in November, came the two PMs – a previous one, John Major, lamenting the dominance of the privately educated; the incumbent, David Cameron, confessing to 'despair' about the situation – but with their interventions soon lost in the relentless news cycle.[9] So, too, with Matthew Parris's *Times* piece in December, when returning to the fray he urged Cameron to grasp his 'clause 4 moment' by compelling private schools to open up 25 per cent of their intake on a means-tested, state-funded basis. 'At a stroke my proposal would neutralise the single most damaging popular perception of the Conservative Party – that they don't care about ordinary people,' argued Parris eloquently if to little visible effect. 'To a party that does not believe in equality of outcome this offers a way to prove that it does believe in equality of opportunity. And it would dish the Labour Party.'[10]

But the winter was still young, and in January 2014 one of the authors wrote with his son George a lengthy cover story in the *New Statesman* about 'Education's Berlin Wall' that over the following weeks generated a flurry of letters and articles in the magazine. Among the latter was a response by Michael Gove (still education secretary) which included his recognition of the dominance of the wealthy in the private sector.[11] Moreover, by the time of his response, he, too, was publicly using the 'Berlin Wall' metaphor – notably in a speech in early February that, calling for state schools to become more like private schools, attracted considerable attention. 'Simply a fantasy' in 'the Britain of 2014', declared the *Guardian* of Gove's ambition to make it impossible to tell the difference between the two sectors, and it noted in passing how the left seemed 'strangely inert about the issue – hostile to private schools, and to the privilege and power that they embody and reproduce, but unwilling to look for realistic ways of addressing the problems'.[12] Most responses, though, came in letters pages, including by four women with a clear sense of practicalities:

If Mr Gove wants to make state schools more like private schools he should concentrate on what really matters – investing in high-quality teaching and facilities, and promoting a culture in which pupils' achievements are recognised. *(Kate Pitcher, Norwich)*

As a teacher with more than 40 years' experience, top of my list to help state schools match the private sector is smaller class sizes. Mr Gove hasn't mentioned that. *(Diana Holl, Clevedon)*

If you visit a school in England, there is no mistaking a comprehensive for an independent school. The comprehensive is required to address the educational needs of children of all abilities. There will never be a level playing field while most independent schools and grammar schools are able to select on ability. *(Marilyn Mullen, Gosport)*

The elephant in the room in the education debate can be summed up as 'discipline' and 'commitment'. Parents in the private sector sign up to an ethos of good behaviour and, in general, their children fulfil their part of the contract; if they persist in unacceptable behaviour they are expelled. Meanwhile, many classes in the state system are disrupted by bad behaviour, albeit of a minority; the school's attempts to discipline these pupils is undermined by similar behaviour by the parents, many view school as free childcare and condone their children's behaviour. *(Marion Hudson, Smarden)*[13]

Another Kentish voice, Linda Karlsen's from Whitstable, supported Gove's aspiration to bring down the Berlin Wall – but 'in the opposite direction': 'Only 7% of young people are privately educated. Let them join the majority in the state system by tearing down the bastions of the privileged few, fee-paying schools – 93% of the nation's young people wouldn't even notice as it would be school as usual for them.'[14]

The usual pause then ensued, before Alan Bennett in June 2014 made at Cambridge his widely publicised remarks about the fundamental unfairness of private schools. Later that summer saw another report from the Social Mobility Commission, with Milburn and his colleagues lambasting what they termed the 'closed shop' of Britain's elite, quoting the increasingly well-known statistics about the dominance in that elite of the privately educated, and calling on companies to reveal the social background of their workforce.[15] Soon afterwards a *Guardian* reader, John Green, took sharp issue with the world-weary reaction to the report from one of the paper's columnists, Simon Jenkins. 'In writing that "most countries are run largely by the products of middle-class education", Jenkins ignores Britain's bloated private education system that is not replicated in any other European country,' asserted Green. While as for Jenkins's dismissal as a timeworn cliché the argument that all social evils start with the education system: 'It is, though, a basic truth that if you allow a wealthy minority to effectively jump the educational queue by paying for the education of their children, you are helping to cement elite structures that dominate all sections of society.'[16]

By autumn 2014, especially after Wilshaw had renewed his attack (urging government to be tougher minded about the schools justifying their charitable status), the sector was back on the counter-charge.[17] 'It is time,' thundered Richard Harman (head of Uppingham, chair of HMC) in *The Times*, 'to stop scapegoating independent schools – to stop using them as lazy shorthand for the social ills of our country and to move beyond resentment.' Claiming that private schools were 'part of the solution' to social mobility, 'not the root of the problem', he went on: 'We are not a laboratory for social engineering. Attacking the excellence of the education we provide will not help solve society's ills.'[18] A smoother operator – but singing from the same hymn sheet – was the ISC's Charlotte Vere, who later that autumn, following Tristram Hunt's cautious policy initiative on behalf of Labour, debated with the *Observer*'s Carole Cadwalladr the issue of charitable status. 'We might as well subsidise five-star hotels,' declared the latter, before soon finding herself powerless to stem a flood of seemingly convincing arguments: the high quality of educational provision 'unencumbered by the cold, stifling hand of government'; the many children benefiting from means-tested bursaries; the savings to the taxpayer; and the folly of the 'cut-off-your-nose-to-spite-your-face argument, that independent schools educate too successfully and therefore should be handicapped in some way'. 'It is time to end the obsession,' concluded Vere. 'It is time to embrace the independent sector, to learn from it, to allow it to learn from the state sector and for us all to work for the greater good of all children in our country.' Cadwalladr was left bloodied and only arguably unbowed. 'OK, you win, Charlotte. You will anyway, so what's the difference? Because that's what going to one of Britain's great public schools amounts to: a Willy Wonka golden ticket to life, the universe and everything.' In short: 'As you were, everybody.'[19]

By this stage, it was the cultural aspect that was starting to take up some of the still ample slack in the wider debate. 'The actresses Julie Walters and Maxine Peake have spoken searingly of how few working-class actors are now coming through, and even reality TV has fallen to the toffs in the shape of *Made in Chelsea*,' noted Julie

Burchill in July 2014, adding that 'a whopping 60 per cent of rock music chart acts are now ex-public school, compared with 1 per cent 20 years ago'.[20]

One of those stars was James Blunt, the Old Harrovian singer-songwriter. Early in 2015 he was cited by the shadow culture minister Chris Bryant as a prime example – in the context of the arts being overly dominated by people from privileged backgrounds – of someone who had benefited from his private education. 'You classist gimp,' began Blunt's open letter to Bryant. But after stating that no one at his school had helped him get into the music business, and accusing the Labour MP of 'populist, envy-based, vote-hunting ideas which make our country crap', he did concede that Harrow had been a help: 'Perhaps it protected me from your kind of narrow-minded, self-defeating, lead-us-to-a-dead-end, remove-the-"G"-from-"GB" thinking, which is to look at others' success and say: "It's not fair".'[21] Feeling similarly put upon was the Old Etonian actor Damian Lewis, who claimed that year that the similar school background of the new wave of male top-of-the-range actors – the likes of Eddie Redmayne (Eton), Dominic West (Eton), Tom Hiddleston (Eton), Benedict Cumberbatch (Harrow) and Rory Kinnear (St Paul's) as well as himself – was 'coincidental and nothing more'. Indeed, he even wondered aloud whether he and his peers had succeeded 'in spite of' that background rather than 'because of it'.[22] An uncomfortable episode followed in early 2016, when Lewis had to face down opposition from alumni of a north London comprehensive, Acland Burghley, over his appearance at the school's 50th anniversary celebrations, with the dissidents claiming that the OE did not 'represent the real Burghley values'.[23]

It only remained for the Rev to weigh in. A few weeks later, Tom Hollander (Abingdon) put the continuing trend purely down to the prevailing zeitgeist, arguing that whereas once there had been 'lots of working-class-hero leading actors', now it was 'fashionable to sound posh'. For good measure, he optimistically contrasted the two eras: 'The barriers most people were facing in that period just don't exist now. There are vestiges, but it's nothing. Things are not as stratified and regimented as they were then.'[24] Whatever the truth, it was undeniably a convenient explanation; and from one sceptical *Guardian* reader, Arthur Gould of Loughborough, it prompted the ironic response (included in a clutch of letters about the 'posh actor posse') that 'there's silly old me thinking Hollander's parents sent him to a posh school to give him a leg-up in whatever career he chose'.[25] But perhaps the last word of this thespian phase should go to Nicholas Hytner. 'The problem is a much wider social problem,' the outgoing artistic director of the National Theatre observed in 2015 in an attempt to dampen down the personal element as well as an undue focus on the arts. 'We have been brought to a place where, whatever you want to do, if you've been privately educated you are going to find it easier to do it.'[26]

The early summer of 2016 witnessed (as we have briefly seen in Chapter 2) arguably the most piquant episode of all, albeit overshadowed by the imminent referendum on Europe. A Tory minister (Matt Hancock) proposed that employers check the socio-economic background of employees; a Tory grandee (Lord Waldegrave) who happened to be Provost of Eton threatened to resign the party whip; the *Spectator* alerted its readers to the spectre of a purge of the posh; and a U-turn was duly if not deftly executed. Again, it was Matthew Parris to the fore. Before the U-turn, welcoming in his *Times* column Hancock's initiative, he was in a self-confessedly 'aggressive' mood, reaching 'a conclusion many fellow-Tories will hate': 'The present public mood of sneering at public-school toffs is healthy. The brand must be trashed. People must be made to feel sheepish about going to Eton or Harrow ... We're in a zero-sum game here. A competitive advantage conferred on 7 per cent is a competitive disadvantage imposed on the rest. And if that isn't about life chances, what is?'[27] A few days later, he noted that 'some readers, posting comments online beneath my column, seem to believe that the upper echelons of society in 21st century Britain are genetically superior to the rest', in other words that 'posh people have got cleverer and cleverer down the generations and the masses stupider and stupider' – a claim that Parris explicitly repudiated: 'On the contrary, a class structure like ours inhibits such a process, trapping many of the genetically better-endowed at a level below where merit would take them, and placing an invisible safety net beneath the caste at the top. The public school system, with the veneer it imparts and the support network into which it initiates its alumni, is part of that safety net.'[28]

Then came the government's U-turn. 'Well, cross that idea off David Cameron's "life chances" agenda,' reflected Parris ruefully. 'I bet somebody from his old school has had a private word, alarmed lest when he talks about "life chances" he might actually mean it. No danger of that. For centuries our poshest schools have been happy enough when names like Eton or Harrow boosted an old boy's prospects. But – horrors! – what if "Bogsville Comprehensive" might give some oik the edge over "Eton College"? How fiercely, then, these gilded institutions' sense of justice kicks in to insist that background should be kept off CVs.' In short: 'Discrimination becomes unfair when it's no longer in your favour.'[29]

Two of the more notable interventions during these weeks were made by a *Financial Times* journalist and a *Guardian* reader. 'This "purge" ought to bother me, since I was privately educated and am now sending my own children to private schools,' wrote Robert Shrimsley (before the U-turn) in his Saturday column after noting the existing dominance of the privately educated:

> But I pay precisely because it offers them the very advantages discussed. People aren't stupid: you don't spend that kind of cash to teach them to play hockey. I don't feel guilty about this. I can think of no better use of my money than maximising my children's prospects. But I cannot pretend it is fair.
>
> Indeed I find myself repelled by the self-declared victimhood of those with all the advantages as they seek to stop the less fortunate getting even a sip from their well. This is the world view of people who think trying to level matters even a notch in favour of those who did not go to Eton is 'punishing' those who did. It is a martyrdom myth; an attempt by the least victimised in society to claim victim status.

There is no purge of the posh; the well-heeled still may safely graze. Fee-paying schools are not being abolished, as many on the left would wish. They will still offer great advantages. There is merely a modest plan to wrest back a small fraction of the advantages enjoyed by a minority.

Yet the disproportionate tone of complaint is proof that, while one day the meek may inherit the earth, those currently in possession would really rather keep it in the family.[30]

As for Peter Slade, from Guildford, his letter asked the big question with seemingly genuine bewilderment: 'Why is there no political debate on how to tackle the grotesque unfairness that results from the public school/Oxbridge escalator to power and influence – which cascades down the generations – or even to acknowledge that there is an issue to tackle? There was not even such a debate during the 13 years of government that claimed to be Labour.'[31]

A tailpiece to the episode came almost two months later, when Peter Wilby interviewed Lord Waldegrave. Wilby rehearsed the usual statistics about Britain's painfully slow progress towards equality of opportunity and greater social diversity in leading positions. 'Aren't targets, even quotas, needed to achieve real change?' he asked. 'Real change is slow,' replied Waldegrave. 'Short cuts end up in worse things. Look at gender; slowly, slowly, we're getting there. If it had been done by quotas, the change might not have been so profound. You don't change what's on the inside. People just tick boxes. We have to be patient.' After Waldegrave had pointed to Eton having recently recruited a full-time director of outreach, the interview finished with him describing as 'not a bad idea' Wilby's *Guardian* suggestion a few years earlier that elite universities should take the two best students from *every* school in the country. 'I am, of course, flattered,' noted Wilby. 'But this must be aristocratic charm and courtesy at work. Eton would be happy with sending just two pupils a year to Oxbridge? I don't think so.'[32]

By this time, not only had Britain voted to leave Europe, but the country was in the middle of a heady if brief 'meritocratic' moment.

'The March of the Meritocrats' was the *Daily Mail*'s jubilant banner headline on 15 July after Theresa May's announcement of her first Cabinet, with its deliberate cull (relatively speaking) of the privately educated and with Justine Greening as the first comprehensive-educated education secretary. Suddenly, and even more so than after the Hancock initiative, the sector's mood was distinctly edgy. 'You may dislike private schools, and that's just fine, but please don't get your hopes up that this new-look Cabinet throws us into chaos and means the end of private schools,' declared within days the ISC's Julie Robinson. 'Independent schools have no interest in running exclusive schools for a "privileged elite", but don't ever expect any of them to apologise for their excellence ... Making the strong weak does nothing to make the weak strong.'[33] That edgy mood continued over the rest of the summer – not helped first by comments about almost one-third of Team GB at the Rio Olympics being privately educated ('there is clearly a massive untapped resource of talent', argued Carphone Warehouse's David Ross, on the board of the British Olympics Association); then by the Social Mobility Commission's urging of employers to ask job applicants for their educational background ('it is risky to see school type as merely a distinction between state and independent', warned Robinson); and finally, on 9 September, by the new PM's 'Britain, the great meritocracy' speech, with its passage, insisting that private schools do more to justify their charitable status, that so upset the heads.[34]

Much of the general focus was on Theresa May's promise to bring back grammars, but her criticism of the private schools did not pass unnoticed. 'She ignores the huge public benefit of children being educated at independent schools at no cost to the taxpayer,' protested Simon Shneerson of Chorleywood in the *Telegraph*. Moreover: 'Most independent school parents make sacrifices to pay fees, and it's unfair to say that they must also donate to state schools or community projects.'[35] What about the speech's bold title? 'Greening and May are going to give us a "meritocracy"? Oh please,' expostulated the children's writer Michael Rosen in the *Guardian*. 'For there to be a meritocracy under capitalism, you would have to abolish any mechanism by which wealth can be passed on from generation to generation (that ain't going to happen), abolish any mechanism by which anyone can avoid tax of any kind (that ain't going to happen), and abolish all forms of private education (that ain't going to happen). All three of these mechanisms are in place precisely in order to avoid us having a meritocracy.'[36]

Consumed by Brexit, the meritocratic moment (for real or otherwise) was already fading by February 2017, when the former education secretary Michael Gove argued publicly in favour of imposing VAT on school fees and ending the sector's numerous other tax advantages. At the heart of his memorable *Times* article was a passage which in its palpable anger and bitterness almost certainly had no precedent from the pen or indeed lips of a Tory MP:

Are the children of the rich intrinsically more talented and worthy, more gifted and more deserving of celebration than the rest? Of course not. But our state-subsidised private schools continue to give them every possible advantage.

Private schools have facilities, and provide opportunities, most state school students could scarcely envisage. And which most five-star hotels would struggle to provide.

Millfield has an equestrian centre and clay pigeon shooting, two recording studios and a 350-seater concert hall. Stowe also has an equestrian centre, a golf course and its own school nightclub – 'kitted out from the remnants of Crazy Larry's in London'. Charterhouse has its own stables, golf course and tennis, squash, racquets and fives courts.

The fees for these schools are all more than £30,000 per year, per pupil. Well above the average annual salary of most Britons. They are out of reach for all save the very wealthiest, or most fortunate. And yet they are all registered charities with huge tax exemptions.

What about the scholarships and bursaries these schools provide to pluck talented youngsters from humble backgrounds and provide them with undreamt-of new opportunities? Well, what of them? How many students from Knowsley, Sunderland, Merthyr Tydfil or Blyth Valley ever cross the thresholds of private schools? And more than that, for every lucky scholarship boy or girl helicoptered out of poverty, for every Oliver Twist who graduates from the streets to Egyptian cotton sheets, how many others are left behind, like the rest of Fagin's gang, not just condemned to second-class status but deprived of the potential example of one of their number encouraging them all to rise together?[37]

Next day the *Daily Mail* turned Gove's piece into a news story, in turn prompting a vigorous online response – mainly hostile, but not entirely – from its readers:

I earn less than £30,000 a year and yet my son is educated at one of these amazing schools by means of a bursary, as are a large proportion of children there. We have very few oligarchs and plutocrats! Most parents are really struggling to pay the fees and sacrificing all other luxuries (car, holidays, eating out, etc) to pay for them, especially as they go up at least 5% a year. I drive a 15-year-old car and haven't had a holiday in years, but I put my son's education first, which, like it or not, folks, is way better than the state education I had.

If all private schools were banned like in Finland, maybe we would have a much better state education system like they do.

I'm working class: my father deserted us when I was 5. My son won a scholarship to a top public school. There is no way that these schools are only for the rich!

Gove you are an idiot if you think only the super-rich send their children to private schools. I earn £4k a month and send my son to private school. Why, because the schools in my area of Wales are abysmal, so it is the only thing I can do for my son, to make sure he gets a good education to stand him in good stead for his future.

'Has Gove taken leave of his senses?' asked a reader from Chester. 'They should focus on bringing up the standards of discipline in state schools (which was the main issue in our decision to switch our children to independent) rather than demonising parents like us who pay double for our children's education – by our taxes and then paying fees also.'[38]

In the event it was Labour that took up Gove's headline proposal, committing itself in April 2017 to charge VAT on school fees in order to pay for free meals for all primary school children. It was a plan with 'a great deal to recommend it', thought the *Guardian*. 'It is clear and uncomplicated and sends a strong message about what a future Labour government would look like: in favour of good universal provision and against privilege for a small minority.'[39] But not so the *Mail*, which in its news pages quoted prominently the HMC's chairman Mike Buchanan ('this policy is based on dodgy maths, myths about independent schools and misunderstandings about the types of parents who typically buy private education these days') and in its editorial accused Jeremy Corbyn of playing 'the politics of envy card'. 'Rising fees,' added the paper of Middle England, 'will force many middle-class parents, who make enormous sacrifices to educate their children privately, back into the state system – at huge cost to the taxpayer.'[40] *The Times* agreed, arguing that if this 'socially divisive' scheme were ever to be implemented, 'the independent sector would become even more exclusive, accessible only by the children of the very wealthy'. In sum: 'Private schools save taxpayers money. The parents who pay the fees should not be penalised for doing so.'[41]

Over the next year, through to spring 2018, the private school issue seldom surfaced in a public discourse dominated week in, week out by all things Brexit. If May had ever been seriously minded to do anything significant, as part of her stated ambition to promote greater equality of opportunity, her straitened parliamentary circumstances seemingly signalled an end to that. The sponsorship issue was a case in point. In May 2017, despite the diffidence with which the call for taking an active sponsoring role had been heeded by most private schools, the Tory election manifesto had renewed the objective that such schools should be helping to improve the state sector, with the aim that at least a hundred should sponsor an academy or start a free school in the state system. Significantly, the manifesto had included as a proposed option the negative incentive strategy that had been advocated the previous year by England's Chief Inspector of Schools – namely, that sponsorship be linked to the retention of the financial benefits of charitable status. However, by September 2017, only three months after May's return to No. 10, all the signs were that this option had been 'rowed back on' by the new Tory government in favour of a conciliatory, voluntarist strategy of encouragement.[42]

One of the very few exceptions to the general invisibility, certainly in terms of achieving any immediate traction, occurred in Scotland. There, the Scottish government's finance minister, Derek Mackay, announced in December 2017 that he had accepted the recommendation of a review of business rates chaired by a prominent former Scottish banker; and that accordingly, the country's private schools would by 2020 no longer be entitled to benefit from business rates relief, a benefit estimated to be worth £5 million a year.[43] Reaction ran true to form. John Edward of the Scottish Council of Independent Schools (SCIS) challenged the SNP's Mackay to be 'honest' and admit that the change was a 'political gesture'; the Scottish Tory education spokeswoman called the move a 'blatant attack' on the private school sector; and Scottish Labour's education spokesman said it was 'unfair' for private schools to receive rates relief while state schools were struggling.[44]

A battle for hearts and minds seemed likely to lie ahead – a battle in which emotion would almost certainly play as big a role as reason. In March 2018 the *Independent Education Today* website posted a piece by Andrea Angus, rector at St Columba's School (fees for sixth-formers approaching £12,000) on the outskirts of Glasgow. It was about how, days after Mackay's announcement, she had attended at Greenock Town Hall the biennial concert given by her pupils in order to raise financial assistance 'to families for whom the outstanding education we offer might well be out of reach':

> There was something deeply moving about watching the accomplishments of pupils whose own performances help to fund the education of those who come after them.
>
> Over the course of the two-hour show there were recitals from soloists, ensembles, choirs, orchestras and our exceptional school pipe band. Through a combination of ticket sales and sponsorship the event raised thousands. This year sponsorship came from local businesses and house builders who understand the importance of supporting 'St Columba's Foundation' and this local charitable event.
>
> For some private schools, the news that they will lose the business rates relief will be potentially damaging.
>
> As one of the leading independent schools in Scotland, St Columba's will continue to flourish and thrive, but what will be threatened is this essential charitable service that we offer – making excellent education accessible for all.[45]

Emotion was also to the fore on a Saturday in June 2018, as the *Daily Telegraph* led with a story titled ' "Purge of the middle class" fears at top firms'. Almost exactly two years after Hancock had been successfully faced down by a mixture of Waldegrave and the *Spectator*, it seemed that the government was trying again. 'Britain's leading employers are asking their staff if they went to public school as part of a government drive to improve diversity in the workforce,' reported the paper. 'Ministers have published a series of questions intended for use by major companies and the Civil Service about workers' socio-economic backgrounds. They include asking staff whether they attended a fee-paying school ...' The sector's reaction was predictable ('methodologically naïve', claimed the ISC chair, Barnaby Lenon), as was the paper's. 'Don't scapegoat a private education' was the title of the *Telegraph*'s main editorial that day, as it rehearsed the familiar arguments: private education as 'often a driver of social mobility'; not every pupil 'the child of a billionaire'; middle-class parents working and saving hard 'so that their children can enjoy an opportunity they never had'; 'many schools' offering bursaries; and, of course, almost as a constitutional requirement and now applied doubly regretfully because it was to a Conservative government, 'the politics of envy'.[46]

As it happened, during this summer of a memorably long heatwave, two more private school stories rapidly surfaced: first, the much-mocked revelation that, at St Paul's Girls School, a meal comprising baked potatoes, baked beans and coleslaw had been designated an 'austerity lunch'; then, the news that all but one of thirty top private schools were refusing to allow their pupils to be guinea pigs for the new tougher GCSEs, so that instead they largely took the International GCSE, viewed by some as an easier test.[47] Soon afterwards, the *Sunday Times*'s deputy editor, Sarah Baxter, offered an incisive overview. She wondered whether, in the light of the government guidelines, 'parents who may have sacrificed their own comforts to pay for their children's education are feeling like mugs', that indeed 'they shudder that in the socially engineered world of the future, young George or Harriet will be shunned by elite universities and employers'. However, she went on: 'Dare I suggest their terror is exaggerated? Private schools, in my experience, are brilliant at finding new ways to game the system.' Baxter's list included canny, well-resourced advice on applications; securing extra exam time; and 'the easy availability in the private sector of mind and character-building drama, art, music and sports lessons'. 'So,' she concluded at the end of a notable, truth-telling piece in an almost unfailingly right-of-centre paper, 'no more sob stories, please, about a purge of the middle classes and how the cards are being stacked against private-school pupils. A more realistic assessment is that they've never had it so good.'[48]

That July saw the publication of *Posh Boys* by Robert Verkaik.[49] Hard-hitting and unsentimental, arguing that a mixture of fiscal measures and positive discrimination could achieve 'a slow and peaceful euthanasia' of the existing system, it was provocatively sub-titled *How the English Public Schools Ruin Britain*. Two of the more interesting early reviews were by Clive Davis in *The Times* and Andrew Marr in the *Sunday Times*. 'Would even a government led by Jeremy Corbyn contemplate those steps?' queried Davis. 'Still,' he added, 'at a time when populism is in the ascendant, you do wonder if the elite schools might overplay their hand, seduced by the temptation to push fees higher and higher to attract more of the pampered offspring of the world's oligarchs.' Marr, after noting that 'quite patently buying access to better education and private, privileged networks ain't fair' and 'never has been', also sniffed the possibility of something in the wind: 'For what it's worth, I think change is coming within a decade – on the tax breaks private schools get, their charitable status, and on the numbers of privately educated people recruited to key institutions.' And at the end of his piece, he held out the tantalising prospect that – at last – 'a political campaign against Britain's private schools is coming'.[50]

Silences and Evasions

Even so, taking the six years 2012–18 as a whole, 'patchy' would probably be the fairest description of the quality of the debate. Yes, there have been enough interventions and flare-ups to suggest that *something* is going on; but there have also been long phases of seemingly indifferent quiescence, as well as a general reluctance on the part of politicians, commentators and public intellectuals to grapple closely with the question in an evidence-based, dispassionate way. Our criticism applies equally to the left and the right. Whether for reasons of policy inconvenience, or personal invidiousness, or just lack of ambition, the overall verdict on the resulting patchiness has to be the one beloved of teachers through the ages: 'could do better'. And this is of course, speaking generally, an all too familiar pattern.

Take in the first place the right. Traditionally the Conservative Party and its supporters have been tepid or even hostile about the pursuit of greater equality of outcome, but in theory much more enthusiastic about the pursuit of greater social mobility and equality of opportunity. Yet, with the partial exceptions of Gove and Parris, it is almost impossible to find from significant figures on the right – whether politicians or otherwise – any sustained attempt to relate that latter pursuit to the issue of private education. When for instance in July 2015 the Social Mobility Commission put forward its highly cogent evidence about how middle-class children benefited from a 'glass floor' protecting them from slipping down the social ladder – a glass floor that, in Milburn's words, 'inhibits social mobility as much as the glass ceiling', and to which, as his Commission showed, the aspirations and self-confidence gained and consolidated at private school contributed crucially – the silence from the right was deafening.[51]

As for the media, the case of the generally right-of-centre *Economist* is particularly illuminating. Quite rightly, that sober paper prides itself on its objectivity and intellectual rigour; and undoubtedly, ever since it began in 1843, greater equality of opportunity has been somewhere near the heart of its world view. Unsurprisingly, then, in October 2016 (soon after May's 'great meritocracy' speech) it tackled the issue of stagnant social mobility, emphasising how if this was to be improved it would inevitably mean not just helping poor children to move up, but allowing rich children to move down; yet although the paper correctly noted that 'well-off parents have many weapons with which to defend their children from this fate', and equally correctly referred to how 'even among children with identical educational qualifications, the privately schooled are more likely to get the best jobs and to take home fatter pay-cheques', it entirely failed to connect the existence of a flourishing private schools sector to the lack of the necessary downward social mobility.[52] In December 2017, in the context of all four members of the Social Mobility Commission resigning in protest at the lack of progress and government action, the paper's 'Bagehot' addressed the social mobility theme. After setting out some familiar facts about 'a calcified society', the columnist pondered solutions, among them 'reaching into Britain's past'. 'Britain,' he/she argued, 'has a distinguished history of elite institutions doing their bit for mobility: Oxbridge colleges creating feeder schools, and private schools setting aside places for poor scholars. Given that so many private schools have forgotten their social obligations in their zeal to fatten their coffers with fees from rich Russians and Chinese, it is time to remind them that they need to earn their charitable status.' And that was it. The possibility of any *intrinsic* incompatibility between the aim of enhancing social mobility and the existence of exclusive, relentlessly credentials-focused private schools ('institutions that once turned out flannelled fools and muddied oafs are now obsessed with exam results') was wholly absent.[53]

What else? On the relatively rare occasions when it does engage in the debate about private schools, the right-leaning media is apt to claim – usually sooner rather than later – that the *real* problem lies elsewhere, above all with the inadequacies of the state sector. In October 2013 one of the authors had a revealing exchange of views with the *Daily Telegraph*. The paper published (somewhat to his surprise) a comment piece by him arguing that crucial to the social mobility blockage was the way in which private schools operated so successfully 'as both formidable exam machines and sophisticated social networks in preventing the nice but dim, or even the nice but indolent, from moving downwards'. Next day an editorial ('Better education for all') more or less ignored that thrust, but instead took the line that 'the tiny number of private schools cannot be blamed for the failure of the enormous number of state schools', citing recent OECD figures showing England near the bottom for both literacy and numeracy. 'This sad state of affairs is the result of a decline in standards within the state system, begun by the assault on the grammars and exacerbated under Labour. The solution is not to punish parents who want the best for their children, but to improve the quality of free education, giving the poorest in society the training they need to make their own way into the elite.'[54]

Or take a subsequent quickfire trio from the *Telegraph* stable. Janet Daley later that autumn lamented how 'pupils who were taught in the Dark Age of British state education are now teachers [i.e. in the state sector] themselves', having 'inherited a professional ethos which, until very recently, was designed not to instruct the young ("instructional" being the most pejorative word in the lexicon) in the accumulated knowledge of the adult world, in the best that their own heritage had to offer'; an editorial in August 2014, responding to the latest Social Mobility Commission statistics about the dominance of the privately educated and the SMC's recommendation that potential employers take educational background into account, declared flatly that 'rather than making employers jump through new bureaucratic hoops, far better to raise the standard of education in state schools to make their graduates more competitive'; and in October 2015 a former editor, Charles Moore, asked ironically, 'If half the students at Oxford come from the independent sector, might that not have a teensy-weensy bit to do with the low standards of too many in the state system?'[55]

More recently, a prominent younger commentator of the right has been Fraser Nelson, editor of the *Spectator*. He has also offered a more unusual take, albeit still reaching the same conclusion that the real problem lies elsewhere. In his 'Purge of the posh' response in June 2016 to Hancock's proposal that employers should check the type of school previously attended by job applicants, Fraser argued that private schools were emphatically *not* the problem. Since 2010 under the Tories state schools had become so good, he contended, that 'parents are today more likely to find academic excellence in the state sector than in the fee-paying sector'; and 'the real inequality' lay not between the two sectors, but instead 'in the scandalous way in which the richest state-school pupils receive the best education, and the poorest, the worst', an inequality in significant part driven (he did not need to add) by the close link between top state schools and top house prices.[56] Whatever the validity of these two large claims, they served the familiar purpose of once more letting the private schools off the hook.

Inevitably, most of the media potshots against private schools tend to come from the left. An 'ongoing offence to any system of morality' is how Will Hutton describes 'widespread private education'; Deborah Orr, lamenting that 'the same people keep on winning, generation after generation', defines 'archetypal success' in England as 'private school, Oxbridge, and, eventually, an honour'; the abolition of private schools is on Polly Toynbee's select wishlist; 'the privately educated reign supreme', notes Owen Jones as he analyses how 'inequality runs through our society like a stick of rock'; and 'as long as private education reigns supreme,' John le Carré tells an interviewer, 'don't talk to me about levelling the playing field – the social contract is bust in this country'.[57] Even Mitchell and Webb join in. 'If there was no independent sector,' speculates David Mitchell, 'it would certainly remove a major cause of social division and undermine a bulwark of both snobbery and inverse snobbery', adding that the sector's obdurate defence of charitable status and other tax breaks 'looks like the establishment taking care of its own, looking after places from which most of the public can never benefit'.[58] As for Robert Webb, discussing the lack of diverse background at the top during the Coalition period, 'I don't mind that George Osborne went to St Paul's School', but 'I mind very much if he shows no sign of reading about, meeting and listening to a lot, and I mean A LOT, of people who didn't'.[59]

All this (and it would not be difficult to find other roughly similar left-of-centre commentators and public intellectuals saying other roughly similar things) adds to the debate – yet at the same time is too often a far cry from systematic, policy-oriented analysis of the great running sore that is the private school issue. Two of the relatively few exceptions to this rule are the educational campaigners Melissa Benn and Fiona Millar: the former writes quite often on the issue (including about a challenging visit to her father's old school, Westminster), while the latter keeps an especially beady eye on the question of charitable status and what the private schools do – and fail to do – to justify that incongruous status.[60] Arguably, though, the blame lies less with individuals than with left-of-centre publications for the fact that substantive analysis is largely confined to inevitably little-read academic studies. Take the *Guardian*, the *Observer*, the *New Statesman* and *Prospect*. All to a greater or lesser extent, it would be churlish not to concede, offer a forum for the issue to be debated. But they relatively seldom sponsor detailed, investigative work, or connect with up-to-date scientific research on the subject; nor do they espouse a consistent, clear and vigorous editorial line – as opposed to the (at best) occasional intervention.

Of the four titles, it is perhaps the *Guardian*, because of its greater reach, which carries a particular responsibility. 'You rightly report Alan Bennett's stirring attack on our educational apartheid,' one of the authors wrote in June 2014 to the paper. 'Will you, please, now,' he went on, 'do what you never do and devote an editorial to the issue? Specifically, does the freedom for the 7 per cent justify the detriment to the welfare of the 93 per cent?'[61] The *Guardian* to its credit published the letter – and six months later, following Tristram Hunt's policy initiative over business rates relief, did indeed devote a leader. Sadly, though, it flattered to deceive. 'No one would design an education policy that included a small, well-endowed selected sector that educated many of the richest and some of the brightest in society' was a promising start, before taking refuge in the European Convention on Human Rights (about the right of private schools to exist) as a way of closing down discussion about the intrinsic rights and wrongs. Instead, the paper pinned its hopes on the spread of state–private partnerships and backed Hunt's proposed method of trying to achieve that. 'Labour should brush aside claims that it's anti-aspiration, or launching a new class war,' the editorial ended. 'Tackling entrenched privilege is nothing to do with the politics of envy. This move could be a small step towards a fairer society.'[62] As to any larger step that might involve doing something else about the private school problem, the *Guardian* was silent – and essentially, in terms of fundamentals, would remain so over the next three and a half years.

What explains the left's general reluctance to engage fully and whole heartedly? For those who have chosen to educate their own children privately (or even have been privately educated themselves), an obvious factor is fear of the charge of hypocrisy being levelled; and in an earlier chapter we have quoted Joris Luyendijk's persuasive interpretation to this effect about the *Guardian*'s unwillingness to put Britain's malign school system centre stage. Another factor is almost certainly the widespread assumption on the part of would-be reformers within the educational world that the priorities lie elsewhere, for example with the need to boost the number of good teachers in those state schools in the most deprived areas; while, related to that, is probably an anxiety, albeit seldom articulated, that to concentrate energies on the private school issue is implicitly to downgrade the importance and worth of the state sector – an anxiety that in turn relates to the phenomenon we call 'the private school denier', in other words refusing to accept the reality (unsurprising, given the huge resources gap) that most private schools provide a better education than most state schools.[63] Yet perhaps the killer factor is none of those things. Instead, it is the feeling, deep down and almost impossible to shift, that the issue is simply too difficult and too problematic, that the schools themselves are too impermeably embedded, for there to be a realistic possibility of serious change. That feeling is compounded by an awareness not only of the powerful forces and vested interests arrayed against change, but of the long history of failure on the part of those who have tried to do something. The prevailing negativity, even hopelessness, is in short all too explicable; and we return to this discouraging theme – but in a less pessimistic frame of mind – in our final chapter, after having considered a number of feasible options for reform.

From neither right nor left, but deliberately bipartisan, have been commissions: the Social Mobility Commission, which under the chairmanship of Alan Milburn produced during the 2010s a series of reports before in December 2017 its members resigned en masse in protest at the lack of backing from Theresa May's government; and the Social Market Foundation's Commission on Inequality in Education, which was chaired by Nick Clegg and reported in July 2017. Each time, the dog that failed to bark – let alone bite – was the private school issue, in other words as an issue *in its own right*. The SMC undoubtedly produced over the years a formidable body of work that among many other things detailed the dominance of the privately educated, including with recommendations about how government and employers could seek to bring about a more level playing field, but it never tackled the fundamental question of the intrinsic relationship as such between private education and social mobility. As for Clegg's body, it deliberately eschewed larger structural matters, focusing instead on teacher quality and parental engagement; and accordingly, despite its 'inequality in education' brief, it had nothing to say on the private school issue apart from the rather tagged-on recommendation that the schools provide more tangible and publicly accountable benefits (including teaching support) to their local communities in order to retain charitable status (with the monetary value of that status to be more transparent).[64]

On the Table

Yet, all that said, the heartening counter-fact is that during recent years a fair amount of substantive proposals for reform *have* been put on the table, unlike in the largely barren 1983–2010 period. Leaving to one side the question of specifically targeted fiscal measures (such as abolition of charitable status and/or imposing VAT on school fees), the rest of this chapter tries to give a sense of what *structural* approaches have been suggested in relation to private schools in order to make Britain's overall education system less grossly unequal.

Starting at the ambitious end of the spectrum, there are the abolitionists (aka full-scale integrationists), including those who surface every now and then in letters to the left-of-centre press:

Simple answer to the problem of the public school 'Berlin Wall': take it down. Like the monasteries, rich, used to power, doctrinally divisive; dissolve them. Use their endowments to fund the common weal. Done it before, do it again. *(Mark Williams, Lewes)*

Only the abolition of private schooling and decent state education can bring about genuine equality of opportunity as the most progressive European nations demonstrate. *(John Green, London)*

The boldest move to build a truly inclusive education system would be to remove the charitable status of private schools, as a first step to abolishing them. Only then will there be enough political will and parental engagement to make the whole system fit for purpose. *(Andrew Colley, Halstead, Essex)*

We need to abolish private education because it engenders inequalities of income, property ownership and social mobility … Would that any government could summon up the courage to begin the abolition. *(Neil Wigglesworth, Forton, Lancashire)*[65]

Among more public, higher-profile figures arguing broadly the same, in effect the nationalisation of the private, fee-paying sector, it is hard to find more than the relatively occasional intervention. We have mentioned Polly Toynbee (who normally stays silent on the issue) and Rachel Johnson. Otherwise, leaving aside those who are best known within the educational world rather than outside it, we are able to identify only a few such figures. 'Private schools add insult to injury,' declared Tim Lott in his 'Family' column in the *Guardian* in 2017. 'If you get rid of them and shift all the pupils into the state system, nothing will guarantee the latter's improvement with more certainty. And the middle-class kids, on aggregate, still come out on top because of their pre-existing advantages – so it is especially egregious that so many people so staunchly oppose their abolition.' 'It is doable, practically,' he concluded, albeit without giving much in the way of detail. 'Shame that it just appears impossible to do politically.'[66] That same year, in a 'What if …?' debate at the Institute of Education, the epidemiologist Kate Pickett (co-author of the best-selling *The Spirit Level*) unashamedly insisted that abolition of private schooling was indispensable for the creation of a more equal society.[67] Then, of course, there has been the doughty Alan Bennett, reiterating in a 2016 interview (two years after his Cambridge sermon) his suggestion that private and state schools should amalgamate at sixth-form level. 'It wouldn't,' he predicted, 'be an enormous social upheaval and, once you've merged them at one level, the others would gradually follow.'[68] Our other abolitionist is the broadcaster June Sarpong, a strong advocate of greater social mobility. 'In Britain, unfortunately, you get the education your parents can afford to pay for,' she argued in May 2018 on Sky's *The Pledge*. 'I think it's time to put an end to our private school system altogether … If all kids are in the same schools, then there will cease to be an exclusive pipeline from private schools into Russell Group universities, and that's how we begin to level the playing field.'[69]

Others – but again, not in any great numbers – have advocated positive discrimination as the best way of tackling the problem. 'Instead of collectively rolling our eyes every time a new report on these statistics comes out, let's introduce quotas,' urged the *Guardian* columnist Ellie Mae O'Hagan in 2017 after citing some of the familiar stats about the dominance of the privately educated. 'If 7% of the population goes to private school, then it seems only fair that 7% of Britain's elite jobs should go to privately educated individuals. This would include chief executives, barristers, journalists, judges, medical professionals and MPs.'[70] Similarly out there was the 2016 suggestion by an *Observer* reader, Jane Duffield-Bish from Norwich, that 'all oversubscribed universities' be required 'to allocate 93% of their places to state school pupils', a measure that, combined with 'the implementation of a ballot system to allocate places in popular state schools', would 'blow a hole in the ability of the rich to buy advantages for their children'.[71] The journalist Peter Wilby has been a particular advocate of positive discrimination, describing it in March 2015 as 'the most promising' of the various approaches to change private education's unfair skewing of life chances and seeing such discrimination as taking three possible forms: 'to persuade or force elite universities to step up their efforts to recruit students from state schools, particularly those in disadvantaged areas; to accept lower A-level grades from such students (justified by evidence that when students from the two sectors have equivalent grades, those from state schools emerge with better degrees); and even to introduce quotas'.[72]

When it came to quotas, Wilby had his own pet scheme, which he had put forward in the *Guardian* three years earlier:

Attempts to widen Oxbridge entry face a chicken-and-egg conundrum. Oxbridge says it can't recruit more from the state sector until schools send them more highly qualified pupils. The schools say the pupils won't go – or won't aspire to go – until the universities appear less exclusive. Bold measures are needed to break this impasse.

Suppose Oxford and Cambridge were to ask every state school to identify, at 15, its brightest pupils academically (one, two or three, depending on size). Suppose those pupils were given every possible support and guidance in A-level subject choice and teaching. Suppose they were invited annually to week-long summer schools where they could form their own peer networks of solidarity and support. Suppose, above all, Oxbridge allocated to this pool of talent a fixed proportion of its places – initially, perhaps 70%, but rising to over 90%, so that its UK intake became representative of the general school population – with those who did best at A-level getting preference.

The outcomes, claimed Wilby, would be wholly beneficial: Oxford and Cambridge having 'access to wider and more diverse talent'; the 'chief incentive' for parents to send their children to fee-charging schools disappearing; and, in the context of 'middle-class parents clamouring to get their children into comprehensives in disadvantaged areas in hope of them grabbing one of those precious places', an 'influx of more aspirational families' who would 'raise standards more effectively than anything governments have done in the past 30 years'.[73] Wilby's idea failed, though, to achieve traction (notwithstanding Waldegrave's kindly approval); and when in September 2015 Tamsin Oglesby's passionately argued play at the Old Vic about education and society, *Future Conditional*, endorsed it, there was again no perceptible shifting of the dial.[74]

The approach best broadly labelled as 'Flemingism' – the provision of a substantive number of state-funded places at private schools – has also had its champions. During 2012 the Sutton Trust's founder and chairman, Sir Peter Lampl, made a significant stir as he pushed hard for what he called 'Open Access', through which (he told the *Financial Times*) 'all places at leading independent schools would be awarded solely on merit, with parents paying a sliding scale of fees according to their means'; and he claimed that such would be the evident boost to social mobility that 'more than 80 leading independent day schools, almost half of the total, would be willing to adopt Open Access'.[75] In the event, however, Lampl failed to persuade the Coalition government to reach into its pocket – a reluctance, in his almost certainly correct view, motivated by political unwillingness to be associated with either academic selection or explicitly putting public money into private schools.[76]

An updated form of Flemingism was also the very visible goal during 2013/14 of Anthony Seldon, high-profile head of Wellington College. Reacting positively in December 2013 to Matthew Parris's proposal that 'all private schools should be forced by law to accept 25 per cent of their intake as scholarship boys and girls, funded by the State on a means-tested basis', he likewise advocated in *The Times* that 'independent schools all take a minimum of a quarter of their students from the most socially deprived 25 per cent of young people in the UK, which includes many bright young people who deserve the best opportunities' – an approach that Seldon formally set out in early 2014 in *Schools United*, his report for the Social Market Foundation. 'Where is the social justice in a country where a privileged few have such enduring dominance and the best chance of success in life?' he appealed that spring to *Daily Telegraph* readers. 'Despite 100 years of attempts to reduce the divide between private and state school performance, the gulf has remained. We need a new tack, and the squeamishness of both Left and Right to use the private sector has to be consigned to the dustbin of history.'[77]

The trail then went cold until August 2016, those challenging early days of Theresa May's premiership, when Shaun Fenton (head of Reigate Grammar School and a future HMC chairman) proposed that 'we should increase social mobility by using state funding to open access to independent schools', though without committing himself to a percentage of such places. 'Is it prohibitively expensive for the taxpayer?' he asked. 'Not at all. State funding of places at independent schools would be the same as for a place at a maintained school. Independent schools must find the rest – from alumni, fundraising and the like.' And he emphasised that 'this is not a return to the old Assisted Places Scheme [of the Thatcher/Major years] which was criticised for benefiting the sharp-elbowed middle classes and required the state to pay full fees'. Instead, 'my proposition is that the partial state funding should be for those who qualify for the Pupil Premium'.[78]

Fenton's initiative presaged a more formal one by the Independent Schools Council. Responding to the government's Green Paper consultation ('Schools that work for everyone') that had asked private schools what they could do to 'support more good school places and help children of all backgrounds to succeed', the ISC put on the table its willingness to support financially, on a joint-funded basis, 'the creation of up to 10,000 free places in independent schools, every year, for families who would not be able to afford fees'. 'There would,' explained the ISC, 'be a range of assessment criteria. The plan is designed to meet the government goal of more good school places and would target children from families with lower income.'[79] In response, Labour's Lucy Powell warned ministers against 'fixating' on private schools as a 'silver bullet' to school improvement, while others detected ulterior motives; but Barnaby Lenon, the ISC's chairman, was adamant that 'it's really got nothing to do with charitable status', while Patrick Derham, head of Westminster School, declared that 'we all want all young people to flourish and to be authors of their own life stories'.[80] In any case, it hardly mattered, because the government – perhaps as with Lampl's scheme sensing a political hot potato – in effect let the proposal lie on the table and quietly gather dust. Flemingism redux would for the moment have to wait.

An alternative channel for reform was proposed by Andrew Adonis, who as schools minister between 2005 and 2008 had been largely responsible for initiating the academies revolution in the state sector. Even then he had had his eye on the private sector, revealing as early as 2006 that he was in confidential talks with various private schools about the possibility of their opting wholesale into the state sector – and that he hoped, by so persuading them, that 'we will re-establish a modern version of the direct grant schools'.[81] Six years later, in June 2012, he hailed as the breakthrough moment – 'perhaps the single biggest breach in the Berlin Wall between the private and state sectors of education in recent decades' – the decision of the prestigious private school Liverpool College (a founding member of the HMC) to become a state-funded academy; or, in his words, 'giving up fees but maintaining independence, ethos and excellence'.[82] What about intake for Liverpool College, the handful of other day schools that had also converted, and any others thinking of doing so? They 'exchange academically selected admissions for all-ability admissions, but with a large catchment area and "banded" admissions to ensure a fully comprehensive ability range,' explained Adonis in his Blairite manifesto, *Education, Education, Education*, published later in 2012; and at the same time, they 'continue with a large sixth form, underpinning continued very strong performance'.[83] By early 2014 these state-private hybrids numbered over a dozen, with Adonis hoping that a mixture of altruism and self-interest on the part of other private day schools would yield another 50 or 100 over the ensuing decade.[84] That hope would seem likely (at the time of writing) to be disappointed: perhaps inevitably so, given that the strategy was always dependent to a considerable degree on private day schools feeling the economic chill – which so far, broadly speaking, has not been the case.

Even as he pursued his idea of direct grant academies, Adonis was also strongly advocating something else. 'Just as the challenge is simple – how to unite state and private schools in a common endeavour – I believe the solution is also simple,' he asserted in his 2012 book. 'Every successful private school, and private school foundation, should sponsor an academy or academies.' He went on:

> Simple does not mean easy, nor does it mean little. By sponsoring academies I don't just mean advice and assistance, the loan of playing fields and the odd teacher or joint activity, which is generally what passes for 'private-state partnership', however

glorified for the Charity Commission. I mean the private school
or foundation taking complete responsibility for the governance
and leadership of an academy or academies, and staking their
reputation on their success as they currently do on the success of
their fee-paying schools.

Adonis then made a direct appeal to 'those in the private schools, and
their governing bodies, who are reluctant to embrace academies' –
declaring that 'the nation seeks your engagement in setting up
new independent state-funded academies in a way which does not
compromise your independence, and which renews for the twenty-
first century your essential moral and charitable purposes' – before
expressing satisfaction that, five years after he had started pushing
the sponsorship idea, some prominent private schools (including
Dulwich and Wellington) had already gone down that route.[85] In
practice, it proved a slow business: by early 2014, only thirty-four ISC
schools (by now including Eton and Westminster) were sponsoring
or co-sponsoring an academy, less than 3 per cent of ISC members,
prompting Wellington's Seldon to call that 'agonisingly slow' process
'the most frustrating challenge of my career', citing resistance among
private school governing bodies.[86] He might also have cited resistance
from heads of middle-ranking private schools, anxious about the
likely time and money involved. Nor did subsequent well-publicised
problems at Wellington's own sponsored academy help the cause;
while as Wilby pointed out more generally in 2015, not only were
'most governing bodies' in the private sector 'not interested', but
'many teachers, on both sides of the divide, argue that the public
schools' expertise in teaching a privileged elite is simply not
transferable to comprehensives that educate the other 93 per cent'.[87]
For the moment, at least, Adonis's sponsorship solution would have
to wait for anything like full implementation.

Mixed-up Confusion

Britain's private schools have been showing their colours now
for many decades. Most provide a high-quality academic and

broad education for those who attend them. Yet looked at from the perspective of the country's whole education system, the concentration of so many resources on one small privileged sector is hugely wasteful: the people who work in private schools, and the extensive facilities, could do so much more for the nation's children if they were spread more evenly among those children. The democratic deficit – those educated in private schools monopolising positions of political, economic and social influence later in life – persists like a childhood scar. Above all, the unfairness of the gilded path, the golden ticket, offends all who believe, deep down, in a reasonably equal educational opportunity for every child brought up in our country.

That, then, is the problem in a nutshell. This chapter has seen the vigorous interventions of a few people, an ignoring or skirting around the issue by many more, and an array of on the whole poorly debated and poorly scrutinised policy prescriptions. Yet there is an overall sense that *something* may at last be stirring even if no one is quite sure exactly what. Chapter 8, setting out our own perspective on possible ways ahead to resolve Britain's private school problem, will attempt to clear the fog. But first, we must deal with arguments invariably brought out by those who defend the system as it is and paper over its shortcomings. After all, if they are right, there is nothing to worry about, and no point in debating solutions. We must also address the views of others who, while acknowledging the problem, think that nothing can or should be done about it.

Defending the Status Quo: Illusions and Propaganda

On the face of it, it may seem a tough ask for the powers that be to try to legitimise the status quo. Yet it is hardly surprising if private school leaders and representatives have some propaganda at hand, given that the schools are deeply embedded within the British establishment's institutional reservoirs of power and money. Most are not the property of wealthy corporations or individuals; but the intricate web of social and economic connections between schools, London clubs, Whitehall, Parliament and businesses – often with City links – involves vested interests with ready access to the necessary resources and connections. In its robust 2017 'manifesto', the Independent Schools Council (ISC) urges that 'all political parties recognise the contribution that ISC schools make to the UK economy and society, and do not propose measures which will inhibit our excellence or ability to extend the work we do in partnership with state schools'.[1] Leave us alone, they are saying.

We should consider their justifications, as well as all thoughtful arguments that might support private schooling being allowed to carry on unchanged. So, how do defenders respond to the trio of major criticisms – economic wastefulness, democratic deficit, fundamental unfairness – that we have levelled in Chapter 1?

Boosting economic performance?

Amid the occasionally simmering public concern and longer pregnant silences of the last decade, one summer's evening in 2014 saw a selection of the great and the good from private schools gather for a reception in the Attlee Room at the House of Lords, to celebrate the fact that the government was about to be questioned in that house on its response to the ISC's publication examining the 'impact' of independent schools.[2] It is tempting to speculate that this choice of venue was a vote of thanks to the private schools' erstwhile saviour. The report, commissioned from consultants, had supposedly estimated private schools' impact on Britain's economy and society. Lord Lexden – in an earlier employment, general secretary of the ISC – asked the government's education spokesperson, Baroness Northover, whether the government had assessed 'the impact of independent schools on the British economy, in the light of the report?' No, they hadn't. But was she impressed by the figure of nearly £10 billion, putatively 'the total amount provided by ISC schools to our national economy'? Indeed she was. Her commentary echoed the self-praise of the sector itself, with the ISC's then general secretary, Matthew Burgess, declaring: 'We can now see how important our schools are to stimulating growth, in contributing our fair share of tax and supporting local communities across the country.' David Hanson, chief executive of the Independent Association of Prep Schools (IAPS), astonishingly used the report to call for tax relief to be granted to the parents of private school children.[3]

If a dispassionate assessment of the report had been made, however, their lordships and the Department for Education might have realised that its conclusions are deeply flawed. It shows that all independent schools (not just those in the ISC) in Britain had an economic 'footprint' of £11.7 billion in the academic year 2011/12, when one includes not only the £5.9 billion gross value added of the schools, but also the additional £2 billion of economic activities of the schools' suppliers that were located in Britain, and the further spending of £3.8 billion that was stimulated by the schools' and their suppliers' staff. So far so good: this is a common type of analysis conducted by regional economists. The flaw arises when 'footprint' is soon rephrased as 'impact'. To quantify properly the schools' impact on the economy, one should compare with a 'counterfactual' – a plausible prediction of what the economic scene would look like in their absence, that is, if all children were educated in state schools.[4]

For a school based in a small community, such as the village of Uppingham where the famous school is located, a school's footprint is a plausible starting point for thinking about its impact on that village – though even there it would be important to consider the counterfactual sensibly. But for the nation as a whole, it is quite wrong to interpret the footprint of the sector as 'impact'. It is not as if all the nation's private school teachers and facilities would disappear if the schools were integrated into the state system; yet that is the implicit – false – assumption behind the report's interpretation, when 'footprint' and 'impact' are equated. *All* we can conclude from the report's quantification of economic 'footprint' is that the size of the private sector is large. The largest element is the estimated turnover, which amounted in 2012 to approximately £14,300 per child. So the report, in effect, only serves to reconfirm the huge amount of resources that are devoured by private schools, in the course of educating roughly 6 per cent of Britain's school pupils plus some foreign pupils. In 2016 the Scottish Council of Independent Schools (SCIS) commissioned its own impact study: there, the sum of all the schools' 'operational impacts' (equivalent to the 'footprint' described and estimated in the ISC study) amounted to £456 million, or £15,068 per child in the schools covered by SCIS.[5]

The same flawed inference is made about tax payments. According to the 2014 report, the tax contributions 'due to the activities of all independent schools' amounted to £2.4 billion in 2012, taking into account not only those paid by the school and its employees, but also the taxes paid by the schools' suppliers and their staff and others indirectly linked economically to the schools. The phrase 'due to' suggests that this amount was supposedly caused by the presence of independent schools, and that if they were to disappear the exchequer would lose that income. Yet it is entirely false, inviting ridicule, to presume a counterfactual in which the taxes of those people and companies would not be replaced, if there were an integrated system with little or no private education. Don't the teachers in state schools pay their taxes? The ambiguity of 'due to' is being finessed in the interests of private school propaganda. Again, all we learn from the report's estimates is some detail about the magnitude of the sector.

The report is on somewhat firmer ground when it comes to estimating the 'savings' to the exchequer that come from not having to fund state education for private school pupils. The extent (nearly £4 billion in 2011/12, approximately 3.8 per cent of the UK's total education budget) would imply a relatively small additional tax burden, less than a penny in the pound, if the state were, hypothetically, to pay the bill for everybody. Obviating the need for this extra tax burden could be promoted as a small efficiency gain in defence of private schooling, in so far as lower taxes are thought to imply better economic incentives (though that assumption begs many questions). The estimate is also potentially helpful for education reformers: it provides a baseline measure of how much extra it would cost, if there were a fully integrated educational system, with all education paid for by the state, and before any additional injections of funding to support a higher-quality national system are factored in.

It is also reasonable to ask whether the money heading into private education is, despite its skewing of the nation's education resources, nevertheless economically beneficial overall because it adds to the sum of educational inputs. Private schools 'are good for the economy and society because they increase the total amount of education and knowledge in Britain', declares, in another common defence of the status quo, journalist David Turner in his book *The Old Boys*. 'In this sense they are efficient.'[6] And it is true that many private schools, because they provide a high-quality education, contribute to the developmental and educational achievements of private school children. The ISC's report estimates that the impact of their educational gains on the economy is to add as much as 0.07 per cent to Britain's economic growth. However, this estimate is far too high. It is based simply on the gap between the maths/science scores of private and state school pupils in tests conducted at the age of fifteen by the OECD in its Programme for International Student Assessment (PISA). The report estimates what would happen if the gap were hypothetically closed, with private school children's test scores levelled down to those of state school children.

Yet, what it fails to address (even while quietly acknowledging it) is that much of the test score gap is attributable to the high prior attainment levels and affluent family backgrounds of the private school children, and not to the schools themselves – as independent scientific study has shown.[7] Although private schools are effective at raising test scores such as the OECD's PISA tests, their causal effect on test scores is much lower than the simple gap in the scores. In truth, the overall impact of the extra resources used in the private sector on the 'amount of education and knowledge', and hence on economic performance, is extremely hard to quantify. Moreover, even if a satisfactory estimate could be agreed, it should be weighed against the very high cost of those resources – which could have been spent much more productively if divided more evenly among all pupils. The defenders of the status quo make no attempt to refute, or even to recognise, the wastefulness that arises from the skewed disposition of educational resources.

Aside from propaganda about private schools' economic impacts, other claims are made about the running of Britain's private schools, notably those concerning the internal efficiency with which schools are managed. We have already examined the grand claims asserting that it is the private schools' independence, per se, that gives them their performance edge – claims which have no evidential support. Private schools do have greater freedom to manage and innovate than in state schools. Turner points with approval to the take-up by a small minority of state schools of new lower and upper secondary exams – IGCSEs, Cambridge Pre-Us and the International Baccalaureate – maintaining this to be attributable to the private schools' earlier initiatives.[8] Nevertheless, the scope for innovation is really not that different, especially when private schools are compared with modern free-standing academies. The big difference relates to the size of the budget and to the freedom to admit only the children they choose to. But are the schools actually run more efficiently? As we have seen, hardly.[9]

Diffusing the democratic deficit?

Against the second charge – the astonishing and persistent dominance of privately educated people in Britain's public life – defenders of the private school system are remarkably quiet. One can easily guess why: the facts, as consistently shown in Sutton Trust reports and elsewhere, are unanswerable. Private school old boys (and occasionally old girls) are ubiquitous at the head of law partnerships, leading newspapers, Westminster, government departments and businesses; take the limelight with influential roles on stage and screen; and star in many of the nation's Olympian events, especially those not associated with traditional working-class sports like football. Criticisms – suggestions that there might be something wrong with this in a mature democracy – are rarely challenged and largely ignored by private school leaders; besides, it's what they do, offering the prospect to parents of a fast-track route to positions of influence and economic success. Just occasionally we see a denial, such as from Damian Lewis's 'nonsense' retort to the accusation of unfairness. Benedict Cumberbatch's drama teacher even holds that his old student has been unfairly held back by being at Harrow.[10] But, in general, it would not do for private school leaders to disavow too prominently the reality of their successes, and risk losing customers.

Turner directly addresses the accusation that private schools' dominance in public life constitutes a democratic deficit, holding it does not matter that political leaders have predominantly been privately educated. 'David Cameron and other Eton boys were given a good political education at a school with a long tradition of educating politicians,' he assures us.[11] Other countries, he notes, are also less than ideally democratic, with political dynasties monopolising power. That's all right then, he implies – it's worse in Pakistan. Why worry about the prominence and dominance of private schools here in Britain? Who cares that, from 1834 to July 2018, every Conservative Cabinet included an Old Etonian?

Following the same line of thought, private school leaders draw up their visions of the education they provide, pushing the idea that their pupils will become both the champions of, and integrated into, the communities which they will serve in later life. 'The children we educate here [Reigate Grammar] will take on future leadership roles,' claims Shaun Fenton, 2018–19 chair of the HMC. 'They will be opinion formers, wealth creators, employers, healthcare providers. They can create employment opportunities and a fairer society.' 'We focus,' he adds, 'on qualities of character, so that they define themselves not just by professional success but by their roles as partners, neighbours and members of a community and family.' 'Yes,' he concedes, 'they are privileged to come here', but 'as long as they pay back in spades, it will be an investment not just for their families but for their country.' Meanwhile, Loren Macallister of Shrewsbury House, a prep school in Surbiton, proposes that 'schools themselves have a duty to instil in children a "healthy" perspective on wealth and not encourage them to pursue material things above all else'; she urges the parents of private school children to 'teach their offspring the value of money and ensure they realise how privileged they are'.[12]

Readers may or may not find convincing these and similar responses – essentially paternalistic – to the charge of the democratic deficit. Civic and political education in an exclusive and luxurious school seems to us a million miles from enabling children to learn, develop and practise civic engagement alongside others from all backgrounds. Prestigious education is, alas, no assurance of virtue in our elites. Nor does upper-class knowledge and culture afford an understanding of the needs and wishes of the bulk of the people in society. Nor is it democratic when the majority's prospects of participation at the top of political and cultural life are systematically diminished.

For the most part, however, apologias such as Turner's for the democratic deficit are rare; private school leaders, along with privately educated people who have achieved positions of influence, tend to keep understandably quiet about it, while visions such as Fenton's and Macallister's are more typically shared with those on the inside rather than broadcast to a sceptical wider public. Better not to stir the hornets' nest; easier, perhaps, to hope secretly that the Sutton Trust will go away and stop producing its annoying reports that remind the world how much our democracy continues to be played out on such uneven terrain.

Mitigating Social Injustice?

Much more energy is devoted to trying to neutralise the perception that private schools are still, in this modern age, at the heart of this country's especially unfair system of educational advancement and life chances. Indeed, the accusation of unfairness is rightly seen as the most crucial charge. Wardens of the status quo understandably spend time and effort not only disputing and colouring the facts about the social exclusivity of Britain's private schools, but also highlighting attempts to surmount the 'Berlin Wall' between the two sectors.

Part of the defence's tactic against the unfairness cry is to mount the argument that the schools' successes are based on merit. In Mark Peel's book on the transformation of private schools since 1979, perhaps the most contentious aspect is his bold title – *The New Meritocracy* – and the attractive gloss on the private school system which follows from that term. The idea that people gain jobs or positions of influence on account of their class background sits uneasily with the modern psyche; most people now believe that where people get to in life should reflect their own efforts and talents – even if this does not necessarily coincide with a humane society in which people of all types and talents are accorded respect. Thus, to proclaim that the private school system has become a meritocracy is to suggest that their pupils are achieving life's prizes on a fair and square basis. An insider's judgement is perceptive here. In an otherwise positive review of Peel's book, Malcolm Tozer of Repton College observes that if, by his chosen book title, Peel 'boasts that their former pupils now form the nation's new meritocracy, then he is overstating his case. Yes, there are more means-tested bursaries nowadays, but private education still remains out of reach of the vast majority of the population. Merit is earned and not bought.'[13]

Philosophers Harry Brighouse and Adam Swift define the meritocratic conception of educational equality as the principle that 'an individual's prospects for educational achievement may be a function of that individual's talent and effort, but they should not be influenced by her social class background'.[14] While the first half of this dictum could be said to apply very approximately in twenty-first-century Britain (even if the meaning and source of 'talent' is debatable), the second half is clearly not applicable. Expensive private schooling, and the cultural resources that come with an affluent family background, both affect educational achievement. Moreover, the routes into post-school education and work are not fully based on merit, even after decades of human resource management policies supposedly democratising entry into the world of work. We have seen how effective the private schools have been at working the system to promote their pupils' access to high-status universities, and how the privately educated continue to gain an edge with higher-paying jobs over those emerging from state education with similar qualifications. Nevertheless, all that said, it is the education itself that mainly makes the difference. And here, the modern-day transformation of private schools means that social class inequality has become *more* aligned with educational inequality – at this very moment of history when educational achievement and qualifications matter so much. In such circumstances, the notion of meritocracy is rendered distinctly hollow.

The main defence against the accusation of unfairness begins by casting doubt on the extent of private schools' social exclusivity. Private schools' pupils 'come from a wide range of socio-economic backgrounds', claims the ISC.[15] 'School type is not a proxy for social advantage,' declares their general secretary in 2018, assuring *TES* readers that private schools cannot be blamed for social segregation.[16] Meanwhile, in Scotland's private schools, the children are said to have a 'healthy and diverse mix of backgrounds', with this 'making for a vibrant and modern community that mirrors the real world'.[17] A common tactic, when aiming to paint a picture of diversity, is to focus on the relatively less wealthy private schools in which, proclaims a former chairman of the HMC, 'there are more families with children benefiting from independent education in the "squeezed middle" income range than from the fabulously rich: aunts, uncles and grandparents as well as working spouses all contribute to the fees of many pupils ...'[18] Alas, there may be no expensive Mercedes depositing children at the gates of some of these poorer schools. 'Have you ever actually been in an Independent school and got to know the children and families?' writes one Dr Pridle in response to journalist Laura McInerney's blog on reforming private schools. 'Most schools are not particularly rich,' he continues, 'and neither are the families that choose to spend their money this way. Many families earn modestly and make huge sacrifices, including working multiple jobs, to have their child in such schools.'[19] Another missive (from Nottingham High School, with senior school fees in 2018 of £14,307) berates Michael Gove for attacking private schools' social exclusivity, with the defence that *that* school is far from exclusive: 'He [Gove] speaks of those attending our schools as the "global super-rich" – I am not sure that our parents would recognise this group in our school.' Indeed, 'our parents are much more likely to be taxi-drivers than hedge fund managers'.[20]

These various descriptions are hard to square with the facts – drawn from the government's Family Resources Survey – which conclusively show how, *overall*, private school participation is mainly concentrated at the top of the income spectrum. While it is true there are some children from low-income families at private schools, the evidence is that there are not that many. Seven out of every ten private school children come from families in the top quarter of the income spectrum, while seven in a hundred come from a bottom-quarter family. It is sufficient to take another glance at the figure on page 2 to conclude that, while private school participation is by no means wholly confined to the very rich, and while the sacrifices of some relatively less well-off families need to be acknowledged, private school families are nonetheless largely drawn from the top end of the income ladder. According to data from the OECD, the socio-economic divide in Britain between the private and state sectors of education is among the highest in the developed world.[21]

If the critique of social exclusiveness is too difficult for the status quo guardians to counter convincingly, the next tactic is to accept quietly that there is an issue to be addressed, while signalling robustly that the schools are on to it. 'HMC members are fully committed to widening access to their schools,' Richard Harman, a former HMC chair, has insisted.[22] Bursaries and scholarships are promoted as aiding access to low-income families, the former being the primary tool. Some affluent schools have indeed genuinely been trying hard to open up to a more socially mixed population – mainly by soliciting donations and otherwise accumulating funds that can be distributed through means-tested bursaries. Lancing, for instance, alma mater of one of the authors, launched in early 2018 a fund-raising campaign for a £6 million bursary endowment. For the purpose of augmenting bursaries, a few schools, such as Dulwich and Harrow, can cream off profits from their East Asian operations; while Eton has tapped financial markets for loans at favourable rates. Some schools proclaim vehemently that they care about social inclusivity, and think they can make a difference. 'It's wrong to say that independent schools simply educate the elite without a care for others, when in reality, we're part of the solution to social mobility' is the optimistic claim of the Master of Wellington.[23] The ISC concurs that private schools in general 'aid social mobility by providing free places for children from lower-income homes and by running partnership projects with state schools'.[24]

Can this be it, then? That private schools are *improving* social mobility?

That there is a good chance of upward social mobility for each child from a lower social class who is granted a fee-free place in a high-quality private school is self-evident; and the well-researched experiences of children who went through the Assisted Places Scheme during the 1980s or 1990s have generally, if not universally, been found to be positive.[25] But how much *overall* difference – in practice – do bursaries make to broadening access? 'A third of our pupils are on some sort of fee reduction' is the mantra commonly brought out, when there is a need to enhance the narrative that effective action is being taken on social inclusivity.[26]

Reading between the lines of hype, it is soon apparent that means-tested bursaries aimed at lower-social-class families are only one part, and a minority part at that, of the help with fees. There are multiple motives and purposes for offering fee reductions.[27] Scholarships are not particularly aimed at low-income families. Fee reductions are offered to siblings, children of staff and to families who find that they are temporarily financially distressed. Across the sector use is regularly and deliberately made of 'the large-number trick', whereby the total amount devoted to bursaries for low-income families – £385 million in 2017 – is declared. Such large numbers are sometimes hard to interpret, and might sound generous at first. However, as we have seen in Chapter 5, for several years *only 4 per cent* of turnover has been devoted to bursaries. In 2018, more funds were spent by private schools on non-means-tested discounts than on means-tested bursaries.[28] When pressed, ISC chairman Barnaby Lenon conceded in 2017 to Parliament's education committee that only 1 per cent of those in ISC schools across the UK – just 6,000 children – had fee-free access.[29] Though more support is talked about, and new groups such as the Springboard Foundation and the Arnold Foundation have emerged to raise funds and manage bursary programmes, there are no signs that access to private schools has been significantly opening up.[30] In reality, because of their small scale, bursaries do not offer a resolution of the problem of the private school system; and there is no evidence that they are likely to do so in the foreseeable future.

Bursaries may also be a bad answer in principle. They are normally linked, if not with scholarships then with some form of academic selection. This filter creates the risk that some more able children are creamed off from the local state schools, with demoralising effects on teachers and other children. 'I do know that the siphoning off of an elite in a school can mean that there are no role models left to be the very makers of excellence for the rest,' relates one honest private school head.[31] Such 'harms' are not the responsibility of these heads, who must each do the best for their own school; and the harms are taken to be only minor, as long as there are only a few children involved. Yet, there lies the problem: if ever the bursary programmes were to be scaled up and become seriously successful, and still skewed towards academically bright children, the problem of an adverse effect on neighbouring schools would cease being 'only minor'. The issue would become acute in particular localities where many private schools are concentrated – such as, for example, the London boroughs of Richmond, Camden and Westminster, where more than three in ten schools are independent. Or take Edinburgh, where a third of Scotland's private school pupils are found. If the schools were to fill up a quarter of their places with the brightest state sector pupils, where would this leave peer effects, not to mention morale, in Edinburgh's other schools?

An alternative way to convey the *impression* that the schools are seriously addressing their problem of social exclusivity is to promote their 'partnerships' with state schools. 'Increasing hostility towards private education is unjustified and ignores partnerships,' insists Julie Robinson, ISC general secretary. Leo Winkley, head of St Peter's in York, goes further by maintaining that, alongside bursaries, partnerships can be viewed as 'part of the solution' to the 'problem of social inequality'. And Barnaby Lenon sums it all up with the extraordinary claim that 'our schools are fully engaged with the state sector'.[32]

Do 'partnerships' substantively mitigate the system's overall unfairness? In support of this claim is the statistic that most private schools within the ISC membership – nine out of ten, amounting to 1,140 schools in 2017 – report that they have a partnership with one or more state schools. The statistic is then typically followed by examples of good practice.[33] At the pinnacle are the small number of schools that have sponsored free schools or academies such as the Folkestone Academy (set up by King's School, Canterbury), Theale Green (Bradfield), or Holyport College (Eton). Sponsored sixth-forms include Harris Westminster (Westminster) and the London Academy of Excellence (Brighton College and five other private schools). At their best, such sponsorships entail some deployment of teaching staff and plentiful resources, sometimes managerial participation, and a range of joint activities. Next level down are the more numerous formal partnerships, involving shared facilities, joint cultural happenings, collective university-preparation events and some academic sharing, sometimes involving multiple schools as with the Southwark Schools' Learning Partnership.

Yet most of the relationships labelled partnerships are really quite minor, such as 'members of staff serving as governors on state schools' (567 schools); 'partner for debating and public speaking clubs/events' (236); 'host joint drama events' (150); invite pupils to attend music lessons or performances (450); share swimming pool (304). By contrast, only 156 schools are involved in the more significant action of seconding academic teaching staff. The most common category of academic sharing is 'invite pupils to attend lessons, workshops or other educational events' (754 schools), while for sport it is 'playing fixtures with or against state schools' (892).[34] Often, though the data do not reveal how often or at what price, the facilities-sharing classed as partnerships involves a commercial exchange. All these arrangements are seen to be beneficial for both parties involved – that is why they are renewed. Yet no proper independent evaluations in relation to social mobility objectives have been made public, and probably none have been carried out – which is unfortunate given that partnerships, along with bursaries, take up so much of the limited air time devoted to private schools in public and political discourse. 'I'm sorry to say, but the ISC's list of activities is hardly evidence of a comprehensive commitment to partnership with state schools' was the verdict of Michael Wilshaw, chief inspector of schools. 'These are crumbs off your tables, leading more to famine than feast.' Educational consultant Joe Nutt agrees that partnerships 'must be more than joint concerts and swimming galas', yet is optimistic that there 'is a growing wish to see ideas, projects and collaboration between schools that produce clear classroom benefits'.[35]

In truth, there are limits to the extension of genuine partnerships – the reluctance on both sides to indulge in old-fashioned paternalistic relationships, financial constraints on the private schools whose governors are unwilling or unable (because of parental reluctance) to share copious resources, and the different skill sets needed in the two sectors. The head of one school remarks that their effectiveness as a sponsor had 'reached the plateau because we were probably at our best looking after their top 40 per cent; we were doing nothing for those children below that'. Another relates that, lacking a major degree of resource transfer, it is hard for a financially constrained sponsoring school to convey a positive ethos to the sponsored school. Indeed, the less affluent private schools have been especially wary of this approach and angry at government plans, advanced in the Conservatives' 2017 election manifesto (though later shelved), which would have obliged them to undertake costly relationships with state sector schools if they wanted to maintain the benefits of charitable status.[36]

In short, the tactic of emphasising the high proportion of schools involved in some sort of relationship with a neighbouring state school, alongside hand-picked snapshots of school sponsorship in those relatively few cases where substantive resources are shared by a few, very affluent schools, gives a misleading impression that most relationships are like these prize exhibits. They are not. It is hard to know the real extent of resource transfer, or of pupil-mixing, that takes place in most 'partnerships', but it would strain credulity to suggest that these activities even begin to surmount the huge resource gap between the two sectors, or engineer any meaningful social mixing between the children of the different educational sectors. Engagement and good relations with one's neighbours? Yes, on occasion. Seriously bridging the divide? Afraid not. Any prospect of scaling up across all private schools? Sorry again.

The last, and perhaps the flakiest, argument surrounding the problem of social injustice is the idea that the private schools are somehow mitigating the unfairness of the system through their charitable and other voluntary activities. Charity fundraising at school has been included since 2014 under the 'public benefit' umbrella in the ISC's annual census, and indeed some heads of schools with charitable status believe that this giving fulfils, at least in part, their regulatory obligations. 'How we do it,' explains one prep school head about her school's delivery of public benefit, 'is fundraising for the girls' chosen charities, so they will choose which charities they want to support. Going out to visit our local elderly people's home – there are two near here ... We go at Harvest and take all the Harvest gifts and sing. We go at Christmas. We go for visits.'

Even if one were to accede to the principle behind noblesse oblige, whereby privilege is thought acceptable as long as the privileged discharge their social obligations, the extent of giving rather pours cold water on this argument from the start. Around £25 per child is raised each year – much more than would be typically raised in state schools, but a drop in the ocean when compared with all the additional resources devoted to private school children themselves.[37] For some schools, the proclaimed vision extends beyond the virtues of giving in the present, and coalesces with the objective that private schools can – and should – help their children grow into people who will serve the community through their adult lives. 'It's not only public benefit, but it's more long-term – opening these things up to children so that they will begin to think about them on their own and what they can do as adults' is how one anonymous head conceives this aspiration. 'It's so that they will make a difference as young adults.'[38] Private schools' charitable activities and associated civic and moral education, it is claimed, ensure that their pupils go out into the world ready to serve and give back to their communities. Implicit is the notion that this contribution is further settlement of what the privately educated owe the rest of society for their advantageous start in life. Underneath is the hidden presumption that private schools do their civic and moral education better than state schools, and that their pupils go on to be better citizens in some way.

Yet, once again, this presumption seems questionable; and no evidence is offered that the privately educated do in fact go on to become more socially responsible citizens than the state-educated. The picture of civic activity and social benefit reported by the twenty-five-year-old participants in a 2015 survey of people educated in England shows little or no difference between the products of private or state schools. With the spotlight on just those coming from managerial or professional families, some 17 per cent of these young adults – whether privately or state educated – did some voluntary work or gave unpaid help to other people at least once a month; and among the privately educated, some 9 per cent attended meetings for local groups or voluntary organisations at least once a month, as compared with 10 per cent for the state-educated. If the privately educated are so much better primed with a moral and civic education, ready to give back in return for their privileged education, how is it we see no difference between them and everyone else from similar backgrounds, just seven years out of school?

The problem lies elsewhere?

Whereas private school insiders typically defend the status quo by talking up their schools' economic and educational contributions to the country, or by claiming that they substantially offset their children's privileges, there are others who might acknowledge the problem of exclusive private education, but nevertheless find justifications for a policy of doing nothing about it.

One such justification we can call the 'rival inequalities' defence: in particular, the view that inequalities within the state school system are a more important concern. 'The major sponsor of inequality in Britain is unequal education, the fact that within the state system that educates 93 per cent of children the poor get so much worse outcomes than the rich. I think that's outrageous and I can't work out why there isn't more anger at this,' declares *Spectator* editor Fraser Nelson, adding that 'instead of discussions about education, you get onto this obsession with state versus private'.[39] As usual, the morality of school choice engenders strong emotions, as for example from journalist Janet Murray:

> By sending your child to private school, you are using the means you have – money – to get the right education for your child. But the state sector is full of parents buying advantage. They kid themselves that what they are doing is somehow morally superior. The truth is that every person who moves house to get into a catchment area is playing the system. So are those who pay private tutors, or consultants to help with school appeals (both booming businesses). Parents who suddenly discover a faith in God to get their children into a certain school are lying and cheating.[40]

The argument goes that indignation about those who choose to pay for privilege through private schooling, an open and honest choice to better their children's prospects, should instead be directed at those who, through whatever means, game the admissions system to exploit variations within the state school system. Such people, continues the argument, are guilty of insincerity or duplicitousness if they simultaneously moralise against the parents of private school children. 'I am fully aware that I paid for an excellent comprehensive with my house, so it would be hypocritical to say that people shouldn't pay school fees!' is how one self-aware parent avoids this ethical trap.[41]

One could, however, question the moral equivalence attributed to varying forms of trying through financial means to do the best for one's own children. Private tuition, for example, is small beer compared with school fees, and might permit filling in gaps not provided by local schools. Likewise, the similarity of paying private school fees with moving house for educational reasons should not be overstated. In financial terms, the costs of moving to be near a top-performing school can be substantial, but still a lot smaller than the average cost of private education over the course of the children's education.[42] And those costs, moreover, are just for the duration of the education. As one Mumsnet commentator advises another who is considering her own 'move or go private' dilemma: 'I would move to the area with decent schools. When the children have finished at school you can move to a cheaper area and pay off the mortgage.'

But to dwell on the relative ethics of rival inequalities is to miss the point. The rights and wrongs of an individual family's choices are an intrinsically unproductive and divisive way to debate and resolve the problem of Britain's private school system. The more significant issue that Nelson raises is the practical comparison between the different sources of educational inequality. His objection interestingly shares something – the realisation that educational inequalities come in multiple forms – with one of the more pessimistic ideas currently in circulation, dubbed 'effectively maintained inequality'. According to American sociologist Samuel Lucas, 'socio-economically advantaged actors secure for themselves and their children some degree of advantage wherever advantages are commonly possible'.[43] Shipped across the Atlantic and applied to the British scene, the idea is that, were our private schools hypothetically to 'disappear', the affluent classes would, sooner or later, amplify the differences among state schools, and secure access to the best for themselves, thereby maintaining their access to the best positions in adult life. 'If they kept their children in British education at all, rather than sending them abroad, [wealthy] parents would ensure that they would attend the best-performing comprehensives,' surmises David Turner. He adds that 'the rich will generally be schooled with the rich and the poor with the poor – whether in Britain or in Finland or Sweden'.[44] Janet Murray similarly reckons that 'abolishing private schools would mean the most affluent would simply create their own "elite" within the state system'.[45]

Yet is it really the case that inequalities within the state system are, or would become, as dire as those between state schools and private schools, or more so? And if so, what would that imply if private education were to be reformed?

On the one hand, Nelson is right to be concerned. Since the peer resources of state schools in different neighbourhoods vary, and since the state system is so large, the differences among its schools are important. Even though the funding of schools is fairly uniform (with some variation remaining), substantial differences in attainment levels between different regions have arisen – London schools, for instance, surging ahead – alongside gaps between girls and boys, between high-income and low-income families, and between ethnic groups.[46] Postcode variation arises because of the concentrations of middle-class families in distinct neighbourhoods, and in some places the presence of grammar schools. Despite pay incentives, schools in disadvantaged areas have difficulties in attracting experienced teachers, and they suffer from higher turnover of staff. All such differences deserve close attention from education policy-makers.

Yet on the other hand the funding gap between private and state schools is of a different order of magnitude to any differences between different schools or areas within the state system. So, too, the private/state gap in the wealth of pupils' families is much greater than the wealth variations among parents at most state schools. And it is simply far-fetched to suppose that such extreme resource gaps as currently exist between private and state would emerge or be tolerated in a universal British state system. Moreover, one 'outrage' does not cancel out another, and the need to level the playing field within the state sector should not be taken as an excuse to forget or ignore the steep slope up to the next suite of fields, where private schools flourish in for the most part splendid isolation. Using state school inequalities to sanction silence or torpor over the private/state inequality is a red herring. As we have seen, the fact that only a small proportion of school children attends a private school belies their much greater significance in Britain's political, social and economic make-up. Political controversy is common about the role of grammar schools, yet it is often forgotten that there are fifteen times as many private schools as there are grammar schools in England. The idea that private schools are, somehow, too small to be relevant for the question of educational inequality is cousin to the perspective of those who choose, despite the evidence, not to recognise the high quality of the majority of private schools. That modern-day private schools do make a difference – to the children who go there; to Britain's educational system as a whole; to society beyond – should be incontrovertible.

Free to choose?

Among those who regard Britain's private school system as a non-issue, the argument with the greatest traction springs from the laissez-faire tradition – so privileged during the last third of a century, as markets have reigned supreme in seemingly ever-more aspects of life. 'I earn a lot of dosh. I spend it. If some of that is on my [child's] education, where's the issue?' asks one father in a social media forum; another insists, 'We don't live in a communist state and people can spend their money as they like. Of all the things to spend your money on, your children's education is by no means the worst'; while a mother has the same point of view: 'Most people seem to have no problem with the concept of luxury goods or hotels or holidays etc – why shouldn't people spend their own money on education if they choose?'[47] It seems that the appetite for school choice so cultivated since the time of Margaret Thatcher, including the consideration of private or state education, has permeated a significant part of the population.

This perspective deserves serious consideration. Paying for private schooling is an expression of individual liberty, and liberty is valued per se, quite apart from the other benefits that the schools bring, especially the high-quality education itself. Yet liberal values are never absolute. They need to be weighed against other, also legitimate values – especially the importance of good and fairly distributed schooling for all our children. So what, precisely, is the 'issue' with private education that outweighs the value of the freedom to spend your money on it without restraint?

The main answer is that the lack of social justice in an exclusive private school system is entrenched across generations in an enduring cycle of privilege. Briefly, to reiterate: the first part of the cycle sees a family's high income enabling their daughters and sons to attend a high-cost private school; in the second part, the advantages of the high-quality education show up in due course in high-earning jobs and privileged access to positions of influence. Neither part of this cycle of privilege is automatic for every individual from an affluent background; but the income and status differences and the identities of one generation are more often than not copied into the next through education. This is the reason why we emphasised, at the very beginning of Chapter 1, that education is *different* from the consumer goods and services people spend their money on. Schooling is for the long term; it is formative, part of the process through which we become who we are. All modern-day societies have cycles of privilege, to varying degrees; but in Britain, where inequality is high and social mobility low, private schooling really does matter. It is hard to imagine a notable improvement in social mobility coming about while private schools as they stand are given full rein. Allowing, as our society does, unfettered expenditure on high-quality education for the small minority of the population with sufficient financial resources to make use of that freedom in turn places a robust limit on that mobility, and thereby condemns our society to an unacceptable degree of social segregation and inequality. Both parts of the cycle are behind the embedding of privilege, reinforcing each other: the schools' degree of exclusiveness interacts with their effectiveness in generating higher subsequent incomes for their pupils.

A second, if subsidiary, argument for restraint on the freedom to spend money on private education stems from the positional character of some of that education. As we have seen, one way in which the private school advantage is secured is through schooling's role as a positional good, that is, something whose value derives from a person's *rank* in life. If private schooling moves one person up that rank, someone else is moved down. If there are capacity constraints in high-ranking universities, or scarce good jobs, then private schools' achievements in gaining a disproportionate share directly disadvantage those from state schools. To the extent that the money spent on private schooling is positional in this way, the laissez-faire defensive argument for freedom to choose is undermined. Like anything else whose use has negative effects on other people – for instance, high-polluting vehicles or loud noise-making after midnight – societies often legitimately constrain them, whether partially through taxation or regulation, or in totality by proscribing them. So indeed it could be with private education. The parents of aspiring children in state schools might be less willing to sanction private school parents' freedoms if, for instance, they were fully aware of the relentless efforts that private schools devote – with considerable success – to snaffling for their own people the best university offers.

For both these reasons – British private schooling's long-term inter-generational and positional effects – a suspension or qualification of the principle of freedom to choose, as applied to education, may be justified. When privilege is locked into society through the private school system, then the principles of social efficiency, decent democracy and above all fairness challenge, or even trump, the liberal values that would otherwise allow people to spend their money on education without restraint.

An End to Fatalism?

Historically speaking, class divisions have been ever-present – and not just in Britain; but that does not mean that education is merely some superficial clothing for a fundamentally and permanently unequal society. No one should doubt that a reform of Britain's private school system would make a difference. The centrality of schooling in both social and economic life is an enduring feature of modern times, which is why the reproduction of privilege is now tied in inextricably with the way we organise our formal education. Other countries manage their educational systems with far fewer private/state inequalities than in Britain, and in some cases the private sector is virtually non-existent. For too long, however, reformers seem to have given up hope of doing anything but scratch at the outer edges of the problem. They seem to have been gripped by fatalism, resigned to defeat by vested interests. Perhaps they are tired. Lives and careers move on, and people go to places where a win seems possible.

What is clear is that failure to stand up to the vested interests and to inaugurate reforms to the system will result in more of the same, for the foreseeable future. Little or no change can be expected from any natural evolution of the private school market. An unreconstructed private school sector in Britain will perpetuate the democratic deficit for generations; continue to over-concentrate teaching resources; hold back the majority who cannot afford to join the high table; and channel the advantages flowing from our affluent private schools to the small minority who attend. It is they who will enjoy the extraordinary sports fields, theatres and music rooms, as well as the great halls of learning and state-of-the-art laboratories – facilities unimaginable to the average school child or even parent. It is they who will get to grow up in an often inspirational environment, among a concentration of other children from affluent families, accustomed to the extensive trips, stimulating guest speakers and other educational add-ons beyond the budget of any state school. And as night follows day, it is they who will gain for themselves the lion's share of the high-status, high-paid and influential jobs later in life.

So far, no system of bursaries, sponsorships, partnerships, or any other attempts to mitigate privilege, have had more than a surface impact. No current defence of the status quo stands up to serious scrutiny. We really do have a problem.

8

Options for Reform

The British public is often credited with a sense of fair play. Asked, in a poll conducted by Populus for this book, whether they think 'it is unfair that some people with a lot of money get a better education and life chances for their children by paying for a private school', 63 per cent of the respondents agreed with that statement, as compared with 18 per cent who disagreed. In other words, *more than three-quarters* of those who expressed an opinion one way or the other agreed that private schooling in Britain is unfair.[1] Faced with this balance of opinion, on top of the moral argument and the evidence, we should be urgently considering how to reform the system. For too long, all the political parties have shied away. Instead, their limited aim has been to use private schools somehow to help state schools improve, as the main part of the private schools' contribution to 'public benefit'.[2] We have seen how minimal these policies can be; how limited they are in the scope of what they could hope to achieve; and how little overall effect government actions have had on the social exclusivity and unhealthy dominance of Britain's private schools.

In this chapter we set out options for serious reform. We evaluate each according to their pros and cons, and whether they could work. A good reform should be both feasible and potentially effective. The main objective for any reform of private education in Britain should be to lead towards a fairer society.

There is no reason why fairness needs to be at the expense of any losses of efficiency within schools; and across the system as a whole, a rebalancing towards the state system would make better use of the nation's resources. In the long term, the reward of good reform would be to diminish the democratic deficit in this country, bringing up a more representative group of people who rise through their education and early employment experiences to become the leaders in Britain's public and commercial life. And, of course, over and above all this, meaningful reform would send out a wholly positive message about what sort of society – equitable, inclusive, released from the class shackles of the past – we are seeking to become.

The proponents of any reform need to be mindful of the missed opportunities of the past and the reasons why they were ducked, including the blocking powers of vested interests who will haul out the usual excuses; to respect and preserve the best of the educational qualities that have evolved in recent decades within these very traditional institutions; and to harness the good motives of teachers who are working in private schools, and of parents who are using them.

There are two types of possible reform. In the first, the aim is to diminish the demand for private schools; this could be done either by lessening the advantages they bring – which in turn would directly lower educational inequality – or by raising their cost, or by a mixture of both. If the reforms are successful, some parents will decide to switch their children to the state sector, and educational inequality is further reduced as the private sector shrinks. In the second type of possible reform, the aim is to diminish the supply of private education, by bringing part or all of the private sector within the state education system; and educational inequality is tackled directly by crossing the sectoral divide – a merging of the private with the state education tracks. These two types of potential reform are not mutually exclusive: we envisage that, if sufficiently thought through, combinations of reform options could be followed to good effect. We are presenting here what we believe to be the fullest discussion for many years of possible – and *practical* – ways forward in resolving Britain's private school problem.

Handicap stakes

One way of reining back some of the advantages that private schools have over state schools is to place restrictions on universities' admissions policies. The prospect of quotas or targets for state school pupils at top universities – a fitting reversal of the guaranteed places for specific private schools that used to prevail at some Oxbridge colleges – is typically considered politically beyond the pale. So too is the idea of quotas at Oxbridge for every sixth form. 'The real killer blow to public schools would be the application of quotas for university entrance,' warned the prominent private school ex-head Martin Stephen in 2017.[3] Yet something similar to quotas is already utilised in British universities as part of the 'access' strategies of successive governments: namely, contextual admissions criteria. These could be expanded in both scope and purpose to include the reform of private schools' stultifying effects on social mobility. Here some background is helpful.

Following the hiking in 2012 of university fees to £9,000, concern has grown about the gap between social classes in university attainment, and in particular about the low proportion of students from disadvantaged families who gain places at high-ranking universities. To encourage participation, universities have been mandated to engage in outreach work to promote higher education among school children from low-income backgrounds. The stimulus for universities has been the government's leverage over funding and fee-setting.

Yet improvement from outreach schemes has been modest, and so the use of contextual data about applicants to inform admissions – and potentially the need for additional support – has been increasing.[4] The contextual data being used can be about the applicant's school, such as its average achievement level; the area where the applicant lives, such as its prevalence of socio-economic disadvantage; or the individual, such as whether he or she has spent time in care. Universities also draw data from their outreach schemes, and the indicator most widely used in top universities is whether applicants have successfully attended and completed one of the university's outreach programmes. So far, however, contextual admissions policies are far from universal, and the use made of them is often not very transparent. If applicants are not properly informed about whether their background will be taken into account, their choice of university is likely to be less ambitious. Typically, contextual data is being used to reduce A-level admissions requirements by at most a grade – for instance AAB rather than AAA; but there are exceptions such as Bristol University's scheme where the potential reduction for contextually identified applicants is up to two grades, and at Edinburgh University even three. As of 2017, contextually driven admissions had had only a small effect on the numbers of students from disadvantaged groups going to a leading university. Yet, where they have made a difference, there is no evidence of universities having suffered higher drop-out rates, or diminished performance in students' final exams.[5]

As the access agenda evolves, universities are being urged to make greater use of contextual admissions indicators, to extend the list of potential indicators of disadvantage, to be more transparent on how they use them, and to offer larger grade concessions. Where the number of high-ranking university places is capped or otherwise limited, any such expansion in the deployment of contextual admissions policies could diminish the success rates for other applicants – including those from private schools – who do not come from disadvantaged backgrounds.

If private school reform were explicitly allied to the access agenda for disadvantaged groups, the effect could in time be striking. Whether a person has been privately educated could easily be added to the list of contextual data and given some weight in admissions policies. Lady Margaret Hall College at Oxford has led the way with an example of how this might be done, starting in 2016 a free foundation year for under-represented students, where 'under-represented' explicitly includes the condition that applicants have never attended a private school; lowered entry grade requirements are built in to the admissions process for the foundation year. In other universities, the typical one-grade concession on offer matches, perhaps by coincidence, the one-grade gap that is warranted by the evidence, noted on p. 12, that state-educated students get better degrees at university than private-educated students with the same A levels. An equivalent way of putting that evidence is to observe that state-educated students admitted with a 'differential offer' involving a one-grade concession will, on average, gain university degrees as good as those of private-educated students admitted with one-grade better A levels.

A government seriously committed to reform could – through incentivised targets, or financial inducements that deliver more funding for state school students than for private school students – persuade universities to adopt differential offers.[6] Simply put, a private school applicant would be expected and required to achieve higher A-level grades or Scottish Highers (or their equivalents at, for example, the International Baccalaureate) than their state school counterparts. Moreover, the level of handicap given to private school applicants could be varied according to the time spent in private school, so that the applicant who had just joined for the sixth-form years would have less of a handicap than the applicant who had been at private school since the age of seven. One could even consider nuancing the criteria according to a private school's fees, with those coming from especially high-fee, well-resourced schools expected to achieve more. And the policy would be devolved to the national administrations, to be applied as appropriate to the different educational environments.

Whether this option for reform would have a substantial impact on parents' demand for private education is hard to predict. The devil would be in the detail, including the extent of any grade differences imposed, and the pace at which such policies were introduced. It is possible that the impact would be significant, even with relatively small grade handicaps, and if so they could become the means for elite universities to achieve targets or quotas for the share of state school students they admit. Contextual admissions would work even better if elite universities were, at the same time, to intensify their outreach programmes. One need not agree with the more extreme version represented by Peter Wilby's proposal, attractive though it is – to choose the large majority of Oxbridge students from among the best one to three pupils in every school, an idea arguably over-reliant on assuming an unrealistically even distribution of talents among schools – in order to welcome his suggestion for a country-wide outreach programme for Oxbridge, extending to *all* children at the age of fifteen.

A successful contextual admissions policy – particularly one that embeds the private/state distinction – puts a barrier in the way of private schooling, reducing its purely *positional* advantage. Highly resourced private schooling would still convey enormous educational benefits, delivering the same broad education and experience as before; but it would cease to be such a reliable ticket to a place further up the ladder of higher educational opportunity at university, and thence to the best-paid jobs and careers. Some parents would shun the private sector and some schools could run into financial difficulties. Indeed, a logical characteristic of all reforms that would diminish the size of the fee-paying private sector is that, if they are successful, they will entail some costs to the exchequer as the number of pupils for the state to educate increases. The parents who switched to the state sector, as a consequence of contextual admissions, would be those who had the least confidence in the private schools to raise their children's grades substantially above what they could achieve for free in the state sector, or who least valued the benefits of the broader education and the luxury facilities.

Yet even in the face of a draconian contextual admissions policy, the most determined and most affluent schools would survive to teach a smaller proportion of the child population. Moreover, there are limits to the constraints that could be imposed on universities. The policy would not, unless effectively explained and marketed, carry very widespread popular support; only a minority – some 30 per cent – in our Populus poll agreed that universities should be *required* to take school type into account. Large grade handicaps could be seen as unfair on the children concerned. Oxford and Cambridge would be likely to defend strongly their ability to attract very bright students, many of whom come from academically selective private schools; through their international reputations and independent wealth, some top universities are less dependent on government funding and ultimately have the option of becoming private institutions, evading the leverage of any reform-minded administration.[7] The private schools themselves would fiercely resist the policy.

Contextual admissions to universities or, similarly, the use of quotas or targets, are potentially the most effective strategies for diminishing the private schools' positional advantages; but they are not the only ones that have been, or could be, considered. Other options entail interventions either earlier or later in the life-course of the privately educated. Political philosopher Harry Brighouse has proposed the prohibition of the use of academic selection by private schools for their own admissions.[8] His idea is that an all-ability private school would be less attractive to fee-paying parents, and that the resultant transfer of bright pupils to the state sector would bring beneficial peer and parental pressures that would improve state schools. While we would expect such a restriction on private schools' independence to be hotly resisted, that in itself is no reason to reject it. Nevertheless, the enormous resource advantages of private schools would still give sufficient reason for parents to pay, and we could expect the schools to bring forth good educational outcomes even without academic selection; the bright children of affluent families would become less concentrated in certain top schools, but most would still find a private school to attend. The example of Ireland – where a thriving private school system persists despite a formal ban on academic selection, which is hard to enforce thoroughly – testifies to the limitations of this proposal as a route to private school reform.[9]

Further along the gilded path to success, another option is 'contextual recruitment' by employers. In April 2018 a former education secretary, Justine Greening, urged employers to take a job applicant's school background into account, and to prefer someone from an under-performing state school over an Old Etonian with the same qualifications. More open recruitment would be good not only for social mobility, she argued, but also for employers, who could thereby cease 'fishing in a talent puddle and start fishing in a talent pool'.[10] Yet would an attempt to persuade employers to alter their recruitment practices *voluntarily* have that much effect? History is not on the side of those who have believed, for example, that ethnic and gender discrimination in recruitment could be ended without legislation; and it is unlikely that a legally mandated requirement on employers would be generally accepted or found to be practical.

Upping the cost

Another strategy for reducing parents' willingness to pay for private schools is to raise the cost through taxation. There are different ways of going about this, with some distinctly more effective than others.

One of the most widely discussed options – though with the least potential to bring about a substantial reform – surrounds charitable status. While many smaller schools (especially those not members of the ISC) are for-profit organisations, in 2017 three-quarters of ISC schools were classed as charities, affording them certain tax breaks.[11] Especially galling for many, in the context of starved local government funding, is the sight of a private school benefiting from the 80 per cent business rate tax relief, yet teeming with the children of rich families enjoying luxury facilities. By contrast, the state schools down the road must pay their local taxes in full, out of the funds they receive from government. For many years, policy has circled around two understandable options: either ensure that the private schools which have the status of charities deliver a proper public benefit to state schools in return for the tax relief; or remove the relief along with the charitable status. In 2014 a YouGov poll showed public opinion to be largely hostile to the thought of charitable private schools, with nearly three-quarters in favour of one or other of those options.[12]

Could a voluntary approach be made to work, somehow to cajole private schools into providing substantive public benefit to state schools? Private schools' charitable status stems from their long-ago historical origins, when most foundation charters specified that they were meant to educate the poor. In recent times, after the passing of the 2006 Charities Act, it could no longer be presumed automatically that, simply by virtue of providing education (seldom to the poor), private schools delivered a public benefit. Subsequent years saw an attempt by the Charity Commission to define public benefit primarily as providing some bursaries for families who otherwise could not afford private education; then came a legal challenge, with the result that from 2011 only an unspecified minimal level of public benefit was ruled to be obligatory – and the schools themselves were allowed to determine how to provide that benefit. In practice, the interests of the school (such as the use of sibling discounts to attract customers) plus a genuine desire to do something for the outside world, however little, have been the more important drivers of public benefit activities, rather than a need to cross an unspecified minimal threshold. Conservative-controlled Taunton Deane council, in Somerset, provides an interesting example of how voluntarism, supplemented by council leadership, can try to influence the contributions that private schools make to a local community. The council in 2017 passed a motion agreeing to monitor and certify the schools' public benefit delivery for the purposes of the schools' reports to the Charity Commission, in return for donations from the schools to a community fund and for some modest contributions of volunteer labour.[13] The aspiration was for 10 per cent of the estimated £340,000 business tax relief to be donated, though no specific sum was agreed by the council. Evidently, an improved voluntary provision of public benefits along these lines, though welcome for a local community, will not have more than a minor impact on the costs and viability of private schools; nor will it bring about a reform of the private school system in any meaningful sense.

One means of trying to conjure up a step-change in the provision of public benefit is the threat of strong regulation: miscreant trustees, found not to be fulfilling their public benefit obligations, might be instructed to increase their public benefit activities; those who failed to do so could in theory face replacement – that is, new trustees would be given control over the school's charitable assets, change the school's policies and deliver a fuller public benefit that actively shares *substantive* resources with state schools, perhaps through widespread sponsorships. But for this option to work, two things would have to happen. Parliament would have to pass a new charity law insisting that where the object of a charity is education, it must be, beyond tokenism, education for the benefit of the majority of families who cannot afford the fees; and the government would need to people the Charity Commission (chaired from 2017 by a former Tory leader of the House of Lords) with those minded to enforce the new, more stringent, public benefit requirement. Even then, fee-paying parents could insist that they are not obliged to subsidise the charitable element by paying above cost; this would limit the value of the public benefit resources available for bridging the sectoral divide. New legislation to change charity law in order to penalise private schools, and the toughening up of regulation, would both face large political opposition; it seems doubtful whether the reform pay-off would be high enough in relation to the prospective political hurdles which would have to be overcome to achieve it.

What about the alternative of simply removing the tax benefits? An authoritative estimate in 2017, from a consultancy specialising in business rates, forecast that private schools with charity status would between them save £522 million in local taxes over five years.[14] For some well-known schools the savings seem large – more than £3 million each for Eton, Dulwich and Leeds Grammar. Averaged over all ISC schools, however, the savings in business taxes amount to approximately £200 a year for each child. Removing the facility for donors to set their gifts against personal taxes would raise this figure, though not by a great deal. Equally, it seems unlikely that removing tax breaks from schools' investments would extract a great deal of extra revenue, given the possibilities for setting any profits against expenses on the school. The overall financial impact would therefore be frankly small in relation to the overall cost of a private education. Indeed, if the loss of tax relief could be recouped by the schools with much less than the cost of an annual fee rise – average £560 over 2014 to 2018 – then the removal of tax reliefs will barely register on the Richter scale of their bursars' anxieties. To avoid the bother of demonstrating 'public benefit' in order to get the tax relief, a trickle of schools have even begun abandoning their status, while new private schools are choosing not to register as charities.[15]

In Scotland, as already noted, the devolved government took the decision in 2017 to go ahead and accept a recommendation from a consultancy report to remove business tax relief for private schools from 2020, at an estimated annual cost to the schools of £5 million. Seen as a move in the right direction by reform supporters, the change drew predictable criticism from the Scottish Independent Schools Council, calling it 'a backwards step' that would 'weaken and narrow the widening access programme'; while ISC chairman Barnaby Lenon threatened that 'all free places for pupils from lower income homes will now be at risk as independent schools are forced to make further cuts in their spending'.[16] Yet, realistically, we should not be expecting post-2020 to witness Scotland's private schools going into decline as a result of a rise of barely 1 per cent on costs; nor is there likely to be a parental exodus to the state sector.

In practice, notwithstanding the implicit subsidy involved in the flows of state-trained teachers from state schools to private schools, and the state's underwriting of school fees for the children of diplomats, army officers and such like, Britain's private schools are among the least state-supported private school sectors around the world.

Of course, charitable status is more than just about money. The conjunction of charitable status and privilege jars the moral compass, provoking an understandable sense of outrage. For many private school supporters and insiders, by contrast, charitable status is something worth having for its own sake. 'In my review of the Charities Act,' declared Tory peer Robin Hodgson in a 2015 House of Lords debate, 'it became very clear what huge advantages charitable status provided. Of course it concerns taxation and taxation privileges but, above all, it is reputational. The charity brand remains very strong in the public mind.'[17] The loss of charitable status, it seems, would have a symbolic value, whether negatively for the schools or positively for reformers. Removing the charitable status of private schools might galvanise public debate around the unfairness of grossly unequal educational opportunities. Yet, as a strategy for private school reform, this option carries the opposite risk that the appetite for reform could be satisfied by a successful removal of charity status, while leaving everything else more or less unchanged. It is, in any case, no simple matter to revise charity law without affecting the many other charities that are not schools. We question, therefore, whether this is an advisable priority for reformers.

By contrast, raising the cost through taxation by an alternative route – and by a substantial amount – would be a much more effective way to start to level the playing field. The Labour Party manifesto of 2017 proposed to levy VAT on private school fees, a tax that would bring in around £2 billion a year, to be allocated to spend on meals for primary school children.[18] Our Populus poll of 2018 found 48 per cent of the population were in agreement with this policy, while 20 per cent disagreed. Understandably, there was a much smaller lead in favour of such a tax among those who had been at private school or sent their children there – but a lead nonetheless.

The manifesto was followed, six months after the election, by an even more radical proposal from a Labour politician. 'The private schools are separating themselves ever more from mainstream society,' lamented Andrew Adonis, long a proponent of private schools sponsoring state schools, in an impassioned speech in December 2017 to the House of Lords. 'Only yesterday, Westminster School, a wholly owned charitable subsidiary of the Church of England, which occupies fabulous charitable premises adjoining Westminster Abbey, announced that it was setting up six elite schools in China. Its social outreach should be to the poor of Bradford, not the super-rich of Beijing.' Later in his speech, about educational priorities generally, he branched out to propose a bigger tax: 'After decades of Government after Government urging private schools to behave like the charities they legally are, but seeing nothing happen beyond tinkering at the edges, we need bold action,' he declared. 'In my judgment, the easiest and most effective intervention is to tax private school fees. An educational opportunity tax of 25 per cent on private school fees would raise around £2.5 billion, which could be used to boost teacher pay in hard-to-recruit areas; fund one-to-one or small-group tuition for children in danger of not getting English and maths GCSEs, the absolutely indispensable passports to skilled work and further learning; and fund free music and sports tuition across state schools, offering the wider curriculum that private school parents and children take for granted.'[19] Adonis's speech came only a few days after the Tory backbencher Robert Halfon, chair of the Education Select Committee, had called for a levy on private schools to support disadvantaged children in the state sector.[20]

Like the Labour manifesto, Adonis and Halfon want to spend the money raised from private school taxation on explicit educational programmes in the state sector. This 'hypothecation' of a new tax, harnessing it for specific uses, can cause problems if the value of those specific uses is questioned, as happened with Labour's proposal.[21] Yet, a commitment to lift the schools budget by as much as the new tax take *does* ensure that, for each pound taken out of private education, an extra pound goes into state education; and that the immediate impact on educational spending as a whole is neutral. It would, in short, be a partial evening out – not a levelling down – of the playing field. Indeed, Adonis's intention was precisely that: to lessen the resource gap directly through taxation.

However, if private schools have to raise fees to pay for the 'educational opportunity tax' or something comparable, possibly by as much as up to 25 per cent, that would induce some parents over time to switch to the state sector. It is hard to say with any precision how many parents might make that move. The only estimate available of how fee-paying demand varies in relation to price suggests that the number of pupils attending private schools would eventually fall by approximately 6 per cent, that is, by around 36,000 – not a hammer blow to the sector, but tough enough that a number of schools would close or join the state sector as academies or free schools, while others would experience some retrenchment of their spending on luxury facilities.[22] This rise in the numbers of state school children would impact on the state's educational costs, though lessening the £2.5 billion fiscal boost to the educational budget by only about £200 million.

Overall, putting barriers in the way of private education, either through a contextual admissions policy at leading universities that has real bite, or through a substantial tax on school fees, or both, would start to make inroads into Britain's private school problem. The barriers would work by taking away from the *net* advantage of private schools, making them less attractive for parents. Contextual admissions eat into the positional advantage, while the tax option leaves the advantages in place but raises their cost. In both scenarios, the pupils who as a result would go to state instead of private schools would probably be the ones with the smallest potential private school advantage; with the tax option, the pupils switching to the state sector would come from the families least able to afford the increased fees. In either case, the state's education budget would have to increase to fund the enlarged sector – though with the tax option, there is a source of extra state revenue which easily covers it.

Yet, neither contextual admissions nor any plausible tax on fees would bring about more than a relatively modest partial reform. While some shrinkage of the private sector would occur, and while more resources would be devoted in the state sector to a fairer opportunity for most children, a smaller but still robust private sector would remain. Or, put another way, there would still be a gaping divide between the two worlds.

Crossing the tracks 1: partially integrated, yet *private* control over admissions

So far we have looked at ways of reducing demand for private schools. But what if, in the cause of greater equality of opportunity, the private schools themselves were to undergo some significant changes? What if they were to become directly integrated, to a greater or lesser extent, with the state system?

The key dimensions of a more integrated system are the degree of mixing – partial or total; the funding balance between parents and the state; and whether there is private or social control over admissions, including whether or not the integrated schools are academically selective. By social control, we mean control by either local or central government, or regional commissioners, or a newly constituted 'national education service'.[23] In practice, private control over admissions would imply, for at least half of private schools, academically selective access; while social control over access might mean non-selective (comprehensive) or selective access, depending on democratically validated decisions taken by national and local governments. Another dimension – whether the governance of integrated schools is private or social – is, in our view, a lesser detail, given that the majority of England's secondary schools are, in any case, now governed as academies responsible to the Department for Education, rather than to Local Authorities. However schools are governed, their management needs to conform to common standards and be regulated uniformly.

A common thread running through the Fleming Report in 1944, the post-war provision of direct grant schools, the Assisted Places Scheme (APS) of the Thatcher/Major years, and several twenty-first-century proposals for reform has been that private schools could admit a proportion of their students paying no or low fees, with the difference made up wholly or in part by the public purse. All these approaches involve a partial integration of private schools within the state funding system, but with private control retained over admissions – and any expulsions – of pupils. The consequence is that the state school pupils become private school pupils, and the state, by funding them, is in effect making a subsidy to the private sector. This would be nothing new in principle. Many of Britain's existing private schools have, in the past, taken a small proportion of state-funded pupils, or evolved from schools that did. According to Sutton Trust research, some two-thirds of private day schools used to take some Local Authority funded pupils.[24] Private schools with partial state funding are also common in other countries' education systems.

The most prominent reform proposal in this tradition of Flemingism, and on the table for the past decade, is the 'Open Access Scheme'.[25] 'Good schools should be open to all, not just those with money or clout,' proclaims Peter Lampl, chairman and founder of the Sutton Trust which pioneered the scheme. The proposal – drawing on the needs-blind admissions policies of Ivy League colleges in the United States – is that all places in the schools that participate in the scheme would be competitively contested by children from all backgrounds, regardless of their financial circumstances. Supplementary measures would ensure that enough applications were forthcoming from children from disadvantaged backgrounds, and that enough of these applications were successful. After places are allocated, families are then to be means-tested, with some paying no fees, some partial fees, and some paying all with no government relief. The exemplar – the proof of concept – behind the scheme was Liverpool's Belvedere School for girls. For many years support for some pupils had come from the APS; but in 2000, not long after new entrants to that scheme had been closed off, the school was declared 'open access' with places paid for on a means-tested basis, subsidised generously by the Sutton Trust. Some 30 per cent of pupils paid full fees, 40 per cent were partly subsidised and 30 per cent paid no fees at all. The school thrived, and at the end of the subsidy period in 2007 became an academy within the state sector.

By 2014, some ninety private day schools with good academic performance had been persuaded to sign up to participate provisionally in the Sutton Trust's proposed Open Access Scheme;

and a switch of 42,000 children from state to private schools was subsequently modelled by the Social Market Foundation. Acceptance of this volume of children through academic selection would, it was estimated, halve the proportion of children at these private schools who come from the richest 10 per cent of families – leaving the ninety schools still socially exclusive, but notably less so.[26] With these numbers, the scheme would cost the state some £215 million a year, as some of the displaced private school parents switched to the state sector rather than to other private schools. Although, as already noted on p. 170, the scheme failed to get off the ground when first proposed to the Coalition government, the principle itself of 'Open Access' remains a wholly relevant possibility.

The National Association of Head Teachers (NAHT), which represents educational leaders from all sectors, also came up in 2014 with an option for a partial integration of private schools. This called for all top schools to give priority to children from disadvantaged backgrounds; in the case of top private schools, the call was more specific – namely, for 10 per cent of places to be made available. This was to be funded partly from the government's pupil premium for disadvantaged pupils, with the rest coming from private schools' bursary budgets. While somewhat less ambitious than the Open Access Scheme with the proportion of pupils to be helped in each school, the call on the state's budget is also smaller, the need for bursary funds that much greater.[27]

Meanwhile, some private school leaders have put forward their own Fleming-type options. The proposal in 2014 from Wellington's Anthony Seldon – that all schools in the sector should take at least a quarter of their pupils from the most socially deprived – is similar in spirit to the Open Access Scheme, in that the available places would by design go to low-income families.[28] Yet it is more ambitious in its intention, in that it would cover *all* private schools, and the state would be expected to contribute a larger amount of funding for each pupil (one and a half times the cost of a state education). Consequently, it could have a greater reforming effect on the sector as a whole than the Open Access Scheme; moreover, it differs from Open Access in that participation would be obligatory. Instead, what Seldon's scheme bears a close resemblance to is the approach advanced at about the same time by Matthew Parris in *The Times*. Crucially, however, the Seldon/Parris approach allows private schools still to control the admissions process, and thus to select on whatever grounds they choose, as long as their pupils come from low-income families. The proposal would therefore still be seen as using taxpayers' money to help private schools fill their places.

The ISC has made its own Fleming-type proposal (formally, in the context of a government consultation on how to improve the education of state school children): namely, that its members would, for an unspecified period, accept 10,000 children a year on a partially state-funded bursary scheme.[29] The proposal has similarities with Open Access; but even though it could apply across more schools, it is on a smaller scale, with the number of state-funded pupils in each school not high enough to alter significantly the dynamics of the school. Long committed to the bursaries model, the ISC proposes that the government would contribute as much funding as it costs to educate a child in a state school, and the private schools would top up the fee from their bursary funds – in effect, a joint funding model. The proposal takes advantage of an assumption that there would be enough spare capacity to accommodate these extra 10,000 children in private schools with no additional capital costs. This assumed saving, along with existing bursary funds, makes the proposition financially feasible for the schools without having to contemplate any great sacrifices from fee-paying parents. Since all schools could be part of the scheme – not just the top-performing academic schools – this option could also be non-academically selective in some cases, even if in practice the participating schools are more likely to have selective admissions than not. 'The scheme is not about choosing the brightest pupils but about providing genuine transformational opportunities for those who need them most,' according to Patrick Derham, head of Westminster School.[30] The obvious attraction for private schools is the increase in demand for places that the grants would stimulate, including in the academically selective schools an influx of a small number of bright children from disadvantaged families. The prospect of additional funds is especially appealing for some schools; but as with the other schemes, the government has so far ignored the proposal, probably for the same reason that it did not warm to the Open Access Scheme, namely the political sensitivity of being seen to support private education.

The proponents of all these schemes are keen to draw dividing lines between their new proposals and the APS – understandably so, since that scheme of the Thatcher/Major years faced continual criticism and opposition throughout its life, largely because it was not properly focused on low-income families. The Open Access Scheme, it is held, would be different because *all* places in a school are to be openly competed for, fundamentally changing the school, whereas typically under APS only a minority of places were filled by the state-funded pupils. Moreover, a more sophisticated, tighter means-testing system is promised, taking into account wealth as well as income, which would prevent the gaming of access by the middle classes that was common with the APS. The ISC scheme looks more like a watered-down version of APS, but differentiates its proposal by stressing how the schools would be contributing to the cost of each child, rather than all the money coming from the state.

Nevertheless, these options are all variants of the same model – a partial integration of private schools with the state system, but with the private schools themselves retaining control over which children join and remain in the school. They differ in important other dimensions, most significantly in the degree of integration – the Open Access Scheme and Seldon/Parris proposal are the only options in this set which could be said to be more than marginal, in that if either could be made to work we should expect to see a notable diminution in the social exclusivity of the top private day schools. Especially among the most academically oriented schools, we could anticipate, with the Open Access Scheme, a significantly increased proportion of very able children from low-income families. The scheme leaves untouched the rest of the population, so that the high-quality education enjoyed exclusively by the large majority of private school children would remain. The ISC offer and the NAHT option are not so explicitly focused on the most able children, but the scale of either proposal would be too small to generate a decisive change in the exclusive access to the schools. The proposed proportion of state-funded children will be too low to change the social dynamic in schools. The co-funding character of the proposals means that these schemes are likely to soak up some of the existing bursary funds, so the net additions to means-tested funding would be less than the amount committed by the state. Most aspects of the system's unfairness would not be affected.

None of the schemes would in themselves address the problem of overall inefficient use of the nation's teaching resources, since it is not envisaged that resources would be transferred away from private schools to where they could have greater effect. Critics fear that the divisiveness brought about by competition for places in the Open Access schools would even make matters worse, by intensifying a sense of inferiority and even hopelessness among those not selected. The reasonable response of the Sutton Trust to that charge is that the scheme does not aim to increase the extent to which academic selection determines school places in Britain; rather, it would open up all existing selective places potentially to everyone, regardless of their means. Yet journalist and educationalist Fiona Millar, focusing on the uncertainty as to how parents would respond to the scheme, is far from reassured about the use of selection in the scheme. 'Once this particular genie is out of the bottle, how could anyone predict where it would end?' she wonders. Rather than being induced to switch to the state system, she maintains that 'a much more likely outcome would be a subtle but pervasive expansion in the selective private sector – new independent schools would be financially viable and existing schools would have a strong incentive to expand'.[31]

The Open Access Scheme if fully implemented could expect to have a palpable long-term effect on the democratic deficit, even if the impact might be hidden. The schools would not have changed, and the top schools would continue to dominate positions of public influence, as they have done for a very long time. Yet the class background of some of the pupils would be altered; it would no longer be axiomatic that a person of influence who had been educated at an Open Access school would have come from an affluent family and neighbourhood. More of Britain's top politicians, judges and businesses might, in the fullness of time, come from less privileged families.

The Open Access Scheme is thus a partial solution to the private school problem, attractive for anyone anxious to see greater social mobility, but less concerned by an extension to, or intensification of, selection in British education. Those worn down by decades of political indifference, and realistic about the low prospects of securing anything like the amount of philanthropy needed to run an alternative, privately driven, open-access reform, may perceive that there is no other way forward. If compared with the alternative of doing nothing at all, with the prospect of yet another generation coming round in a decade's time to look aghast at the way the education system is organised in this country, we the authors would take it as a modest gain worth having. For many objectors to private schools' social exclusivity whose views are on the right of the political spectrum, the risk of an extension to selection would hardly keep them awake at night. The difficulties with putting the scheme into effect are as much political as anything else, and could potentially be surmounted; the proposal also appears to have the support of a large number of leading private schools.[32]

Crossing the tracks 2: partially integrated, with *social control over admissions*

Nevertheless, the conversation most certainly does not end at this point. The Open Access Scheme still falls well short of what is needed to reform the system thoroughly. The troubling problems of academic selection that accompany the Fleming-type solutions for partial integration so far considered, and the rather small effects that these solutions would have on the overall fairness and efficiency of Britain's education system, can be avoided if a key element is altered. Rather than allowing private control over admission and retention of state-funded pupils, alternative schemes for partial integration should allow some form of social control, in which admission and retention protocols in relation to the state-funded pupils would be determined by government, whether local, regional or national. After all, social control over something that the state funds is easily justified.

An important consequence is that no reform that entails social control of admissions could be introduced on a purely voluntary basis, any more than a tax on school fees; an element of compulsion, using primary legislation, would be necessary. In what we call a 'Fair Access Scheme', the government would require, after passing suitable legislation, that all private schools accept a significant proportion of pupils chosen by the state, after means-testing, funded at the same rate as everybody else in the state system. As with the Open Access Scheme, each school would have to make up the rest of the cost of educating the children from its own bursary funds and any surpluses. Fee-paying parents would bear at least some of the additional costs of a Fair Access Scheme through fee increases; these would come in gradually, through the years following the first intake of students under the new policy. In the richest schools the difference to be made up would be substantial, while in the less affluent schools not so much is required; hence, the increases in fees would be proportionate to their starting level. Especially in the wealthiest schools, we would expect that some of the spending on de luxe accommodation, and other excessive if splendid facilities, would be cut back. In all private schools, there would have to be some drop in the value of resources spent on each private school child.

What do we mean by 'a significant proportion' of state-funded places? The initial percentage – as applied to each year's new intake – should satisfy two criteria: first, that it must be large enough to be a game-changer, that in other words there is sufficient critical mass to begin to change decisively the social composition and thus character of the schools; second, that it is not so large that it fails to allow for an adjustment process on the part of the schools themselves. In addition, the decision on the chosen initial percentage will have to take account of the financial consequences for both the schools and government. So what might that starting percentage be? Surely not below 25 per cent, if this is really going to be an attempt to achieve meaningful reform. And surely not above 50 per cent, if we are going to keep the goodwill of the schools, allowing them time to adapt, through the transition period. For ourselves, a proportion of 33 per cent – one-third – feels about right. Nevertheless, this book is not a manifesto, so we are disinclined to insist dogmatically on a specific initial percentage; moreover, we would expect that the proportion could be above the minimum in some schools, and that the regulated minimum would rise over time.

Social control over admissions would allow governments, present and future, to choose the extent of academic and other selectivity in allocating the minimum 33 per cent of places in each school to state-funded pupils. Selection might be appropriate and allowed for some schools, while not for others. For example, a government might want to require that, in the transition to the reformed system, there was no overall increase in the amount of selection in the education system; this could be achieved by ensuring that private schools do not change their admissions protocols. It would have to consider, in any case, the financial costs and short-term disruption of any change in the procedure for allocating places in a school; these costs could be high in the short run if a socially mixed cohort were introduced suddenly in an academically selective school whose teachers were experienced primarily in teaching only the children of the well-heeled.

Places in some schools will be in high demand and, where not by academic or other form of selection such as musical or sporting, there will need to be a system of allocation. A purely postcode-based system carries the well-known risk of social inequalities, as affluent families are able to move into the favoured localities. 'Without strong local oversight the potential for sharp practices and backdoor selection is huge,' observes Fiona Millar.[33] To counter this, one might follow education journalist Laura McInerney's idea: learning from India's experience, selection of the 33 per cent state-funded intake could be done via a random lottery.[34] A random lottery, however, would need considerable promotion to garner enough political and public support. A yet more radical idea proposed by Melissa Benn is that the places should be allocated to children who have been in care or who have spent extensive periods of time eligible for free school meals.[35] Whatever the chosen allocation criteria, a substantial degree of social control over schools' admissions policies, to ensure those criteria are met, would need to be put into place; while this is not always straightforward, the overly cynical knee-jerk reaction, which assumes that the privileged could simply defend all or most of their advantages by gaming even a well-thought-through admissions policy, is hard to sustain. Among other safeguards, the means-testing to be used for the state-funded places would be part of the armoury that ensures a balanced intake. The schools could then be required to allocate places for the 33 per cent, following the means-testing, according to the Schools Admissions Code (SAC). Although imperfect and in continual need of amendment, the SAC is designed in principle to ensure fair and transparent admissions processes; if private schools were to resist that, they would be flying the flag for being allowed to run an unfair, non-transparent system. Attention would also need to be paid by the Department for Education to the regional and local balance of new state school places becoming available through a Fair Access Scheme.

Control over the composition of the state-funded places does not entirely end with the admissions process. Also important – and in effect the other side of the admissions coin – is the issue of who controls exclusions. Where they can expel pupils with complete freedom, schools do not have to take into account the interests of the excluded children, and they can shift onto other schools or institutions the harms caused by disruptive behaviour. Before 2010 those excluded from state schools could go to an Independent Appeals Tribunal, and potentially be reinstated if the tribunal considered that the child's interests, when balanced with those of other children in the school, had not been fairly and properly accounted for. In private schools, however, there is no external right of appeal against exclusions; and since 2010, even in state schools, there has been no right to reinstatement after review. If there were a return to the pre-2010 review system, including a proper right to appeal and be reinstated if necessary, its scope could easily be extended to cover all private schools. In fact, though private school heads would no doubt resist any such restrictions on their freedom to exclude, an expansion of the scope for appeal rights could be implemented through amendments to the Statutory Instrument concerning Independent Schools Standards.[36] This could be done even as a stand-alone policy, whether or not it was accompanied by a Fair Access Scheme.

Once a system is established – with a significant proportion of children in every school being funded by the state, and with their composition controlled at some level outside the school itself – in effect these school places will have become attached to, and de facto part of, the state system. Over time, as and when society comes fully to recognise the value of education for what it is, and therefore to devote more resources to it, the state funding for the 33 per cent of children in private schools would increase, and the gap to be made up by other parents would fall. Future governments could decide to increase the proportions that are state-funded, and could mould the degree of selection as thought best, with the possibility that all schools could be made comprehensive in their intake. Diversity among schools would remain as with the current unreformed system, and parents could continue to be offered some choice between schools.

A scaled-up partially integrated system would undoubtedly need detailed planning from both above and below, and close regulatory monitoring of admissions procedures. No blueprint has yet been produced, in similar detail to that set out for the Sutton Trust's Open Access Scheme, for a Fair Access Scheme that is also open, but with admissions and retention socially controlled. Nor are there any twenty-first-century examples, proofs of concept, of partial integration that one can point to. Yet there are precedents, which have worked satisfactorily, in the hybrid, partly state-funded schools of the last century – the direct grant schools. Occasionally, as we have seen in Chapter 6, private schools in the present century have also turned to the state for funding in full, and been accepted as fully funded state schools with socially controlled admissions. The Belvedere School was one case in point, while some fifteen schools altogether had become free schools or academies by 2014; prominent other examples were Liverpool College, Queen Elizabeth's Grammar School in Blackburn, Chetwynde in Barrow-in-Furness and Holy Trinity School in Cumbria. Schools that switch to the state sector are typically ones that have failed to attract enough fee-paying pupils. After the transition they retain the independence of governance afforded to free-standing academies and free schools; some have found ways to maintain a more affluent intake of pupils by privileging access from local feeder schools, so these are neither harbingers of, nor ideal models for, a larger migration across the private/state tracks.[37]

The Fair Access Scheme would be less congenial for private school leaders than the Open Access Scheme, not least because of its compulsory element and because it would be more far-reaching, affecting all schools; there would also be more schools having to stretch their resources and retrench, in order to meet the challenge of having a significant portion of their intake with only the state per capita funding for income. Yet, we believe, Fair Access would stand a greater chance of *political* acceptability. It is hard to persuade politicians that giving money to private schools, which are disliked as unfair, would be popular – this, more than anything else, probably explains the fact that no Open Access Scheme or similar has to date found its way into a political manifesto.[38] But since, with a Fair Access Scheme, the state would retain *control* over whom the money is spent on, it would involve, in effect, an extension of the state school system to include the available allocated places at otherwise private schools. The diversity of private schools currently open mainly to the affluent would be made available to all. Secondary schools need to expand until at least 2025, in order to accommodate the rising volume of pupils going through education; introducing the Fair Access Scheme would thus also be going with the grain of total demand. Those committed strongly to the improvement of state education should be able to see the scheme, not as putting money into private schools, but as offering improvement to the expanding state system.

As for the money, would a Fair Access Scheme be affordable? Given that Anthony Crosland, half a century ago, justified his lack of action by reference to the potential cost involved at a time of difficult economic circumstances, when the maintenance of dilapidated Victorian state school buildings was high up his priority list, this is a relevant question. With a Fair Access Scheme, the funding for the children at the formerly fully private schools would be no more than the state would incur in any other school – meaning that for these children the main extra cost is zero. If the schools maintain the same level of resourcing per student (some of which is educationally unnecessary), the fee-paying parents would have to pay higher fees, just as they would if their fees were subject to an educational opportunity tax; if they had to shoulder the full burden for a third of pupils in the school, fees would rise by around a third. As a consequence, some 52,000 pupils could be predicted to switch out of the private and into the state sector, and so the state would eventually have to find an additional £300 million annually – less than 1 per cent of its overall schools budget and nothing like enough to deter or postpone such an urgently needed and beneficial reform.[39]

A Fair Access Scheme would be – of the options so far considered – the most serious and extensive response to Britain's private school problem. Not only would it contribute to making the system overall far less unfair, it would also begin to make better use of the nation's teaching resources and facilities; more children would be benefiting directly from the resources, some of which would transfer over time into the state sector, where they would be better utilised by children who otherwise make do with far fewer resources than private school children. And in the long term, as the proportion of state-funded places increases, the democratic health of the country, as shown by the diversity of backgrounds of the people who wield political, cultural and commercial influence, could only improve.

Crossing the tracks 3: fully integrated

But what if, instead of requiring that schools admit at least one-third of their pupils as state-funded pupils, as with the Fair Access Scheme, that proportion were increased to 100 per cent? Could, or should, any government ever go as far as outright prohibition of fee-paying schools?

Contemporary calls for the 'abolition' of private schools echo similar pleas down the ages, but the meaning of what abolitionists are proposing can be unclear. Sometimes, what is envisaged is conceived, metaphorically at least, as 'sending in the bulldozers' – an evocation of creative destruction comparable to Thomas Cromwell's dissolution of the monasteries, in which the school names and even buildings become history, and where there is no intention of using the facilities and staff to good effect in a reformed system. A more common meaning, however, is that, while the names, facilities and buildings remain, the schools are fully incorporated into the state education system. An expansion of the Fair Access Scheme to all pupils would be just that – a matter of full integration, and with no places left for fee-paying pupils. In effect, the private schools would have been nationalised. The same outcome – no more fee-paying – could alternatively be reached by raising the cost with such prohibitive taxes that all demand is choked off, with schools surviving only by switching to the state system. This option of complete nationalisation, integrating private schools fully into the state system, would not solve all the problems of Britain's education, but it would remove a substantial chunk of its inequalities and inefficiencies. Over the long term, with all citizens using the same system, all energies (including parental energies) would be brought to bear at both local and national levels to improve Britain's schools; and democratic pressures could make it harder for governments to deprive schools of the needed resources for truly developmental education.

A policy of nationalisation would face moral, practical and legal hurdles. From the moral perspective, we have weighed in Chapter 1 the positive freedom of the many to receive a good education and a fair chance in life against the negative freedom of the few to spend their money on educational advantage as they like. Yet, once private schooling has diminished to insignificance – using some combination of substantive but less earth-shattering reforms, with the great majority of places at the high-quality schools becoming part of the state system – we would have gone beyond the point where the rest of society is harmed. In other words, *complete* abolition is not needed to resolve Britain's private school problem. Children's educational needs are both universal and varied; a well-constructed state system respects the need for, and provides, some diversity, but a *small* amount of private not-for-profit enterprise could help to serve that need, while not adversely impinging on others' life chances. It would thus be hard to justify banning *all* forms of private spending on education, including all forms of private tuition that could be suited to children's particular needs; and if we were to ban only some forms of private spending, it is not clear how one could decide which ones these should be.

From the practical perspective, a strategy for total abolition of fee-paying education could expect to face intense and concerted resistance from the private schools, along with their friends in high places; the full weight of hostile opposition would come from several quarters, much more so than for other strategies for radical but less obviously dramatic reform. There is also a serious issue of legal constraints. The nationalisation of private schools – requiring them to admit only state-funded children and to conform to state-controlled admissions and expulsions procedures – would require primary legislation in Parliament. But the 1998 Human Rights Act, which sets out how Britain conforms with the European Convention of Human Rights (ECHR), under Article 2 of Protocol 1, expressly 'guarantees the right to open and run a private school'. Prior to Brexit, the European Union could indirectly prevent Parliament from passing a law that counters this convention. After Britain has left the European Union, Parliament could pass a law that, in effect, nationalises private schools. This might be in contravention of the ECHR, but since that is a convention, not in itself a constraint on Parliament, a legal challenge could at most lead to the court making a 'declaration of incompatibility' under the Human Rights Act 1998; that would not stop Parliament legislating, or make the legislation ineffective. Such legislation might not be the first or only area where a breach of the ECHR happens in the coming years; abolition of private schools would follow on more smoothly if the ECHR had already been breached elsewhere.

Nevertheless, a law which ushered in private school abolition would not only be seen by some as the end of the world, but would also (not unlike the fox-hunting ban) be daunting to implement. Full nationalisation would, therefore, be a difficult option to follow, albeit not impossible if a government were so minded and had sufficient support in Parliament and more widely. Whether it would be the best option should be weighed against pursuing a combination of other, less extreme, options, whether for taxes and other barriers to private schools' operations, or for their partial integration within the state system. The diminution of private education – to a point of insignificance – is enough of a prize for those who value equity and fair play. Given Britain's collective failure over the last three-quarters of a century to do anything significant about the problem, we as authors would not favour a perfectionist, all-or-nothing reform strategy.

What won't work and what could

Some proposed options are really not worth pursuing. We have already explained our view on the option of seeking to use the schools' charitable status to persuade or threaten trustees to raise their game in the delivery of public benefit. There would be considerable hurdles to be encountered in passing new charity legislation, and in the strengthening of the regulator. Yet the gains for state education and communities from dragooning the charitable schools into being properly charitable would not do much to level the resources gap – given that so much of it comes from parents' willingness to pay exorbitant fees, which they could insist were not used to subsidise other children. Similarly, though it might be easier to enact, the impact of ending the tax relief that derives from charitable status would be hardly noticeable, and almost one in two private schools would be entirely unaffected; even the larger schools would not be too concerned.

There are also other non-fliers around, which occasionally surface. Proposals to open chains of ultra-low-cost private schools in Britain have emerged, built on an extreme free-market ideology and drawing on some positive experiences of private schools in developing countries, typically with weak state education sectors for competition; these would be 'no frills' schools, using low-paid, inexperienced teachers, with at least thirty pupils in each class, renting cheap premises and facilities, and charging no more than £50 a week.[40] Previous attempts at very low-cost private schools in Britain, many spawned by the Christian Social Trust (CST), have served poor working-class families who wanted more spiritual and religious education than the state offered; they have survived with the help of many teachers giving their time free or for very low pay. With precarious finances, the number of CST schools declined from sixty-five to forty between 1992 and 2010.[41] In May 2018 a new ultra-low-cost school, the Independent Grammar School: Durham, was given government permission to open; *The Economist* had already expressed its doubts, observing dryly that 'the experiment will be a big test of the school's leaders'.[42] Ultra-low-cost schools are neither likely to be a viable alternative for the main mass of children in Britain, nor will they compete for the affluent clientele of other private schools charging very much higher fees.

Building up the bursaries of private schools from private philanthropy is another idea with little prospect, except for a few favoured schools, of coming to fruition sufficiently to be a game-changer. A fund of between £100 million and £300 million would have to be raised for each school, in order to run sustainably a privately funded open access scheme.[43] Another hope, sometimes voiced, is that state schools will be able to catch up in the amount of resources that private schools have, and thereby provide a comparable quality of education; Anthony Seldon, when he was head of Brighton College, suggested this could be achieved by allowing private funding into state education – in our view just another kite in the wind.[44] More broadly, concentrating reforming energies on improving state schools across the board has, time and again, served as in reality an excuse for leaving the private sector untouched; not least, it is a strategy that has underestimated the capacity of the private school industry to adapt, with enough money behind it, to the last half-century's increasing demands for academic success and for a general high-quality education.

Some options are, however, potentially workable candidates for reforming schools, in part or in full. And here, given the paucity of detailed public discussion about options for change, it is worth briefly recapping.

Contextual admissions for universities, and taxing private school fees (whether through VAT or an 'educational opportunity tax'), would both be viable ways of affecting the demand for private school places, because parents would see that the net advantages had been diminished. They would in increasing numbers start to prefer the state school system; while not only would some private schools go out of business, but others would be obliged to retrench with smaller numbers and larger class sizes, as well as making do without some of their luxury facilities. Yet, overall, these effects would be containable for the sector rather than catastrophic.

Options for partial integration would also work, and are arguably preferable because these directly cross the different educational tracks that divide our society. The Open Access Scheme of the Sutton Trust starts to solve the access problem for especially able children who are born into low-income, disadvantaged families, giving them a chance of a lift-up in life through a highly resourced education. Yet its beneficial effects would be mainly for just those relatively few children who could compete for academic places at the top ninety or so private day schools. The majority of children would not be affected, nor would the elite dominance of many of these schools in our national culture; and, of course, the historic boarding schools (Eton, Winchester et al.) would be untouched. The scheme is likely to be most attractive for those policy-makers and commentators who have the least aversion to the principle of selection in school admissions. The alternative option for partial integration that we have proposed, a Fair Access Scheme, would aim to be larger in scope, taking in all private schools; and because the state, at some level, would control who takes up the places, the beneficial effects would reach children of all abilities. Over time the educational resources we devote to our children would become less unequal.

While each of these broad options has its drawbacks, and has practical details to be resolved, they are all *serious* possibilities. Any one of them would have some effect, and be much better than doing nothing. In some combination or another they could amount to very substantial reforms. Contextual admissions to universities could, for example, supplement options for partial integration, as long as the admission protocols were suitably nuanced to take account of the altered character of any reformed private schools. While all options imply less educational inequality, none involve the loss of valued historic institutions or a 'levelling down' of educational resources. Rather, these previously inaccessible places of educational excellence would be opening up; where schools are to be partially integrated, they would still be the same recognisable schools; where school fees are to be taxed, the raised money would be channelled into the education of all children.

So what, in a satisfactorily and fully reformed system, involving a significant degree of integration, would remain of the old private schools? There would *not* be the luxurious extras – hardly necessary for a high-quality education and no longer required to convince pupils and parents of their sense of entitlement; nor the layers of staff skilled at gaming places for their pupils at elite universities, and the undue preponderance of teachers with degrees from those universities; nor would there be the socially exclusive collection of pupils drawn so narrowly from professional and managerial families, or the merely super-rich. Other current ingredients of a high-quality education, however, could and should remain. The schools could retain a high degree of autonomy of management. They could at last adhere as appropriate to their founders' wishes, and most decisions could be taken by heads, with accountability to governing bodies. Any schools that became fully integrated could join a chain of other academy schools if they so wished, and inter-school partnerships could be encouraged where parties find them to be mutually beneficial. Improvements could be made in their regulation, including requiring that teachers – especially heads – are trained; indeed, partially or fully integrated private schools could and should contribute to teacher training. No doubt there would have to be a compromise on class sizes, a position in between the private sector's current super-low class sizes and the level currently sustained in the state sector.

Where schools met a need for boarding, this would continue to be served as before; and where schools took in some paying pupils from abroad, again this demand could, within the limits of each school, be met. As we have seen, boarding in the private sector has, after a sharp decline in the late twentieth century, broadly stabilised in the early twenty-first. The most recent ISC Census shows just over 13 per cent of places to be on a boarding basis.[45] Given the probability of a general continuing parental reluctance not to be separated from their children for more than the odd day, and the availability nowadays of good schools in most of the countries where British subjects are working, the demand for boarding is unlikely to increase significantly. Even so, there will still be an ongoing need for boarding for some children according to their circumstances. Those coming from families without sufficient means, currently accommodated by a small number of state boarding school places, would have their options enlarged when, under a Fair Access Scheme, at least a third of the boarding places at private schools become available as de facto part of the state system. These boarding places, underwritten by the state, would presumably not be allocated on a narrowly geographical basis; but whatever criteria are adopted, *any* basis for determining intake is better than depth of parental chequebook. The reforms would have broadened or even transformed the social intake at boarding schools.

Reformed schools would also continue to meet the needs of foreign students, who comprise roughly 10 per cent of the modern private school population. Schools are entitled to argue that they bring money to British education, while enhancing its global brand.

If in a reformed system there is partial integration of the state and private sectors, involving, for instance, a stipulated minimum of British students going to private schools on a subsidised, non-fee-paying basis, then foreign students could still attend, though treated (and counted) on a fully fee-paying, non-subsidised basis, rather like foreign patients using the NHS for significant medical treatment. What overwhelmingly matters in the issue at large is the nature of the intake of the mainly British pupils who will live out their lives as part of British society.

In short, the needs of boarding students and of foreign students (to some degree overlapping) are practical issues that will require some consideration, but in neither case present any sort of insuperable challenge. Back in the 1960s, the Newsom Commission set up by Anthony Crosland got itself into a horrible, disabling tangle by conflating the question of boarding need – admittedly much greater then, in an era of still large armed forces and a relative absence abroad of international schools – with the much more fundamental question of private education itself. Now, half a century later, there is no need to repeat that fateful mistake.

An altogether weightier practical problem than either boarding needs or foreign students is that of the *pace* of change for any package of reform. Adjustments to changed intakes will need to be made within the private schools, and it is recognised that most adjustments will bring costs in the short run. In our view, Goethe's famous maxim '*ohne Hast, aber ohne Rast*' (without haste, but without rest) should be the watchword: steady, purposeful, year-on-year reform (cohort by cohort in, for instance, the case of a scheme for partial integration), and always bearing in mind the importance of complete transparency in relation to parents, children and teachers, the key individual stakeholders. Over the lifetime of a Parliament? That seems a reasonable time-scale to introduce and start to entrench substantive reform – but a realistic aspiration only if three important riders are fulfilled: that the detailed thinking and preparatory work have been done well in advance of those five years of potentially momentous change; that from the outset of implementation, even allowing for certain concessions and a degree of gradualism (in part to minimise adjustment costs), there is no half-heartedness or loss of nerve; and that the whole reform project is underpinned by substantial public support for action towards a fairer and better national education system – even if this support will not be universal and even if resistance to change is inevitable.

Viable reform policies versus the shaming game

That there are valid, well-founded policies which would address, in varying degrees, Britain's private school problem is our key optimistic conclusion. The solutions we have canvassed – contextual university admissions, taxation of school fees and forms of partial integration (including both the Open Access Scheme and the Fair Access Scheme) – are all workable, in that none of the practical issues that might be raised can in any remote sense be seen as deal-breakers.

The time is ripe for a concerted debate about reform policies: not running away from the problem any more, not just a wringing of hands about depressingly stagnant social mobility, not just another solutions-free exposé of social and educational divisions. An equally sure way of getting nothing done, even now in the twenty-first century, would be to adopt a name-calling strategy, calling out and stigmatising the supporters of reform among 'insiders' – those who are themselves privately educated and/or who decide on private for their own families. Strikingly, among those *insiders* with an opinion either way, there are many more who agree than disagree that the system is unfair – 64 per cent to 36 per cent, according to our Populus poll. This is not in itself an indication of hypocrisy, and it is quite consistent that insiders could view the system as unfair. The 'politics of hypocrisy', as we have termed it, effectively closes down the debate rather than opening it up. People have to make the best of the world as it is, not as they wish it to be. To hope to persuade all parents who think the system unfair to choose accordingly a state education, and thereby starve the private sector of demand, is an unrealistic expectation. Many are unlikely to respond in that way when their children's interests (which they may well consider have, for them, a higher moral value) are at stake. Instead, it would be more productive to empathise with their current position and to harness the energies of all those who hold that the system itself is unfair, *whatever* their personal circumstances and choices. The only consequence of name-calling is the silence of many; and those many include influential opinion-formers, who could otherwise contribute effectively and creatively to finding the best ways forward.

9

We Need to Talk

As and when politicians, opinion-formers and the public at large begin – we hope – to grapple closely with the range of possible approaches to doing something meaningful, it will be important not to be distracted. 'Ah, but what about the private tutoring industry?' 'Ah, but what about the role of grammar schools in the social mobility mix?' 'Ah, but what about the profound inequalities within the existing state system?' 'Ah, but what about the need for extra educational resources to make up for the long tail of social disadvantage?' We do not deny the significance of any of these issues; but they are separate issues. This is a book specifically about Britain's *private school* problem. Some repetition no doubt, and perhaps also some hesitation – but definitely no deviation.

Entrenched, formidable and thoroughly modern

We have canvassed and discussed at some length possible reform options to the existing status quo. Yet what follows in this and the next section is something in the nature of a reality check. 'That's a hard one you've taken on there,' Gordon Brown wryly remarked to one of the authors in 2014 after he had published an article on the issue; another prominent figure of the New Labour era, Alan Milburn, indicated more recently much the same to both of us.[1] The private schools have long enjoyed – and felt able to rely on – the well-nigh unquestioning support of friends in high and influential places. But now, compared to, say, half a century ago, they have truly got their own act together on an industry-wide basis.

'The independent schools have not in the past been their own best advocates,' declared an internal report on their behalf back in 1971. 'They have had little common organization and have left prospective clients to find out about them individually as and when they could. This is a weakness which should be remedied ...'² Remedied indeed it was over the ensuing decades, above all through the highly focused efforts of what became the Independent Schools Council (ISC), sleepless champion of the sector. The ISC is a non-profit organisation that promotes the interests of its private school members and serves as a well-oiled PR machine for the private school industry: it produces instant rebuttals of any whisper of criticism, particularly political criticism; specialises in supplying carefully chosen statistics (including the large-number trick), for example about bursaries; tries to make the schools seem like part of the solution, not the problem; and has no qualms about lobbying hard in the sector's interests. Take, even as we are drafting this chapter in May 2018, an interview in the *TES* with the ISC's general secretary, Julie Robinson. Regretting the existence of what she calls an 'anti-privilege mood', she deplores the 'lazy caricature' of private schools ('our little sector') as 'full of one type of child'. 'It's a shame,' she concludes in pained tones.³

More broadly, the schools' links with powerful vested interests are close and continuous. London's main clubs (dominated by privately educated men) would be one example;⁴ the Church of England (closely connected with many private schools, from Westminster downwards) would be another.⁵ Or take the City of London, where in that historic and massively wealthy square mile not only do individual livery companies have an intimate involvement with a range of private schools (the Fishmongers and Gresham's, the Grocers and Oundle, the Haberdashers and Haberdashers' Aske's, the Leathersellers and Colfe's, the Mercers and St Paul's, the Saddlers and Alleyn's, the Skinners and Tonbridge, and so on), but the City Corporation itself supports a trio of elite private schools in Surrey and London to the tune of £4 million a year (compared to the barely £½ million it spends on five City academies).[6] While as for the many hundreds of individual links between 'top people' and private schools, often in the form of sitting on governing bodies, it only needs a glance at *Who's Who* to get the gist. The term 'the Establishment' can be a tiresome one, too often loosely and inaccurately used, but in the sense of complementary networks of people at or close to the centres of power and wealth, it actually does mean something; and given the dominance of the privately educated in our national life, and the matter of one's schooling as a ubiquitous reference point, it would be calling black white to deny the importance of private schools in the continuing smooth functioning of that Establishment – an Establishment that is, as Owen Jones has convincingly argued, as much as anything about shared assumptions.[7]

All of which leaves the private schools almost uniquely well placed to make their case and protect their corner. They have ready access to prominent public voices speaking on their behalf, especially in the House of Lords; they enjoy the passive support of the Church of England, which is distinctly reluctant to draw attention to the moral gulf between the aims of ancient founders and the socio-economic realities of the present; and, of course, they have no qualms about utilising all possible firepower, human as well as media and institutional, to block anything they find threatening. A couple of revealing episodes – from around the same time, and both of them destined for the history books – make the point eloquently.

The first involved the aftermath of the Labour government's Charities Act of 2006. Although, as we have seen, far from as radical as some had hoped, it did nonetheless mean that private, fee-paying schools were no longer automatically entitled to charitable status and that they would need to demonstrate that they provided 'public benefit'. The arbiters of that benefit were to be the Charity Commission, chaired by Dame Suzi Leather (rapidly characterised by the right as a Labour-supporting 'quango queen');[8] and by 2009 it was starting to inspect and rule on individual private schools, with a particular focus on whether they provided adequate bursaries for pupils from deprived backgrounds. This did not go down altogether well. 'The Charity Commission has clearly decided to define the notion of "public benefit" in order to suit its own political agenda,' declared a comment article in the *Daily Telegraph* that autumn. 'The Commission doesn't like private schools, so it rules they don't benefit the public.'[9] In January 2010 the ISC's chief executive, David Lyscom, weighed in. 'We feel the emphasis on poverty and means-tested bursaries is politically driven,' he told the ever-willing *Telegraph*. 'It is a political interpretation of public benefit as being to do with poverty.' In short, he asserted, the Charity Commission had 'defined public benefit in much too narrow a way'.[10]

The denouement came relatively swiftly. Later in 2010 the ISC decided to take the Commission to court and was granted a judicial review; the ensuing tribunal heard a range of evidence and opinions, including very forcibly from the private school lobby; and in October 2011 the tribunal ruled in the ISC's favour, to the effect that the Commission's guidelines had placed undue emphasis on bursaries for poor students, which could mean schools having to increase fees. 'The tribunal has recognised the crucial independence of schools to pursue a panoply of public benefit strategies,' acclaimed the victorious Matthew Burgess, the ISC's general secretary.[11] Yet, in the long term, was it really such a victory? 'Sadly there are quite a lot of people who want the benefits of charitable status without the responsibility,' reflected Stephen Lloyd, a lawyer prominent in the charitable sector. 'The Tribunal's decision puts the obligation of recognising that responsibility firmly on the trustees' shoulders [that is, the shoulders of the private schools' governing bodies]. Will they be up to it? Or will a future Labour government go for real reform? If so, this could prove a Pyrrhic victory ...'[12]

By this time the other episode had already played out, in a very English way behind closed doors. It concerned the proposal, which Labour's Andrew Adonis had been strongly pushing during the second half of the 2000s, that private schools should start to sponsor – in a proactive, whole-hearted way – state academies. When the Tory-dominated Coalition government came to power in May 2010, it was an idea that elicited a considerable degree of enthusiasm from the new education secretary, Michael Gove, and a milder degree of enthusiasm from the new prime minister, David Cameron, who saw it as perhaps fitting in with his 'Big Society' vision. That autumn, in the Cabinet Room at No. 10, both men were present, along with the trusted Adonis, for a meeting with a group of private school chairs of governors and heads. From the start the visitors spoke vehemently against the proposal, largely on the grounds that it represented wholly unwarrantable interference with their autonomy. Then, with the politicians suitably softened up, came the *coup de grâce*. A knock on the door, and it was Lord Waldegrave, Provost of Eton. After apologies for lateness, he was soon giving his view. 'Looking at the problem through the wrong end of the telescope' is the phrase that Adonis recalls about how Waldegrave – quietly and authoritatively, as one Old Etonian politico to another – persuaded Cameron that his government should tread with the utmost circumspection in this whole fraught area of private school reform; and with a clear sense on Adonis's part, and apparently Gove's also, that the moment for doing anything significant had decisively passed, the meeting broke up soon afterwards.[13] Yet, as with the court case over the obligations of 'public benefit', only time will tell whether it was likewise a Pyrrhic victory. Or put another way, whether the private schools had, perhaps because of an unimaginative and defensive mindset, missed their chance to help shape a serious reform agenda – to be, in fact, on the right side of history.

Meanwhile, it is instructive to see the private schools in day-to-day action looking after their own. In 2015, Wellington College launched 'the Wellington Community', open to Old Wellingtonians (OWs), parents, staff and children. 'We had a fantastically enjoyable Lent term,' noted its head three years later:

> We were incredibly excited to host our inaugural Entrepreneurs' Exchange which saw around 100 OWs, parents and students come together to share ideas, give advice as well as generating

some investment opportunities with a number of OW start-ups benefiting from advice and crucially funding – which was tremendously exciting. The Entrepreneurs' Exchange was one of the biggest business networking events that we held last term and is part of our plan to continue to build more business networking and entrepreneurship opportunities for OWs and parents.

As part of this programme, Wellington Connect [launched in 2016] continues to grow and we currently have over 2,600 members. We are thrilled that over 200 offers of work experience have been made available and over 88% of all members have offered some form of mentoring. If you haven't already had a chance, join today and get networking!

So it went on during summer 2018: the Blues Kitchen in achingly well-connected Shoreditch as the venue for a five-year reunion; meetings at the Naval and Military Club and the House of Lords for different Career Opportunity Groups ('set up to provide support and networking opportunities for OWs'), with the former meeting focusing on law, the latter on politics; and, open to anyone in the Wellington Community, a drinks function at the Waterloo Sports Bar & Grill ('rapidly becoming the must-attend event for those looking to extend their business network').[14]

Understandably, most of this networking goes on below the radar. By contrast, in the sphere of public discourse, the sector is happy to present itself – and earn kudos – as an authority not only on educational matters, but also on broader social issues. 'In the private system, headship still seems to spark a lifetime urge to be Dr Arnold or Albus Dumbledore, speaking *ex cathedra* to the hoi polloi', rather caustically observed Libby Purves in April 2018, contrasting them with the 'target-haunted, ministerially harassed' state school heads. And she went on: 'Here's Mr Belfield of Ruthin School condemning teenage love as leading to "underachievement," Mr Robb of Gresham's saying young people lack "grit" and Sir Anthony Seldon pointing the finger at "clueless narcissist" parents …'[15] Back in the 1960s or 1970s, it was the state sector that was generally at the educational cutting edge and attracted most of the attention, until some private school heads, led by John Rae at Westminster, initiated in the late 1970s a deliberate policy of seeking to lead rather than follow educational debate.[16] The key figure of more recent years among the private school 'headocracy' has undoubtedly been Seldon, head of Wellington between 2006 and 2015: there, quite apart from becoming famous (and deservedly praised) for promoting emotional 'wellness', he started an annual Festival of Education ('two days of celebration, discovery, learning and networking') in which, hosted by the school, many significant players from the educational world have taken part. In short, an audacious coup. Yet, as one of the authors has personally found, to suggest in this forum that the very existence of a fee-paying sector might not, in the big picture, be helpful to educational and social wellness is a somewhat uncomfortable experience.

There has also been a skilful makeover, to bring their public image more into line with their transformation on the ground. Whereas once the schools were legitimately seen as cruel, repressive, reactionary and generally antediluvian, now they convincingly present themselves as modern, caring, cultured and socially liberal – while also, at the same time, disciplined and ambitious, with a golden ticket for life beyond. Take an almost random clutch of advertisements from spring 2018:

A strong community where pupils are known, nurtured and challenged to the best of their ability. *(Hurstpierpoint College)*

Outstanding academic results ... Extensive co-curricular programme ... Exemplary pastoral care and nurturing environment. *(Mayfield)*

A breathtaking range of opportunities in a school small enough for everyone to know and support each other. *(Cranleigh School)*

Building confidence, inspiring success. *(Shoreham College)*

Happy and high-achieving. *(North Bridge House)*

Unlocking each child's full and unique potential. *(Dolphin School)*

The ad for King's School, Canterbury, covers all the bases. Historic setting creating a spiritually aware, historically informed and aesthetically appreciative community? Cheque. Unique annual festival of music, drama, art and recreation? Cheque. Over twenty sports on offer, from rugby and hockey to fencing and equestrianism? Cheque. Scholarly excellence supported by a caring pastoral and tutorial system? Cheque. Oxford, Cambridge, the Russell Group of universities, and American colleges as the most popular leaver destinations? Cheque, cheque, cheque and cheque again.

All these selling pitches come from two magazines. One, called *A+ Education*, is published twice a year as a supplement to the three magazines *Surrey Life*, *Sussex Life* and *Kent Life*; the other, the trendily lower-case (and title beyond parody) *angels & urchins*, is billed on its front cover as 'Indispensable to London Parents', appears four times a year, has a print run of 50,000 copies, and is distributed free across London in places like schools, nursery schools, shops and museums. Their similarities are striking: glossy, with high production values; page after page of advertisements for private schools, usually featuring photographs of happy, attractive, engaged children, more often than not mixed-sex and ethnically diverse; fully supportive editorial matter which never even faintly questions whether a fee-paying system of education is a good concept; and a fundamental if never explicitly stated assumption that going down the private route is the *only* feasible thing for a parent in London and the South-east to be doing.

A casual half-hour with these magazines leaves the reader with an unmistakable sense of a deeply entrenched service industry, brilliantly and persuasively marketing itself, amidst a largely compliant media. Or take the *Guardian*, which in its Saturday edition periodically includes 'an independent promotional supplement' called 'Modern Family'. Typically, as in the issue in February 2018, this includes twenty pages on 'Education &

Schooling', dominated by advertisements for private schools and accompanying advertorial. The *Guardian*!

A final example, from around the same time, is the main feature one day in the *Oxford Mail*: about how its sister paper, the *Oxford Times*, had teamed up with the city's leading private school, St Edward's ('Teddies'), to offer free places in the sixth form to two lucky local state school pupils. 'It is a stepping stone to success,' acclaims the paper's reporter Sophie Grubb. And to reassure potential applicants (family income not exceeding £50,000), she quotes two current sixth-formers. There is, insists Pippa, 'nothing snobby' about Teddies (boarding fees in excess of £36,000 a year, day fees almost £30,000), and students do not differentiate between those from private and state backgrounds. 'It's really inclusive here and you really feel a part of it,' agrees Kitty. 'There are so many people from different backgrounds.'[17]

Whispers and Cries

A mood of fatalism, accompanied by collective reluctance to engage in a serious and sustained national conversation on the subject of private education, is all too understandable. 'Yes, I do think they've been favoured,' the working-class Glaswegian actor James McArdle has remarked of the high-profile Etonian actors. 'But, actually, I think they've been favoured throughout all of time, and will be favoured throughout all of time.'[18] Complexity – in addition to the intimidating aura of the vested interests – contributes to the fatalism: for all the fundamental simplicity of the moral argument about unfairness, the issue is undeniably a complicated one taken in the round; it is not straightforwardly easy to grasp and evaluate the merits of alternative reform proposals; and too often emanating from the media is a fog of confusion or worse. Take, as a case of mixed messages, a single issue in early 2018 of *The Times*. 'Why it pays for a trainee to be posh' was the title of a revealing and implicitly condemnatory article in the main section, reporting in some detail on a survey showing that in the previous year 'half of all trainees joining leading law firms were privately educated and will earn more than those from state schools as they progress up the career ladder', that indeed the law firms with the strongest bias towards privately educated graduates paid twice as much as the firms most open to state-schooled graduates; by complete contrast elsewhere in the paper, the cover story in *Times 2*, entirely laudatory in tone, was about some sixth-formers at Rugby School – 'hallowed turf ... castellated brown brick buildings ... £35,000 a year ...' – paying regular visits to Rainsbrook, a nearby secure training centre for young offenders.[19] Socio-economic facts and human interest stories are not, of course, mutually exclusive; but the conjunction (presumably inadvertent) was telling as well as piquant, leaving the casual reader wholly uncertain about whether private schools are a 'bad' thing or a 'good' thing.

More generally, as we have tried to show earlier in the book, a host of elements contribute to the absence of an adequate national conversation, with a particular responsibility attached to politicians, editors and the broad commentariat. Many of them have been privately educated; and many have decided, often for understandable reasons, to educate their children privately. The upshot is a significant degree of inhibition in openly talking or writing about the issue. Are they underestimating the pervasive influence of private schools? Do they have a natural wish not to upset the apple cart? A sense of guilt? A concern that to push for change is to invite the uncomfortable charge of hypocrisy? Or, quite likely, a mixture of these things?

We do not underestimate the invidiousness. The role of head of Ofsted is not a political or media one, but it is perhaps the most senior position in the educational field, automatically conferring considerable clout on every opinion and judgement. Amanda Spielman was interviewed in February 2018 by Peter Wilby, to whom she explained that she had attended a state primary and then two private schools (including St Paul's Girls) before going to Cambridge. 'As for her two daughters, she won't answer. "I don't think you're entitled to ask," she says, which I assume means they have been educated privately.'[20] It is not to criticise Spielman herself to assert that this type of evasiveness is unhelpful: the 'activators', those individuals who go a long way to determining the scope of what society engages with and talks about, *should* in a grown-up democracy be able to discuss private education – including their own involvement – freely, publicly and honestly.

So, more generally, should those well-off people who have the means to educate their children privately choose to do so? Instead, the issue tends to provoke emotions ranging from embarrassed justification at one end of the spectrum to combative bluster at the other, with an awkward silence somewhere in the middle. Few people find it easy to stand back from their own personal situation – in which they have a considerable emotional and usually financial stake – and instead try to look at the issue objectively and dispassionately in the round. This is, of course, in human terms almost entirely unsurprising, and we make the point with a note of regret, not accusation.

Another evasion, similarly unhelpful but not exactly morally heinous, is the retreat to some sort of comfort zone. The commentator Jenni Russell describes best the key psychological background. 'In a cold, competitive world, the lucky and privileged – that's me, and most probably you – will fight to preserve our own and our children's advantages,' she has written in *The Times*, 'because we know that the rewards for success and the penalties for failure are large and getting larger.'[21] Why in that context, if one is sending one's child to a private school or thinking about doing so, would one voluntarily *want* to look at the wider issue, including the cost to the children of less affluent parents of one's decision? Far more natural to stay in one's reassuring, mutually supportive, 'Wellington Community' bubble. 'The inhumanity of much modern life, in schools, hospitals and in urban planning, is no concern of the elites because they (we) don't have to experience it,' is how the one-time Tory guru Steve Hilton has nicely evoked that syndrome as a whole. 'Our children go to private schools, we supplement our NHS care with private insurance and we eat organic food from Waitrose ...'[22] Similarly, for those many privately educated people who have flourished in their post-school lives, it is difficult to take on board – let alone discuss the implications of – the strong possibility that a significant part of that success may be down to the size of their parents' bank balance and the accompanying positional advantage bought by going to a private school. Altogether, as T. S. Eliot so memorably reflected, 'humankind cannot bear very much reality'. But the ineluctable fact remains that that reality is not going to change unless collectively we begin to examine and confront it.

Three potent but misleading cries – mainly from defenders of the status quo – also contribute to closing down the issue. The first is 'social engineering', the cry so often uttered when any form of positive discrimination is discussed, for instance whether top universities should apply a contextual admissions policy, or even outright quotas, in order to ensure a more equitable distribution of places between the privately and the state-educated. This is a mindless cry – for what could be a more blatant form of social engineering than the existence of a thriving private school sector which strives might and main to improve the life chances of its clientele? Then there is the time-honoured cry of 'the politics of envy', one that has become a particularly familiar trope in the modern era. 'Envy is dangerous, destructive, divisive,' Margaret Thatcher told her party shortly before coming to power; 'I have no time for the politics of envy,' Tony Blair declared likewise, again just before entering No. 10. A rejoinder came in 2001 from the influential philosopher John Rawls, who in his book *Justice as Fairness* insisted on the importance of society establishing, among other things, 'equal opportunities of education for all, regardless of family income'. And going further, two years later, the educational academics John Ahier and John Beck argued cogently that some circumstances legitimately give rise to what they called a politics not of envy, but of 'justified resentment'; and we would claim, as far as our own approach to Britain's private school problem is concerned, that justified resentment, not envy, lies at the heart of the matter.[23]

The final defensive cry is the emotive one best summed up as 'don't punish the children', that is, the privately educated children. Take an article, entirely well-meaning, by the *Daily Telegraph* columnist Judith Woods in October 2017, when she worried about the possibility of leading universities in the future making wholesale 'contextualised' offers (a potentially viable option discussed in the previous chapter):

> Figures just published show that 82 per cent of Oxbridge offers are currently made to applicants in the top two social classes ... They also revealed Oxbridge makes more offers to applicants from four of the Home Counties than the whole of the north of England.
>
> That can't be right, by any measure. But it raises a quandary. Is it fair to redress the balance by penalising young people for attending top schools? No, it is not. Yet what of those who attended inadequate state schools? Should they be expected to suffer the educational consequences? No, that's not right either.

She concluded at the end of her piece that 'the truth is, until we have something approaching a level playing field, a bit more contextualisation is going to be the least worst option, even though it's an essentially obfuscatory term ripe for satire'.[24] That did not prevent, a few days later in the same paper, a prominent private school head, Chris Ramsey, citing her approvingly and declaring that 'there is a paradox at the heart of "differential offers" (the mechanism by which lower university offers are given to those from disadvantaged backgrounds)' – namely, 'by being "fair" to the underprivileged student and giving him or her a lower offer, you risk being unfair to the student who after all cannot do any more than get top grades, and didn't themselves choose their background or school'. In short: 'You can only run the race set in front of you.'[25] Which begs the question of what should be the terms and conditions of that race.

There is, finally, one further important reason why the national conversation on the private school issue is so often patchy and/ or unfocused: namely, the fact that in whole swathes of Britain, especially working-class or lower middle-class areas, private schools are so thin on the ground – and so remote from daily lives – that they might as well exist on a different planet. The veteran journalist Christopher Hird has recalled a Nottingham MP describing how only 2 per cent of her constituents were privately educated, so that the issue simply failed to register there.[26] Taken as a whole, the 'different planet' reality goes a long way to explaining why the issue has failed over the years to achieve national traction (as exemplified by a 2010 survey showing the majority of respondents neutral or having no opinion on the question of whether the state system would benefit or suffer if there were fewer private schools).[27] A recent episode eloquently if unwittingly made the point. 'The son of a supermarket worker raised in one of Britain's most impoverished areas is following in the footsteps of royalty after winning a scholarship at Eton,' reported the *Daily Mail* in December 2017. 'Stephen Geddes, 16, from Dingle, in Liverpool, left his teacher and his mother in tears after he was selected to study at the £38,000-a-year school in Windsor, Berkshire.' Among the 500 or so comments over the next few hours going up online, there was barely a critical or analytical voice. Instead, the dominant mood was one of touchingly genuine pleasure at his almost fairytale good fortune in going to such a famous, semi-mythical institution that might as well have been in El Dorado as in Berkshire:

> Well done young man. Keep at it. The world is your oyster.
>
> Well done to this lad, his family and teachers. Go and achieve your dreams and have a fantastic life but never forget your roots.
>
> Good lad and bloody well done!
>
> Well done lad. Be yourself and don't let Lord Snooty and his pals get you down.

'The rich kids generally have class and treat people with respect,' reassured a reader from Henley, 'he won't have any problems.'[28]

A Fair Shake

The great historian E. P. Thompson wrote over half a century ago about 'The Peculiarities of the English'.[29] Historically, those peculiarities have been various, but the most important – and pervasive in its consequences – has been social class. Industrialisation and urbanisation in the nineteenth century entrenched class deeply; and during that long and painful period of British economic decline – between the late nineteenth and late twentieth centuries, even as 'the Gentlemen' and 'the Players' (the amateurs and the professionals) continued to play each other at cricket until the 1960s – it became increasingly clear to observers and historians that class divisions (with their accompanying 'gentlemanly capitalism') had been and were still a major contributor to Britain's sluggish economic performance and obstinately backward-looking institutions. To watch or to listen to Tony Hancock's classic comedies of the 1950s is to be struck repeatedly by the ubiquity of class distinctions – and how much they meant to everyone, above all Hancock himself. Of course, things to a degree have changed during the half-century or more since then. The visible distinctions of dress and speech have been somewhat eroded, if far from obliterated; the obvious social manifestations of a manufacturing economy have been replaced by the more fluid forms of a service economy; the increasing emphasis of reformers and activists has been on issues of gender and ethnicity; and a series of politicians and others have sought to assure us that we are moving into 'a classless society'.

Yet the fundamental social reality remains profoundly and obstinately otherwise. Britain is still a place where more often than not it matters crucially not only to whom one has been born, but where and in what circumstances one has grown up. Survey after survey, including on an almost annual basis from the Social Mobility Commission, has revealed in painful detail the profound and systemic unevenness of the great British playing field.

It would be manifestly absurd to pin the blame entirely on the existence over the last few centuries of a flourishing private school sector. Even so, given that these schools have been and still are places which – when the feelgood verbiage is stripped away – ensure that their already advantaged pupils retain their socio-economic advantages in later life, common sense places them squarely in the centre of the frame. Cut off from normal life yet providing a high proportion of the nation's rulers, hoarding educational and other resources, symbolising unfairness, bequeathing on successive generations a sense of entitlement, handing out golden tickets to those with sufficient parental funds – the charge sheet is lengthy and incontrovertible, even if by this stage of our book wearingly familiar. We would not deny for a moment that the overwhelming majority of people who teach in these schools, giving their lives to their work, are sincere and honourable, very far from deliberately seeking to entrench privilege. Indeed, when one researcher, Saskia Papadakis, recently interviewed teachers at a girls' independent day school called 'Stonecroft', she found that 'nearly all criticised the role private education plays in preserving the privilege of a small elite at the expense of the state-educated majority'.[30] But that very fact makes it yet one more reason why the larger situation has been – and continues to be – not far short of tragic.

Elsewhere, they tend, as we mentioned in Chapter 1, to arrange matters somewhat differently. France, Germany, the United States – in none of those countries is there the same inextricable connection between private schooling and privilege-cum-power that there is here. 'Their alumni do not stand out in the same way they often do in Britain,' accurately noted a letter to *The Economist* in 2015 about the products of American private schools. 'Walk down a street in St Andrews or Durham and you will see what I mean.'[31] India is also a suggestive case – over the last decade, requiring that all of its private schools ensure some 25 per cent of their intake comes from the poorest children in a given area[32] – but the classic exemplar of taking a different path is undoubtedly Finland.

There, in 1963, at a time when the quality of education in that country was barely at international average, the Finnish Parliament reached a decision in principle for comprehensive school reform, involving a long-term commitment to a common basic school for all and in effect the phasing out of private schools. This was duly implemented, on a basis of widespread consensus, in the course of the 1970s. Inevitably, however, there *was* opposition, mainly from businessmen and right-wing politicians, who then and through the 1980s and 1990s forcibly argued that the new path would jeopardise the country's economic prospects by holding back the most talented, and they demanded greater choice and competition. Then in 2001, the first PISA (Programme for International Student Assessment) comparative study of educational attainment was published, sensationally revealing that Finland had, in the three key disciplines of reading, mathematics and science, outperformed all other OECD countries; thereafter, opposition became more muted.[33] Sixteen years later, in 2017, a range of international indices ranked Finland the most stable, the safest and the best-governed country in the world; it was also ranked the second most socially progressive and the third wealthiest, least corrupt and most socially just; while in March 2018 the UN declared Finland no less than the happiest place to live on the planet.[34] Looking back on what has been a truly remarkable success story, with education at its heart, the world-renowned Finnish educationalist Pasi Sahlberg has concluded that, back in the crucial 1960s, 'equality, efficiency and solidarity' were 'the essential principles' that 'merged into a consensus that enriched each other'.[35] It has, somewhere near its very core, been a story of equal educational opportunities for all – and the greater good, whether educational or social or economic, that has flowed from the steady, determined application of that keystone principle.

But perhaps we are just talking about 'The Peculiarities of the Finnish'? In our view, not so; we would argue that, however different Britain and Finland are in their respective historical formations, there are significant lessons from the Finnish experience. In part, yes, about the ambition of the reform route that was chosen – though as we contend in the previous chapter, other reform routes, less ambitious than Finland's, also need to be considered and evaluated carefully. Yet arguably, just as important a lesson concerns not so much the Finnish route itself as the way in which the whole reform exercise was undertaken there: patient, long-term and, as much as possible, consensus-establishing, with the consequence being that not only has it proved irreversible, but that it was easier to implement in the first place than might well otherwise have been the case.

Is it possible in Britain over the next ten or twenty years to build a similar and sufficiently widespread consensus for reform? Or, at the very least, to begin to have a serious, sustained, non-name-calling, non-guilt-ridden national conversation on the subject of private education? The Populus poll we have cited, showing a virtually landslide majority for a perception of unfairness about private education (when the context of that education is accurately described), shows that public opinion is potentially receptive to grappling with the issue and what to do about it. Moreover, and at the risk of repeating ourselves because the finding is so suggestive, the poll reveals that *even* those who have been privately educated, and/or have chosen to educate their own children privately, are more likely to have a perception of unfairness. The issue is undeniably hard, often invidious; the forces on the side of the status quo are formidable; free and open debate is subdued; but at some point it is surely time for the waves – of discussion, of regret, of outrage – to start pounding relentlessly, not spasmodically or apologetically, on Britain's deeply embedded rocks.

Looked at in a strictly educational sense, it is easy to understand that the question of what to do about a sector educating only 6 or 7 per cent of our school population can seem relatively marginal, and difficult to prioritise (especially in challenging economic circumstances), compared to, say, the challenges of quality teacher recruitment across the state sector or the whole vital area of early-years learning. Yet it would be a huge mistake to underestimate the seriously negative educational aspects of the current dispensation and to continue to marginalise the private school question. The private schools' reach is very much broader than their minority share of school pupils implies. A disproportionately large proportion of our teachers are engaged with this minority of pupils, and overall as much as one in every six education pounds goes on this sector. As we have seen, a wholly disproportionate share of the influential and well-rewarded positions in British society fall to this privately educated elite. Even a partial resolution would start to bring into the state education system the energies, enthusiasms and experience of very many parents and teachers. Unless some radical reform is set in train, an unreconstructed private school system, with its enormous resource superiority and exclusiveness hanging over the state system as a beacon for unequal treatment and privilege, would make it hard to sustain a fully comprehensive and fair state education system.

Ultimately, the issue is at least as much about what kind of society one might hope the Britain of the 2020s and 2030s to be. A more open society in which upward social mobility starts to become a real possibility for many children, not just a few lucky ones? A society in which the affluent are not educated in enclaves, and in which schooling for the affluent is not funded at something like three times the level of schooling for the less affluent? A society in which the pursuit through education of greater equality of life chances, seeking to harness the talents of all our children, is a matter of real and rigorous intent? A society in which there is a just relationship between the competing demands of liberty and equity, and in which we are, to coin a phrase, all in it together? For the building of such a society, or anything even remotely close, the issue of private education is pivotal, both symbolically and substantively. The reform of private schools will not alone be *sufficient* to achieve a good education system for all, let alone the good society; but it surely is a *necessary* condition. At this particular moment in our island story, the future seems peculiarly a blank sheet. Everything is potentially on the table. And, for once, that has to include the engines of privilege.

A significant strand of this book has concerned the failures of the past, especially the political failures. It is time to learn from those failures: the patchy dialogue; the lack of consensus-building; the loss of nerve; the reluctance to see the big picture. It is time, in short, to get it right. For if not now, when?

Postscript: Moving Ahead?

Private schools did not exactly disappear from view between late summer 2018 (when we finished writing the book) and spring 2019 (as we write this additional chapter).

Toffee, a high-profile dating app, was set up – exclusively for the privately educated; figures showed that, after the introduction of charges in Scotland, private school pupils there are three times as likely to appeal exam results as those at state schools; a hastily withdrawn advertisement for Vinehall School (£23,000 a year) in East Sussex depicted going to that prep school as the indispensable route to becoming 'very successful in business' and thereby acquiring a 'beautiful dark blue Jaguar'; the mushrooming number of British private schools abroad prompted accusations of poaching science and maths teachers from British state schools, aggravating already serious shortages; BBC Radio 6 Music's Cerys Matthews imposed, in the cause of social mobility, a temporary ban on playing records by the privately educated; the Institute of Student Employers found that the leading graduate schemes are dominated by the privately educated; the security minister, Ben Wallace, warned private schools against facilitating money-laundering; a Sutton Trust report revealed the sheer extent of dedicated specialist support at the top private schools for pupils aspiring to leading universities; the latest Coutts shopping basket of luxury products costed five years of private education at an average of £156,000; Ruby Wax advocated that, to instil empathy across the great divide, 'all posh schools should take children twice a week to play with kids who have nothing'; ahead of the UCAS deadline for personal statements, *The Tab*, a network of student news sites, set up a free helpline 'to give some state school applicants the kind of help that posh schools offer'; Hasan Patel, a youthful Corbynista living on a Leyton council estate, was branded a hypocrite for taking up an Eton scholarship; a former Harrow head, Barnaby Lenon, observed the increasing tendency of Old Etonians and Harrovians to speak in mockney to seem less posh; Canford School (£36,000 a year) sought to keep ramblers off its playing fields by saying they could be hit by balls from its nine-hole golf course; the *Daily Telegraph* celebrated how 'Britain's top public schools are revamping with help from superstar architects' (Eton's 'sleek' new tennis pavilion 'clad in charred timber', Wellington's new Performing Arts Centre 'clad in fine ribs of stained birch', Brighton College's new music school 'as finely acoustically attuned as a musical instrument'); state schools – educating 93 per cent of British children – encountered a severe funding crisis; and fees went up another 3.7 per cent.[1]

Three relevant books also appeared during these months, starting with Melissa Benn's *Life Lessons*, subtitled *The Case for a National Education Service*. 'We urgently need to renew the conversation about the private–public divide, and move beyond the superficial, profoundly apolitical debates of recent years,' she argues. 'These have chiefly been characterised by the rolling out of the same information again and again, almost as if the private schools were not human creations but unchallengeable phenomena like the weather or religious deities.' Her main solution is strongly integrationist: 'At a time of growing divides and damaging inequality, we urgently need public institutions that bring the nation together, not further separate and divide us. For many in the UK the idea of a unified education system to which all subscribe is too great a leap of the imagination, too daring a proposition, yet the benefits of a common schooling could be immense.' And while accepting that 'proposals for outright abolition are likely to raise an unproductive political outcry followed by years of legal wrangling', she wants private schools to be compelled to take, on a state-funded basis, a 25 per cent quota of 'children who have been on free school meals for an extended period of time, children who have been in care or children who struggle to attain basic levels of attainment'.[2]

The other two books focus mainly on social mobility. *Social Mobility and Its Enemies*, by Lee Elliot Major and Stephen Machin, devotes a chapter to 'Britain's Privately Educated Elite', spelling out in detail its dominance while gloomily asserting that 'on current evidence' it 'will continue to prosper in Britain for the foreseeable future'. Indeed, the authors are generally somewhat low key about possible ways ahead for resolving the private school problem. The Sutton Trust's Open Access Scheme 'is a difficult sell to Ministers on both sides of the political divide'; and potentially 'more palatable' to politicians might be 'to demand that private schools form genuine and accountable partnerships with state schools or relinquish the charitable status they enjoy'.[3] *The Class Ceiling: Why It Pays to Be Privileged*, by Sam Friedman and Daniel Laurison, is a rich sociological study (including the private school aspect) of social class in contemporary Britain and its disabling effects on the great majority, but sadly even lighter on what to do about our favourite issue. Their book ends with an epilogue called '10 ways to break the class ceiling': it contains some valuable practical suggestions (including 'Find out whether an organisation has a class ceiling' and 'Start a conversation about talent') – but of the private school issue *as* an issue, systemic and pervasive, not a word.[4]

Barely a word either from the commentariat when one might have expected – or at least hoped for – something more. Taking what she terms 'the dispiriting data' of *The Class Ceiling* as her starting point, *The Times*'s Clare Foges (a former speechwriter for David Cameron) calls for more day-to-day 'mixing of private and state school pupils', but otherwise has nothing to suggest beyond society getting better at helping those from 'less advantaged backgrounds' to 'emulate the ease and studied informality of the privileged'. Her fatalism becomes all-consuming. 'We can rail at the bastions of privilege all we like,' she concludes in justification of an if-you-can't-beat-them strategy, 'but the privileged will always pull every string going to get their children the breaks, recruiters will always gravitate to people like them, fit and polish will always give some candidates the edge. We can as easily fight all this as turn back the tides.'[5] Or take *The Economist*. In September 2018 it marked its 175th anniversary by publishing a lengthy manifesto, designed to reinvent liberalism for the twenty-first century. There was nothing on the question of private education, even though the editorial summary of the manifesto declared that 'in all sorts of ways, the liberal meritocracy is closed and self-sustaining'.[6] Three months later the paper's 'Bagehot', assessing the British political crisis over Brexit, wrote scathingly about the disastrous 'rule of the chumocracy'. Yet of the role of private schools in the formation of that 'introverted and self-regarding' chumocracy, only the familiar silence.[7]

What about the sector itself? Often it remained in stubbornly defensive mode – typified by the alarmist, over-the-top battle waged by the Scottish Council of Independent Schools against the prospective stripping away of business rates relief.[8] Yet there were some signs of trying to get more on the front foot for a post-Brexit world when (so the conventional political wisdom ran) the socio-economic causes of Brexit would be thoroughly addressed. No major new initiatives for broadening the social composition across the sector were announced – with the ISC's 'up to 10,000 free places every year' offer of 2016 still on the table gathering dust – but a cluster of moments is worth recording. Westminster School launched a fundraising campaign with the ambition of becoming 'truly needs-blind'; Millfield announced it was cutting its fees by 10 per cent; Mike Buchanan, executive director of the HMC, hailed bursaries as 'socialism in action', by which 'relatively well-off, fee-paying parents are funding the free and assisted places for others' (and adding, naively or otherwise, that 'few object'); Emma Hattersley, head of the Godolphin School in Salisbury, urged that scholarships for exceptionally talented pupils be 'phased out' in favour of bursaries for pupils from less well-off families; and Stowe's head, Anthony Wallersteiner, lamented in heartfelt fashion how most of his school's bursaries were going to 'the squeezed middle' rather than being effectively targeted at genuinely low-income families.[9] Undeniably, though, all this at best amounted to early steps on a long, long road from social exclusivity to social breadth – a road with few signposts and no real indication of a collective will to travel along it.

The political class, meanwhile, was as economical as ever with its interventions. Even so, half a dozen episodes deserve noting, with the first in October 2018 as Philip Hammond prepared his Budget. As reports circulated that he was considering imposing VAT on school fees (Labour's policy), not only did the sector move into predictably robust action about the 'folly' of doing so, but Tory backbench voices were sufficiently loud and hostile to prompt Hammond to scrap the idea – though suggestively enough, an Ipsos MORI poll found 54 per cent in favour, more than double the 26 per cent opposed.[10] Then came the pre-Christmas launch by an education minister, Nadhim Zahawi, of a national scheme between some private schools and local authorities to offer more places to children growing up in care. According to Zahawi, it was a scheme ensuring that Labour would 'never be able to abolish' private schools – a bold claim, especially given the numbers were still relatively small and no one could know how the scheme was going to work on the ground.[11] It was just after Christmas that Labour, following detailed analysis by Manchester Central MP Lucy Powell, called for an inquiry into the question of whether private schools, through strategic use of internationally recognised GSCEs (IGCSEs), were gaming to their own advantage the fact that GCSEs as taken by state school pupils were now harder. In the event, Ofqual's Roger Taylor ruled in March that there was indeed 'a disturbing issue in terms of the fairness of the system'. He was speaking to the education select committee, whose Conservative chair, Robert Halfon, made his feelings plain: 'Basically, what we are saying is that if you are wealthy enough to afford to go to private school, not only that, you're going to get an easier exam, which is called the same name and recognised by employers. But if you're not wealthy, you go to state school and do a higher-quality, higher-standard exam that is called GCSE, and you get potentially lower grades even though that person from private school is getting all those advantages.'[12]

The other three episodes were also in March 2019 and likewise featured Tories, all of them strong Brexiteers. 'What about our brilliant independent school sector?' asked Dominic Raab in a speech setting out his vision for 'the Opportunity Society', before advocating implementation of the Sutton Trust's Open Access Scheme – 'a first step,' he added, 'to opening up all independent schools on a means-tested and meritocratic basis'.[13] Liz Truss's contribution, in a *Times* interview, was to push the idea of the top 100 pupils from each region's state schools being automatically offered a place at Oxbridge, with no need for an entrance interview. 'Incredibly offputting for a lot of students from state schools,' she described the interview process, 'compared to those who have got private education who have had training to do it.'[14] 'I would have hoped', Michael Gove had meanwhile told the *Evening Standard*, 'we would have been able to make sending your children to a private school, as it is in Europe, an increasingly eccentric choice.' Did he therefore, he was asked, want to end private education by stealth? 'Well, yes,' he replied. But as to how he was going to achieve that, he could only fall back – with no mention of disparity of resources – on the old hope (as espoused by Ellen Wilkinson some seventy-three years before and many education ministers since) that the state sector should be improved until most parents did not even consider going private.[15]

Critics have their say

That Britain's private school problem should persist in fizzing only intermittently, and for the most part inconsequentially, is hardly surprising given that this is what had been happening for several years. When our hardback was published in February 2019, we were grateful for the amount of attention it received.

The reviews in the mainstream press covered most of the bases. Alex Renton in the *Spectator* predicted that our arguments would be tolerated and absorbed as a classic example of establishment

survival strategy; Anne McElvoy in the *Evening Standard* similarly
had confidence in the infinite capacity of the private schools 'to beat
the rap'; Janice Turner in the *New Statesman* wrote candidly from
the perspective of 'a girl from a crap northern comprehensive' who
was now a critical private school parent; *Private Eye*'s anonymous
reviewer invoked Orwell but took refuge in stale irony; the
Guardian's Kate Clanchy had a problem with the book being by
two privately educated 'chaps', and not more about state schools;
the *Sunday Telegraph*'s Allison Pearson had a problem with the book
not being about grammar schools; *Standpoint*'s Jamie Whyte, a
free-market economist in outright denial about the very concept of
unfairness, had a problem with the book full stop; Hugo Rifkind in
The Times concluded triumphantly that the lesson of the book was
that 'maybe it's time to remortgage the house and start googling open
days'; Harry Mount in the *Catholic Herald* agreed that sufficiently
well-off parents will always turn 'to St Custard's, chequebook in
hand'; Maggie Fergusson in the *Tablet* came to the book undecided,
but concluded 'not just that change is urgently needed, but that
the options for change are more varied, imaginative and realistic
than I'd dared imagine'; Dominic Sandbrook in the *Sunday Times*
called our Fair Access Scheme 'bonkers'; and Miranda Green in
the *Financial Times* anticipated 'the manifesto-writers at the next
general election' looking 'magpie-like' at our policy prescriptions.[16]

Our preface to the book called for a more sober, more evidence-
based, more objective debate. And while uncomfortably aware
that authors complaining about reviews is only marginally less
productive than sailors complaining about the sea, we have to
admit to being – with exceptions, of course – largely disappointed
on this front. Too much overheated language; points of refutation
implied as the reviewer's own when in fact they are already
rehearsed in the book; frequent deflective resort to variations on
'the problem lies elsewhere'; and a tendency to play the man (men),
not the ball. Our real frustration, though, is in the relative paucity
of serious and accurate engagement with our core arguments,
especially those going beyond the more obvious and familiar
ones like socially exclusive composition, huge resources gap and

undue dominance of the privately educated in the top echelons of national life. In particular, there are four arguments which we hoped to see a high degree of engagement with: that the purchase of education is fundamentally different from most other types of purchase, thereby involving considerations of equity as well as liberty; that we do not blame parents who choose to go private, and accordingly the politics of hypocrisy represent a dead end; that we need as a society to discuss the private school issue dispassionately and detach ourselves from our own particular circumstances; and that the Fair Access Scheme we propose represents a worthwhile way forward. Yet if one takes the four reviews with probably the greatest reach (Clanchy in the *Guardian*, Pearson in the *Sunday Telegraph*, Rifkind in *The Times*, Sandbrook in the *Sunday Times*), there was generally a poor or even non-existent level of engagement with these four arguments, irrespective of whether they agreed or disagreed. Put another way, we were pleasantly surprised by the number of column inches in the mainstream press devoted to our book; but by and large it was a lost opportunity to move the debate forward.

Three contrasting reviews came from the world of education, including two thoughtful comments in less prominent mouthpieces. Bringing in the comparative position of private schooling in other countries would enhance an already-strong argument, suggested Richard Lofthouse in Oxford University's *Quad* magazine.[17] Higher education expert Nick Hillman reckoned that our argument 'comes a little unstuck' because 'it treats the most elite, autonomous and well-resourced schools as an embarrassing stain on society that should be removed, but simultaneously assumes our elite, autonomous and well-resourced universities are a welcome fact of life'.[18] Here we should set the record straight and confirm that, if we treat our hierarchical university system uncritically, it is not because we somehow 'welcome' or endorse it; rather, it is because we see that there are feasible private school reforms that do not entail rebooting Britain's entire university system as well.

The third educational review came from the private sector itself, in the form of Patrick Derham (head of Westminster) in the *TES*. Broadly hostile, including an implied slur on the integrity of the book's research, it amounted in effect to little more than run-of-the-mill private school propaganda. It made the familiar assertion that partnerships with state schools were 'making a real difference'. What Derham failed to offer was any substantive, validated evidence of the resource transfers that might or might not be made through partnerships nationwide; or about the extent of any substantial educational gains for state school pupils. There is little to go on, other than a few carefully chosen exemplary cases – and we are entitled to ask whether partnerships, taken in the round, are making more than a minor difference to the life chances of state school pupils. Instead, in a breathtaking leap, Derham offered, seemingly as proof of partnerships' value, the ISC's latest study of the sector's 'impact' on the economy. This study is just as deeply flawed in its conception as the earlier one in 2014. Derham misrepresented our argument, before going on to his own version of the 'the problem lies elsewhere' game, calling for an entirely different book – about wealth inequality.[19]

What about the political response to our book? It was welcome but also sobering when one of us was invited on to the *Reasons to be Cheerful* podcast hosted by Ed Miliband and Geoff Lloyd. Although Miliband himself was brave enough subsequently to write an article for *Metro* praising our book and calling for change, he characterised the private school problem as a 'third rail' issue – in other words, touch it as a politician and you're dead.[20] Nevertheless, our hope remains that *Engines* may have a value if and when, at some point, politicians and policy-makers do start seriously to get to grips with the subject. More encouraging have been editorials, sparked directly by our book, in two key left-of-centre organs, the *New Statesman* and the *Guardian*. The former endorsed the main thrust of our arguments, before noting that at one level the Brexit vote of 2016 had been 'a protest against a stratified society' in which 'a self-segregated elite has captured the benefits of globalisation while leaving others to bear its costs'. Accordingly, 'without significant educational reform' (not only in relation to private schools), 'the only certainty is that further revolts will follow'.[21] For its part, the *Guardian* similarly backed our 'timely' book and wryly referred to its own 1968 cartoon looking ahead to an obstinately unchanged 2068 (a date now closer than 1968 is). 'School funding, failing academies and technical education all require attention more urgently than private schools', the editorial fairly enough concluded. 'But it is possible to do more than one thing at once', it equally fairly went on. 'The sharp elbows of fee-paying parents don't just serve to shield their own children, but also push others out of the way. Countering such behaviour is in the interests of the country as a whole.'[22]

In Search of Fairness

Comforting myths continue to abound, perhaps none more so than about social composition. 'Private education is no longer the preserve of the privileged,' insists the *Daily Mail* in a February 2019 double-page spread about parents who are 'digging deep' for the sake of giving their children a better education. 'There's an assumption that people who are privately educating their children have pots of money, but we've made huge sacrifices,' explains one such parent. 'We're not frivolous with money and rarely go out or buy clothes, and if things get financially tricky with fees, then we'll make further cutbacks such as not having holidays.' Unsurprisingly, the private sector itself takes every opportunity to put such parents in the spotlight. Shane Fenton, head of the HMC, pays public tribute to the 'many' parents who 'sacrifice and save' to pay for fees; while in our own conversations with private school leaders, they dispute our understanding of the reality of modern private schools, but instead draw a picture of schools across the country that have a very varied composition and are fundamentally different animals from the Etons and the Harrows and the Winchesters.[23]

Of course it is true that there are some – if not that many – private school attenders from low- and middle-income families. Yet, while a fraction of these gain access via bursaries, the rest draw on family wealth that puts them relatively much higher up the ladder than their current income – enough to cover the high school fees

What middle-income families with children aged 5–15 spend per week on recreation and culture (including package holidays), restaurants and hotels.

	Private school families	State school families
Spending (£ per week at 2015 prices)	£179	£136
Proportion of their disposable income	26%	20%

Source: ONS, *Living Costs and Food Surveys*, 2004–2015. A 'private school family' is one with at least one child aged 5 to 15 in a private school; a 'state school family' has one or more children aged 5–15, all at state school. A 'middle-income family' is one that is between the 40th and 60th rungs of the income ladder. Disposable family income is the family's gross income minus taxes and national insurance.

without any obvious sacrifices. As the table above shows, middle-income families with children at private school spend *more* – not less – on their holidays and other recreational activities than similar families with children at state schools.

Such is the reality – albeit, as yet, the wholly unpublicised reality.

In their hearts, we suspect, most private school leaders recognise this to be true and know that they have a serious problem with social exclusivity: in the context partly of ever-rising fees; partly of external criticism just starting to show signs of achieving some sort of critical mass; and partly because at least some would genuinely wish it otherwise. Indeed, the official line is that there exists a new generation of progressive-minded heads, many of them not privately educated themselves, who are passionate about opening up their schools to a much broader range of pupils. One such, for all his unsympathetic review of our book, would be Westminster's Derham. 'There's nothing wrong with an elite education, but we're trying to stop it being elitist', he tells *The Times*, about his ambition to move to a needs-blind basis. 'It's not healthy,' he adds, 'just to have a small cross-section of society.'[24]

Can reality match the talk? Left to its own devices, can the fee-paying, resource-heavy private sector somehow magic a transformation from social exclusivity to social diversity? We remain sceptical. To achieve this in anything like a substantive and permanent way, presumably through a hugely enhanced provision of bursaries, is far beyond the financial means, even allowing for generous private philanthropy from alumni and others, of all but a handful of the richest, most elite schools – and even for them, probably not until some very distant point in the future. The HMC's Mike Buchanan may talk optimistically of 'socialism in action', but is he really imagining that fee-paying parents will be happy to see a high proportion (much higher than now) of ever-greater fees devoted to the children of parents unable to pay fees? There remain, moreover, two other problems. Is it truly the case, as some private school leaders claim, that the modern-day fee-paying parent values social diversity over social exclusivity when choosing the type of school they want their children to go to? And, one might add, the type of parent they want to stand next to on the touchline on a Saturday morning? We seriously doubt it. The second problem concerns the allocation of places in these vastly expanded bursary schemes. Private school heads – certainly at the top private schools – tend to combine means-testing with the selection of academic potential: in short, a creaming-off process – and the bulk of those who work in, care about and philosophise about state schools would, entirely understandably, be profoundly suspicious.

Ineluctably, the route to social diversity lies through state-funded places, in effect involving a significant degree of integration with the state sector and, given who is paying for them, *social* control over admissions criteria. When we have put this proposition to private school leaders, and specifically asked them about two key issues which flow from it, they have responded with a perhaps surprising degree of flexibility. The first is selection. Any serious scaling-up of state-funded places at private schools would be most unlikely to gain cross-party political support – and possibly not even support from the right – unless it was made clear from the outset that this would involve no increase in the total number of children who are academically selected within each catchment area. The places in hitherto all-private schools would become part of the state sector funded by government. As far as we could tell, this political reality seems to be something they could live with. What about the second issue, the time-honoured one of independence of governance? This matters a lot to private school leaders, but even here the discussion can be constructive, with talk of a neutral body or agency being able to hold the ring between the state and the private sector, thereby ensuring that the day-to-day relationship remained an arm's-length one. Nevertheless, there would have to be social representation on governing bodies, able to represent the interests of the state-funded children. We are conscious that a handful of private school leaders do not necessarily represent the views of the sector as a whole; conscious, too, of a possible charge of naivety. But it does not seem out of the question that some common ground could emerge.

All that said, the lesson of history is that meaningful change through internal reform almost invariably requires focused and relentless external pressure in order to make sure it happens. Here, the means of holding the schools' feet to the fire are obvious enough: on one hand, the threat-cum-reality of fiscal pressure, for example VAT on school fees; on the other hand, the increased use of contextual admissions, or other forms of positive discrimination, at leading universities. Both these approaches are, quite apart from any tactical or strategic purpose, good in themselves – especially if all money derived from taxing the private sector goes direct to desperately underfunded state schools.

Which raises the specific issue of the state sector and the not altogether easy matter of its relationship to private school reform. How, we were asked by a state school teacher at our launch event at the LSE, would any of the proposed reforms make a significant difference to her daily task?[25] A good question. There are no overnight solutions to the funding drought, other than immediate relief from the exchequer. Yet private school reforms would have benefits for state schools, both in the short and the long term: in the short term, at a time of ever-rising fees and an ever-widening resource gap (new evidence from Bristol shows a private/state resource ratio as high as approaching 4 to 1),[26] not only a substantive boost to funding through fiscal transfer, but also a gradual, partial integration of the state school sector into existing private schools would take some of the pressure off rising numbers in the state school system; while in the long term, not only would a good reform staunch the flow of teachers away from state schools and spread the parental drive for improvement across the board, but eventually a reformed system could help to produce a breed of politicians and opinon-formers who more commonly identify with having a robust, inclusive school system. Ultimately, it is a false choice to suggest that we can *either* address the state schools' problems *or* find solutions for private schooling. These are not real alternatives, but inherently interlocking issues. And the chances of doing something about the private school problem will be materially enhanced if more state school leaders – pursuing, we fully acknowledge, hard-pressed and difficult lives – are more willing to stick their heads above the parapet, acknowledge its relevance and say something about it.

Overall, we remain hopeful. The issue has an appreciably higher salience in 2019 than it did at the start of the decade; there seems to be an increasingly widespread acceptance that the educational apartheid we have is fundamentally unfair to the great majority of children, as well as severely disabling to any notions of an equitable and inclusive society; and the scope for campaigning, arguably local as much as national, is considerable. The time is at last at hand for a critical mass of sober and sustained hard thought about the best way ahead. 'Those who cannot remember the past are condemned to repeat it,' the Spanish philosopher George Santayana famously pronounced. In this case, we do know the past; and happily, therefore, the future can be different – but only if the anger, resolve and focus are there to make it different.

Notes

1

1 Green, F., J. Anders, M. Henderson and G. Henseke (2017), *Who Chooses Private Schooling in Britain and Why?*, Centre for Research on Learning and Life Chances (LLAKES), London, Research Paper 62.

2 Independent Schools Council (2017), *ISC Census and Annual Report 2017*, ISC.

3 The UK has one of the most socially stratified private school sectors in the developed world. See Fig. 2.4 in OECD (2012), *Public and Private Schools: How Management and Funding Relate to their Socio-economic Profile*, OECD Publishing. http://dx.doi.org/10.1787/9789 264175006-en

4 Kirby, P. (2016), *Leading People 2016*, The Sutton Trust, London.

5 Reeves, A., S. Friedman, C. Rahal and M. Flemmen (2017), 'The Decline and Persistence of the Old Boy: Private Schools and Elite Recruitment 1897 to 2016', *American Sociological Review*, 1–28.

6 Haroon Siddique, 'Old school tie still counts as route to elite, study shows', *Guardian*, 31 October 2017.

7 Pages 39 and 55 in Kirby, *Leading People 2016*.

8 Ed Smith, 'No family ties, no emotional inheritance: who would want "perfect" social mobility?', *New Statesman*, 6 February 2015; M. Tozer (2013), '"One of the worst statistics in British sport, and wholly unacceptable": the contribution of privately educated members of Team GB to the summer Olympic Games, 2000–2012', *International Journal of the History of Sport*, 30(12), 1436–54.

9 Tim Wigmore, 'Why England's sports teams are dominated by the privately educated', *New Statesman*, 15 October 2015.

10 Green, F., S. Machin, R. Murphy and Y. Zhu (2011), 'The Changing Economic Advantage from Private Schools', *Economica*, 79, 658–79.

11 Green, F., G. Henseke and A. Vignoles (2017), 'Private schooling and labour market outcomes', *British Educational Research Journal*, 43(1), 7–28.

12 McKnight, A. (2015), *Downward mobility, opportunity hoarding and the 'glass floor'*, London, Social Mobility and Child Poverty Commission.

13 Green, F., G. Henseke, Samantha Parsons, A. Sullivan and R. Wiggins (2018), 'Do private school girls marry rich?' *Longitudinal and Life Course Studies Journal*, 9(3), 327–50.

14 Kevin Jefferys, *Anthony Crosland*, Politico's, London, 2000, p. 108.

15 Ashley Kirk, 'Top independent schools GCSE results: How did your school rank?', *Daily Telegraph*, 2 September 2017; Camilla Turner, 'Exam results gap between state schools and private schools is narrowing, figures show', *Daily Telegraph*, 26 August 2017.

16 Ysenda Maxtone Graham, 'The truth about private school admissions', *Spectator*, 14 March 2015.

17 Parsons, S., F. Green, G. B. Ploubidis, A. Sullivan and R. D. Wiggins (2017), 'The influence of private primary schooling on children's learning: evidence from three generations of children', *British Educational Research Journal*, 43:5, 823–47.

18 Ndaji, F., J. Little and R. Coe (2016), *A Comparison of Academic Achievement in Independent and State Schools*, Centre for Evaluation and Monitoring, Durham University. For a study of value-added from Key Stage 3 up to GCSE in the two sectors, see also E. Malacova (2007), 'Effect of single sex education on progress in GCSE', *Oxford Review of Education*, 33(2), 233–59.

19 Smith-Woolley, Emily, et al. (2018), 'Differences in exam performance between pupils attending selective and non-selective schools mirror the genenetic differences between them', *npj Science of Learning*, 3:3; much was made of this study when released since, unusually, it also controlled for genetic characteristics; however, these genetic factors were rather less important than the socio-economic background, prior abilities and achievements in explaining the GCSE gaps between children from private schools and comprehensive schools.

The significance and implications of the study were over-interpreted in public debate.

20 Schooldash, 'State or private? Part 3: All subjects are not equal'; see https://www.schooldash.com/blog-1603.html#20160324.

21 Henderson, Morag, Jake Anders, Francis Green and Golo Henseke (2018), 'Private schooling, subject choice and upper secondary academic attainment in England', mimeo, UCL Institute of Education.

22 Green, F., S. Parsons, A. Sullivan and R. Wiggins (2017), 'Dreaming Big? Self-Evaluations, Aspirations, Valued Social Networks, and the Private School Earnings Premium in the UK', *Cambridge Journal of Economics*, 42(3), 757–78.

23 Gurpreet Narwan, 'Private pupils better placed to get help for special needs', *The Times*, 10 November 2017; Laura McInerney, 'It's time to confront A-level marking's dirty little secret', *Guardian*, 16 August 2016; Eleanor Busby, 'Independent schools successfully challenge more GCSE results, leading to "double disadvantage" for state pupils', *TES*, 24 August 2017; Sally Weale, Richard Adams and Helena Bengtsson, 'Going backwards; richer students from the south-east still dominate Oxbridge intake', *Guardian*, 20 October 2017; Oxford intake (HESE figs); Nicola Woolcock, 'Fewer state pupils winning places at Oxford', *The Times*, 3 February 2017.

24 The basis for the calculation of this resource gap is shown in Chapter 4.

25 Josie Gurney-Read, 'Independent school pupils "twice as likely to attend elite universities"', *Daily Telegraph*, 27 January 2015; Ed Cumming, 'Top Marks All Round', *Daily Telegraph Magazine*, 5 September 2015.

26 ISC Annual Census, 2018.

27 Gurney-Read, 'Independent school pupils "twice as likely to attend elite universities"'.

28 Social Mobility and Child Poverty Commission (2014), *Elitist Britain?*, London, Social Mobility and Child Poverty Commission.

29 Britton, J., L. Dearden, N. Shephard and A. Vignoles (2016), *How English domiciled graduate earnings vary with gender, institution attended, subject and socioeconomic background*, London: Institute for Fiscal Studies, IFS Working Paper W16/06.

30 HEFCE (2014), *Differences in Degree Oucomes: Key Findings*, Higher Education Funding Council; Smith, J. and R. Naylor (2005),

'Schooling effects on subsequent university performance: evidence for the UK university population', *Economics of Education Review*, 24(5), 549–62.

31 Green et al. (2017), op. cit.

32 Alan Bennett, 'Fair Play', *London Review of Books*, 19 June 2014.

33 The proportion of private school teachers is calculated using the Quarterly Labour Force Survey, and cross-checked against estimated numbers from the ISC Census, scaled as appropriately for England, with a small addition for non-ISC schools, together with official data – DfE Statistical First Release SFR 21/2015 for teacher numbers in state schools. The share of education spending that goes on private schooling is calculated from spending data at https://www.statista.com/statistics/298910/united-kingdom-uk-public-sector-expenditure-education/, together with private spending estimated as fees times number of pupils; this is cross-checked against the national participation rate, and the per pupil spending data shown in the table in Chapter 4.

34 Peter Wilby, 'Shami's hypocrisy, the pound plummets, the *Guardian*'s mea culpa and my Trump nightmare', *New Statesman*, 14 October 2016.

35 Source: The *Next Steps* study, Wave 1, parent interview, authors' analysis, University College London, UCL Institute of Education, Centre for Longitudinal Studies (2017), *Next Steps: Sweeps 1–8, 2004–2016*, [data collection], 13th Edition, UK Data Service, SN: 5545, http://doi.org/10.5255/UKDA-SN-5545-5

36 Tim Lott, 'Why I want to see all private schools abolished', *Guardian*, 22 April 2017.

37 Social Mobility & Child Poverty Commission (2014), *State of the Nation 2014: Social Mobility and Child Poverty in Great Britain*, p. 47.

38 Institute for Fiscal Studies, Living Standards, Inequality and Poverty Spreadsheet.

39 World Inequality Lab, *World Inequality Report 2018*, Figure 2.3.1 at www.wid.world/world-inequality-lab.

40 Blanden, J., A. Goodman, P. Gregg and S. Machin (2004), 'Changes in Intergenerational Mobility in Britain', in M. Corak (ed.), *Generational Income Inequality*, Cambridge, Cambridge University Press; Goldthorpe, J. H. and M. Jackson (2007), 'Intergenerational class mobility in contemporary Britain: political concerns and empirical findings', *British Journal of Sociology*, 58(4), 525–46.

41 Nicholas Watt and Sam Jones, 'Nick Clegg vows to tackle Britain's lack of social mobility', *Guardian*, 22 May 2012.

42 James Kirkup, 'Well done, David Cameron: Social mobility and equal opportunities are Conservative ideas again', *Daily Telegraph*, 7 October 2015.

43 Jeremy Corbyn, 'Rebuilding the Politics of Hope', Ralph Miliband public lecture, 17 May 2016. http://www.lse.ac.uk/website-archive/publicEvents/miliband/2015-2016-Lecture-Series.aspx; Andrew Lilico, 'Theresa May's "meritocracy" is a recipe for Darwinian dystopia', *Daily Telegraph*, 12 September 2016.

44 'Room at the Top', *Prospect Magazine*, October 2013.

2

1 Maurice Kogan, *The Politics of Educational Change*, London, Fontana, 1978, p. 148.

2 Ted Tapper, *Fee-Paying Schools and Educational Change in Britain: Between the State and the Marketplace*, Woburn Press, London, 1997, pp. 42–3.

3 Colin Shrosbree, *Public Schools and Private Education: The Clarendon Commission 1861–64 and the Public Schools Act*, Manchester University Press, Manchester, 1988, pp. 3–4.

4 T. W. Bamford, *The Rise of the Public Schools: A Study of Boys' Public Boarding Schools in England and Wales from 1837 to the Present Day*, Nelson, London, 1967, p. 276.

5 Jonathan Gathorne-Hardy, *The Public School Phenomenon, 597–1977*, Hodder & Stoughton, London, 1977, pp. 99–100.

6 Ibid., p. 98.

7 Shrosbree, *Public Schools and Private Education*, pp. 126, 182, 187.

8 Ibid., p. 114.

9 J. A. Thomas, *The House of Commons, 1906–1911: An Analysis of its Economic and Social Character*, University of Wales Press, Cardiff, 1958, p. 20. We are grateful to Duncan Marlor for this reference.

10 Rodney Barker, *Education and Politics, 1900–1951: A Study of the Labour Party*, Oxford University Press, Oxford, 1972, p. 98; Geoffrey Walford, *Privatization and Privilege in Education*, Routledge, London, 1990, p. 24.

11 Barker, *Education and Politics*, pp. 104–5.

12 R. H. Tawney, *Equality*, George Allen & Unwin, London, 1931, pp. 96, 204–5.

13 Barker, *Education and Politics*, pp. 107–11; Brian Simon, *Education and the Social Order, 1940–1990*, Lawrence & Wishart, London, 1991, pp. 38–9.

14 Graham Greene (ed.), *The Old School Tie: Essays by Divers Hand*, Jonathan Cape, London, 1934, pp. 7–8.

15 Bamford, *Rise of the Public Schools*, pp. 287–8.

16 Cyril Norwood, 'Public Schools and Social Service', *Spectator*, 13 November 1926.

17 Frank Fletcher, *After Many Days: A Schoolmaster's Memories*, Robert Hale, London, 1937, p. 278.

18 Nicholas Hillman, 'Public schools and the Fleming Report of 1944: Shunting the first-class carriage on to an immense siding?', *History of Education*, March 2012 (41/2), p. 238.

19 P. H. J. H. Gosden, *Education in the Second World War: A Study in policy and administration*, Methuen, London, 1976, pp. 332–4.

20 Simon, *Education and the Social Order*, pp. 40–41.

21 John Campbell, *Edward Heath: A Biography*, Jonathan Cape, London, 1993, pp. 18–19.

22 T. C. Worsley, *Barbarians and Philistines: Democracy and the Public Schools*, Robert Hale, London, 1940, p. 237; Simon, *Education and the Social Order*, p. 81.

23 Sonia Orwell and Ian Angus (eds), *The Collected Essays, Journalism and Letters of George Orwell*, vol. II, Secker & Warburg, London, 1968, pp. 121, 98–9.

24 Edward C. Mack, *Public Schools and British Opinion since 1960: The Relationship between Contemporary Ideas and the Evolution of an English Institution*, Columbia University Press, New York, 1941, pp. 462–3.

25 Barker, *Education and Politics*, pp. 111–13.

26 Hansard, *Parliamentary Debates: Fifth Series, Volume 358* (1940), House of Commons, 5 March 1940, cols 270–71.

27 Simon, *Education and the Social Order*, p. 42; Anthony Howard, *RAB: The Life of R. A. Butler*, Jonathan Cape, London, 1987, p. 119.

28 Paul Addison, *The Road to 1945: British Politics and the Second World War*, Jonathan Cape, London, 1975, p. 72.

29 Howard, *RAB*, pp. 119–20, 122–3; Hansard, *Parliamentary Debates: Fifth Series, Volume CCLXXIII* (1966), House of Lords, 23 February 1966, col. 229.

30 Gosden, *Education in the Second World War*, p. 345.

31 Gabriel Gorodetsky (ed.), *The Maisky Dairies: Red Ambassador to the Court of St James's, 1932–1943*, Yale University Press, New Haven, 2015, pp. 523–4; 'The New Plan of Education', *Sunday Times*, 18 July 1943.

32 Hansard, *Parliamentary Debates: Fifth Series, Volume 396* (1944), House of Commons, 19 January 1944, col. 234.

33 Lord Butler, *The Art of the Possible*, Hamish Hamilton, London, 1971, p. 121.

34 Nicholas Timmins, *The Five Giants: A Biography of the Welfare State*, HarperCollins, London, 2001, pbk edn, pp. 85–6; Hillman, 'Public schools', pp. 241–2.

35 Gosden, *Education in the Second World War*, pp. 355–6.

36 *New Statesman*, 29 July 1944, 5 August 1944.

37 Hillman, 'Public schools', pp. 243–4; Tapper, *Fee-Paying Schools*, p. 105.

38 Orwell and Angus (eds), *Essays, Journalism and Letters of George Orwell*, vol. III (1968), p. 226.

39 Rodney Lowe, 'The Second World War, Consensus and the Foundation of the Welfare State', *Twentieth Century British History*, 1/2 (1990), p. 175.

40 Hillman, 'Public schools', pp. 247–8, 251–4; Michael Sanderson, *Educational Opportunity and Social Change in England*, Faber and Faber, London, 1987, pp. 66–7.

41 Denis Healey, *The Time of My Life*, Michael Joseph, London, 1989, p. 153.

42 *The Times*, 29 June 1946.

43 D. W. Dean, 'Planning for a Post-war Generation', *History of Education*, June 1986, p. 114.

44 Barker, *Education and Politics*, p.118.

45 Simon, *Education and the Social Order*, pp. 138–9; Fred Blackburn, *George Tomlinson*, William Heinemann, London, 1954, p. 193.

46 *Observer*, 1 August 1948.

47 *The Times*, 15 December 1990.

48 Vivian Ogilvie, *The English Public School*, B. T. Batsford, London, 1957, p. 216.

49 *Socialist Commentary*, August 1958, p. 12; *New Statesman*, 27 September 1958.

50 Anthony Sampson, *Anatomy of Britain*, Hodder & Stoughton, London, 1962, p. 194.

51 *Spectator*, 20 June 1958; Robin Pedley, *The Comprehensive School*, Penguin Books, Harmondsworth, 1969, p. 180; Nicholas Hillman, 'The Public Schools Commission: "Impractical, Expensive and Harmful to Children"?', *Contemporary British History*, December 2010 (24/4), p. 513.

52 Hillman, 'Commission', p. 514.

53 Anthony Crosland, *The Future of Socialism*, Constable & Robinson, London, 2006 edn, p. 218.

54 C. A. R. Crosland, *The Conservative Enemy: A Programme of Radical Reform for the 1960s*, Jonathan Cape, London, 1962, pp. 174, 180.

55 Maurice Kogan, *The Politics of Education: Edward Boyle and Anthony Crosland in Conversation with Maurice Kogan*, Penguin Books, Harmondsworth, 1971, p. 155.

56 John Thorn, *The Road to Winchester*, Weidenfeld & Nicolson, London, 1989, p. 93.

57 Susan Crosland, *Anthony Crosland*, Jonathan Cape, London, 1982, p. 149.

58 Kogan, *Politics of Education*, pp. 196–7.

59 Kevin Jefferys, *Anthony Crosland*, Politico's, London, 2000, pp. 107–8.

60 Hillman, 'Commission', p. 514.

61 A. H. Halsey, *No Discouragement: An Autobiography*, Macmillan, Basingstoke, 1996, p. 131.

62 John Dancy, *The Public Schools and the Future*, Faber and Faber, London, 1966 edn, p. 184.

63 Nicholas Lloyd, 'How facts took second place', *Sunday Times*, 21 July 1968; Hillman, 'Commission', pp. 515–16.

64 Simon, *Education and the Social Order*, pp. 324–5.

65 Hillman, 'Commission', p. 517.

66 A. H. Halsey, 'The Public Schools Debacle', *New Society*, 25 July 1968; Hillman, 'Commission', p. 518; John Vaizey, 'If The Public Schools Go Bust So Be It', *Sunday Times*, 21 July 1968.

67 John Vaizey, *Scenes from Institutional Life and Other Writings*, Weidenfeld & Nicolson, London, 1986, p. 154.

68 Kogan, *Politics of Education*, p. 197.

69 Simon, *Education and the Social Order*, p. 325.

70 *Daily Telegraph*, 23 July 1968.

71 *Daily Telegraph*, 23 July 1968; *Guardian*, 23 July 1968, 26 July 1968, 25 July 1968.

72 Simon, *Education and the Social Order*, p. 326; Hillman, 'Commission', pp. 518–19.

73 *The Times*, 3 October 1968; *Daily Telegraph*, 3 October 1968.

74 Hillman, 'Commission', p. 522; Rachel Reeves, *Alice in Westminster: The Political Life of Alice Bacon*, I. B. Tauris, London, 2017, pp. 97, 163.

75 Hillman, 'Commission', p. 522.

76 Stuart Maclure, 'Public Schools after Newsom', *Spectator*, 23 February 1968.

77 David Kynaston, *Modernity Britain, 1957–62*, Bloomsbury, London, 2015 pbk edn, p. 243; Halsey, *No Discouragement*, p. 131; '67% say hands off public schools', *Sunday Times*, 10 March 1968.

78 Kogan, *Politics of Education*, p. 197; John Rae, *The Public School Revolution: Britain's Independent Schools, 1964–1979*, Faber and Faber, London, 1981, p. 44.

79 Clive Griggs, *Private Education in Britain*, Falmer Press, Lewes, 1985, p. 148.

80 Thorn, *Road to Winchester*, p. 156.

81 Mary Warnock, 'The wrong target', *New Society*, 23 April 1970.

82 Simon, *Education and the Social Order*, p. 330.

83 Warnock, 'The wrong target'.

84 Tapper, *Fee-Paying Schools*, p. 143.

85 *The Times*, 8 September 1973.

86 *The Times*, 26 September 1973.

87 *The Times*, 25 September 1973; Roy Hattersley, *Who Goes Home?: Scenes from a Political Life*, Little, Brown, London, 1995, p. 122.

88 Rae, *Revolution*, p. 54.

89 Gathorne-Hardy, *Public School Phenomenon*, p. 415.

90 Walford, *Privatization and Privilege*, p. 32.

91 John Rae, *The Old Boys' Network: A Headmaster's Diaries, 1972–1988*, Short Books, London, 2009, pp. 38, 78, 81; Ben Pimlott, *Harold Wilson*, HarperCollins, London, 1992, p. 630.

92 Tony Benn, *Arguments for Socialism*, Jonathan Cape, London, 1979, p. 162.

93 Email from Melissa Benn to authors, 10 February 2018.

94 Gathorne-Hardy, *Public School Phenomenon*, p. 407.

95 http://www.politicsresources.net/area/UK/man/lab79.htm

96 John Rae, 'The challenge to freedom if we lose our public schools', *The Times*, 28 May 1973.

97 Kynaston, *Modernity Britain*, pp. 545–6; Griggs, *Private Education*, p. ix.

98 Hillman, 'Commission', p. 523.

99 Mark Peel, *The New Meritocracy: A History of UK Independent Schools, 1979–2015*, Elliott and Thompson, London, 2015, p. 13; David Turner, *The Old Boys: The Decline and Rise of the Public School*, Yale University Press, London, 2015, p. 221.

100 Griggs, *Private Education*, pp. 138–9.

101 Christopher Tyerman, *A History of Harrow School, 1324–1991*, Oxford University Press, Oxford, 2000, pp. 563–4.

102 Andrew Neather, 'Will Milliband do his bit to grow the middle class?', *Evening Standard*, 20 November 2013; Harry Eyres, 'An English tragedy', *New Statesman*, 16 September 2016.

103 Christopher Hope, 'Major hits at elite in corridors of power', *Daily Telegraph*, 11 November 2013; Patrick Wintour, 'Preposterous: Gove's view of Old Etonians' influence on Cameron', *Guardian*, 15 March 2014; Rosamund Urwin, 'Minister for Girls', *Evening Standard*, 22 July 2014; Oliver Wright, 'Warsi calls on Javid to be the voice of ethnic minorities', *Independent*, 11 August 2014.

104 'Minister wishes to end state-private divide', *The Times*, 3 February 2014; Michael Gove, 'Our segregated education system perpetuates inequality and holds our nation back', *New Statesman*, 14 February 2014.

105 Elizabeth Rigby and Andrew Bounds, 'Concerns over UK Conservatives' "posh" manifesto', *Financial Times*, 23 February 2014.

106 Anthony Seldon, 'Build character and you close the class divide', *The Times*, 9 December 2014; Fraser Nelson, 'Purge of the posh', *Spectator*, 4 June 2016; Christopher Hope, 'Matt Hancock signals U-turn on forcing former public school pupils to disclose backgrounds to employers', *Daily Telegraph*, 8 June 2016.

107 Theresa May, 'We can make Britain work for everyone', *The Times*, 30 June 2016.

108 Ruth Sylvester, "'I'm sure Theresa will be really sad that she doesn't have children ...'", *The Times*, 9 July 2016.

109 Philip Collins, 'Her speech unspun', *The Times*, 14 July 2016; Rowena Mason, 'State-educated but mostly male', *Guardian*, 15 July 2016.

110 Prime Minister's Office, 'Britain, the great meritocracy: Prime Minister's speech', 9 September 2016.

111 Peter Dominiczak et al., 'Theresa May takes on private schools as she warns institutions must do more to help poor children', *Daily Telegraph*, 9 September 2016.

112 Michael Gove, 'How Britain can help reinvigorate the West', *The Times*, 27 January 2017; 'Put VAT on school fees and soak the rich', *The Times*, 24 February 2017.

113 *Forward Together: The Conservative and Unionist Party Manifesto, 2017* (2017), p. 50.

114 Martin Westlake, *Kinnock: The Biography*, Little, Brown, London, 2001, p. 154.

115 Walford, *Privatization*, pp. 32–3.

116 British Social Attitudes Surveys, authors' analysis of data.

117 Walford, *Privatization*, p. 33; Peel, *New Meritocracy*, pp. 12, 16, 23.

118 Andrew Adonis, *Education, Education, Education: Reforming England's Schools*, Biteback, London, 2012, p. 155.

119 Peel, *New Meritocracy*, p. 18.

120 Geoffrey Walford, *Private Education: Tradition and Diversity*, Continuum, London, 2006, p. 8.

121 Peel, *New Meritocracy*, pp. 19–22; Sam Freedman, 'State schools don't need private sector advice', *Observer*, 30 November 2014; Wilde R., F. Green, P. Taylor-Gooby and S. Wiborg (2016), 'Private Schools and the Provision of Public Benefit', *Journal of Social Policy*, 45(2), 305–23.

122 This account is based on: 'Public schools face end to charitable status', *Daily Telegraph*, 27 May 2004; Fiona Millar, 'Ed Miliband ought to re-start the debate about charitable status for private schools', *fionamillar.com*, 13 January 2012; Alice Faure Walker and Stephen Lloyd, 'The Charities Act: Charity law finally enters the modern age', *Third Sector*, 22 November 2006; interviews with Andrew Adonis, 14 May 2018, Alan Milburn, 23 May 2018.

123 Harry Brighouse, *A Level Playing Field: The Reform of Private Schools*, Fabian Society, London, 2000, p. 4.

124 Adonis, *Education, Education, Education*, pp. 23–4.

125 Tony Blair, *A Journey: My Political Life*, Hutchinson, London, 2010, p. 572.

126 Peter Mandelson, 'The rise and flaw of Gordon Brown', *Evening Standard*, 9 November 2017.

127 Andrew Sparrow, 'Labour could strip some private schools of charitable status', *Guardian*, 20 July 2012.

128 Patrick Wintour, 'Labour's assault on private schools', *Guardian*, 25 November 2014.

129 Mark Beard, 'Did you learn nothing from us, Tristram?', *Daily Telegraph*, 26 November 2014; 'The school of envy', *Daily Telegraph*, 26 November 2014; Margaret Drabble, 'Feeble Hunt has lost Labour my vote', *Guardian*, 1 December 2014.

130 For an example of someone from the left wanting a bold policy on the issue from the new leadership, see Steven Longden, 'It's time to phase out elitist education', *Left Foot Forward*, 20 January 2016.

131 Frances Perraudian et al., 'Corbyn defends free school meals policy despite warning that benefit is unproved', *Guardian*, 7 April 2017.

132 Robert Verkaik, 'Why is Corbyn so unambitious on education?', *The i*, 22 May 2017.

3

1 Arthur F. Leach, *Educational Charters and Documents: 598 to 1909*, Cambridge University Press, Cambridge, 1911, pp. 321, 323, 407, 499.

2 David Turner, *The Old Boys: The Decline and Rise of the Public School*, Yale University Press, London, 2015, pp. 13–14, 30, 39–40; Jonathan Gathorne-Hardy, *The Public School Phenomenon, 597–1977*, Hodder & Stoughton, London, 1977, p. 27.

3 Ted Tapper, *Fee-Paying Schools and Educational Change in Britain: Between the State and the Market-place*, Woburn Press, London, 1997, p. 37.

4 Christopher Tyerman, *A History of Harrow School, 1324–1991*, Oxford University Press, Oxford, 2000, p. 48.

5 T. W. Bamford, *The Rise of the Public Schools: A Study of Boys' Public Boarding Schools in England and Wales from 1837 to the Present Day*, Nelson, London, 1967, pp. 6–7. For his full analysis, see his 'Public Schools and Social Class, 1801–1850', *British Journal of Sociology*, 12/3, September 1961, pp. 224–35.

6 Tapper, *Fee-Paying Schools*, p. 37.

7 Ibid., pp. 52–3.

8 Anthony Quick, *Charterhouse: A History of the School*, James & James, 1990, pp. 59–60.

9 Colin Leach, *A School at Shrewsbury: The Four Foundations*, James & James, 1990, p. 44.

10 Turner, *Old Boys*, p. 43; Edward Gibbon, *Autobiography*, Routledge & Kegan Paul, London, 1970, p. 26; Leach, *Shrewsburg*, p. 38; Anthony Trollope, *An Autobiography*, Oxford University Press, Oxford, 1953, p. 15.

11 Turner, *Old Boys*, p. 73.

12 Alex Renton, *Stiff Upper Lip: Secrets, Crimes and the Schooling of a Ruling Class*, Weidenfeld & Nicolson, London, 2017, pp. 132–3.

13 John Chandos, *Boys Together: English Public Schools, 1800–1864*, Hutchinson, London, 1984, p 7; Turner, *Old Boys*, p. 61.

14 Chandos, *Boys Together*, pp. 37, 156; Renton, *Stiff Upper Lip*, p. 146.

15 Edward C. Mack, *Public Schools and British Opinion: An Examination of the Relationship Between Contemporary Ideas and the Evolution of an English Institution*, Methuen, London, 1938, p. 154.

16 Colin Shrosbree, *Public Schools and Private Education: The Clarendon Commission 1861–64 and the Public Schools Act*, Manchester University Press, Manchester, 1988, p. 7.

17 Anthony Fletcher, *Growing Up in England: The Experience of Childhood, 1600–1914*, Yale University Press, London, 2008, p. 198.

18 Tyerman, *Harrow*, p. 285.

19 Brian Simon, 'Introduction', Brian Simon and Ian Bradley (eds), *The Victorian Public School: Studies in the Development of an Educational Institution*, Gill and Macmillan, Dublin, 1975, p. 3.

20 T. J. H. Bishop and Rupert Wilkinson, *Winchester and the Public School Elite: A Statistical Analysis*, Faber and Faber, London, 1967, p. 86.

21 Bamford, *Public Schools*, p. 30; Vyvyen Brendon, *Prep School Children: A Class Apart Over Two Centuries*, Continuum, London, 2009, p. 30.

22 Turner, *Old Boys*, pp. 127, 151–3.

23 Andrew Gimson, 'Strange death of the English gentleman', *Standpoint*, September 2012, p. 53.

24 Fletcher, *Growing Up*, pp. 201, 204.

25 David Newsome, *Godliness & Good Learning: Four Studies on a Victorian Ideal*, John Murray, London, 1961, p. 83.

26 E. M. Forster, *Abinger Harvest*, Edward Arnold, London, 1936, p. 5.

27 Graham Greene (ed.), *The Old School: Essays by Divers Hands*, Jonathan Cape, London, 1934, pp. 112, 97–8, 119, 201, 214.

28 J. A. Mangan, *Athleticism in the Victorian and Edwardian Public School: The Emergence and Consolidation of an Educational Ideology*, Cambridge University Press, Cambridge, 1981, p. 136.

29 Edward C. Mack, *Public Schools and British Opinion since 1960: The Relationship between Contemporary Ideas and the Evolution of an English Institution*, Columbia University Press, New York, 1941, pp. 247, 253–4.

30 For two very different perspectives, see Peter Parker, *The Old Lie: The Great War and the Public-School Ethos*, Constable, London, 1987; Anthony Seldon and David Walsh, *Public Schools and the Great War*, Pen & Sword, Barnsley, 2013.

31 Mangan, *Athleticism*, p. 68.

32 Daphne Rae, *A World Apart*, Lutterworth Press, Guildford, 1983, p. 27.

33 Tyerman, *Harrow*, p. 398.

34 Bamford, *Public Schools*, p. 82.

35 Donald Leinster-Mackay, *The Rise of the English Prep School*, Falmer Press, Lewes, 1984, p. 193.

36 Mangan, *Athleticism*, p. 110.

37 Gathorne-Hardy, *Public School Phenomenon*, p. 350.

38 Bamford, *Public Schools*, p. 277.

39 Ross McKibbin, *Classes and Cultures: England 1918–1951*, Oxford University Press, Oxford, 1998, p. 244.

40 David Ward, 'The Public Schools and Industry in Britain after 1870', *Journal of Contemporary History*, 2/3, July 1967, p. 42.

41 J. R. de S. Honey, *Tom Brown's Universe: The Development of the Victorian Public School*, Millington Books, 1977, p. 129; Gathorne-Hardy, *Public School Phenomenon*, p. 350.

42 Tyerman, *Harrow*, p. 285; Shrosbree, *Public Schools*, p. 9.

43 Bishop and Wilkinson, *Winchester*, p. 87.

44 Tyerman, *Harrow*, p. 376.

45 McKibbin, *Classes and Cultures*, p. 237.

46 Cyril Norwood, 'Public Schools and Social Service', *Spectator*, 13 November 1926.

47 McKibbin, *Classes and Cultures*, p. 246.

48 Greene (ed.), *Old School*, p. 11.

49 Ibid., p. 214.

50 Tyerman, *Harrow*, p. 436; Honey, *Tom Brown*, pp. 153–4.

51 Evelyn Waugh, *Decline and Fall*, Penguin Books, Harmondsworth, 1937, pp. 28–30.

52 Mangan, *Athleticism*, p. 170.

53 Tyerman, *Harrow*, pp. 395–6.

54 McKibbin, *Classes and Cultures*, pp. 249, 238; Bishop and Wilkinson, *Winchester*, p. 34.

55 George Smith, 'Schools', in A. H. Halsey with Josephine Webb (eds), *Twentieth-Century British Social Trends*, Macmillan, Basingstoke, 2000, p. 188.

56 Irene Fox, *Private Schools and Public Issues: The Parents' View*, Macmillan, Basingstoke, 1985, pp. 23–4.

57 Smith, 'Schools', in Halsey with Webb (eds), *Social Trends*, p. 188.

58 George Snow, *The Public School in the New Age*, Geoffrey Bles, London, 1959, p. 19.

59 Nicholas Hillman, 'Public Schools and the Fleming Report of 1944: shunting the first-class carriage on to an immense siding?', *History of Education*, 41/2, March 2012, pp. 250–51.

60 Hillman, 'Public Schools', p. 251; Tapper, *Fee-Paying Schools*, p. 164; John Rae, *The Public School Revolution: Britain's Independent Schools, 1964–1979*, Faber and Faber, London, 1981, p. 28.

61 Daphne Rae, *A World Apart*, p. 148.

62 Bishop and Wilkinson, *Winchester*, pp. 85–6.

63 John Wilson, *Public Schools and Private Practice*, George Allen & Unwin, London, 1962, p. 80; Peter Wilby, 'A parents' guide to private education', *Sunday Times*, 22 November 1981.

64 Turner, *Old Boys*, p. 206.

65 Ibid., pp. 195–8.

66 Mallory Wober, *English Girls' Boarding Schools*, Allen Lane, London, 1971, p. 284.

67 Ysenda Maxtone Graham, *Terms & Conditions: Life in Girls' Boarding Schools, 1939–1979*, Slightly Foxed, London, 2016, pp. 255–8.

68 H. L. O. Flecker, 'Character Training: The English Boarding School', in *The Year Book of Education, 1955*, Evans Brothers, London, 1955, p. 263.

69 Wilson, *Public Schools*, pp. 120–21.

70 Ibid., p. 113. For the fullest guide to the realities of public school life by the 1960s, see Royston Lambert, *The Hothouse Society: An Exploration of Boarding-school Life Through the Boys' and Girls' Own Writings*, Weidenfeld & Nicholson, London, 1968. On the psychological legacy of that life (before, during and after the 1960s), see Nick Duffell, *Wounded Leaders: British Elitism and the Entitlement Illusion*, Lone Arrow Press, 2014. On the difficult subject of physical abuse, see Renton, *Stiff Upper Lip*; Charlotte Santry ' "We are deeply sorry" – boarding schools apologise for child abuse', *TES*, 1 May 2018.

71 Jeremy Paxman, *Friends in High Places: Who Runs Britain?*, Michael Joseph, London, 1990, p. ix.

72 Turner, *Old Boys*, p. 196.

73 Wilson, *Public Schools*, pp. 77, 84.

74 A. H. Halsey, A. F. Heath and J. M. Ridge, *Origins and Destinations*, Clarendon Press, Oxford, 1980, pp. 211–12.

75 Smith, 'Schools', in Halsey with Webb (eds), *Social Trends*, pp. 212–15; Anthony Sampson, *Anatomy of Britain*, Hodder & Stoughton, London, 1962, p. 198; Anthony Sampson, *The New Anatomy of Britain*, Hodder & Stoughton, London, 1971, p. 139.

76 Sampson, *New Anatomy*, p. 140.

77 Geoffrey Walford, *Life in Public Schools*, Methuen, London, 1986, p. 13; Clive Griggs, *Private Education in Britain*, Falmer Press, Lewes, 1986, p. 46.

78 Alisdair Fairley, 'Tom Brown's High-Yield Schooldays', *Listener*, 1 November 1973.

79 Wilson, *Public Schools*, pp. 76–7; John Rae, *The Old Boys' Network: A Headmaster's Diaries, 1972–1988*, Short Books, London, 2009, p. 42.

80 Sampson, *Anatomy*, pp. 194, 347.

81 Wilfred De'Ath, 'What they told me', *Oldie*, March 2017, p. 49.

82 Gathorne-Hardy, *Public School Phenomenon*, p. 407.

83 Turner, *Old Boys*, p. 207; this figure does not include pupils at the direct grant schools, which had just joined the private sector.

84 Anthony Sampson, *The Changing Anatomy of Britain*, Hodder & Stoughton, London, 1982, p. 122.

85 Rae, *Revolution*, pp. 177–8.

86 Walford, *Life in Public Schools*, pp. 204–5; Turner, *Old Boys*, p. 217; Mark Peel, *The New Meritocracy: A History of UK Independent Schools, 1979–2015*, Elliott and Thompson, London, 2015, p. 2.

87 Peel, *New Meritocracy*, p. 35.

88 Rae, *Revolution*, p. 170; Griggs, *Private Education*, p. 34; John Rae, 'Portrait of a public school', *Listener*, 13 September 1979.

89 Dearden, L., J. Ferri and C. Meghir (2002), 'The effect of school quality on educational attainment and wages', *Review of Economics and Statistics*, 84(1): 1–20; Parsons, S., F. Green, G. B. Ploubidis, A. Sullivan and R. D. Wiggins (2017), 'The influence of private primary schooling on children's learning: Evidence from three generations of children living in the UK', *British Education Research Journal*, October 2017, 43(5), 823–47; Green, F., S. Machin, R. Murphy and Y. Zhu (2011), 'The Changing Economic Advantage from Private Schools', *Economica*, 79, 658–79.

90 Gathorne-Hardy, *Public School Phenomenon*, p. 409.

91 James Sabben-Clare, *Winchester College: After 606 Years, 1382–1988*, P&G Wells, Winchester, 2nd edn, 1989, p. 50.

92 Irene Fox, *Private Schools and Public Issues: The Parents' View*, Macmillan, 1985, Basingstoke, pp. ix, 115–18, 136, 138, 142, 154.

93 Harry Brighouse, *A Level Playing Field: The Reform of Private Schools,* Fabian Society, London, 2000, p. 17.

94 Anthony Heath, 'What difference does the old school tie make now?', *New Society*, 18 June 1981.

95 John Thorn, *The Road to Winchester*, Weidenfeld & Nicolson, London, 1989, pp. 171–2.

96 Turner, *Old Boys*, pp. 235–6; Peel, *New Meritocracy*, pp. 97–8, 179.

97 Brighouse, *Level Playing Field*, pp. 4–5.

98 Peel, *New Meritocracy*, p. 99.

99 Parsons et al., 'Private Primary Schooling'; Green et al. (2011), 'Economic Advantage'; Sullivan, A., S. Parsons, R. Wiggins, A. Heath and F. Green (2014), 'Social origins, school type and higher education destinations', *Oxford Review of Education* 40(6), 739–63.

100 Turner, *Old Boys*, p. 223; Tyerman, *Harrow*, p. 561.

101 Ed Smith, *Luck: What It Means and Why It Matters*, Bloomsbury, London, 2012, p. 23.

102 Brighouse, *Level Playing Field*, p. 4.

103 Paxman, *Friends*, pp. 165–6.

104 Angela Wintle, 'David Hare: "All good dramatists are scared of the audience"', *Observer*, 18 February 2018.

105 Schumpeter, 'A very British business', *The Economist*, 18 April 2015.

106 Peel, *New Meritocracy*, pp. 118–19.

107 Turner, *Old Boys*, p. 249; Peel, *New Meritocracy*, pp. 36, 50; School Census for England, data from https://www.gov.uk/government/statistics/schools-pupils-and-their-characteristics-january-2016.

108 Turner, *Old Boys*, p. 223.

109 Peel, *New Meritocracy*, p. 14.

110 Griggs, *Private Education*, p. 41.

111 Tapper, *Fee-Paying Schools*, p. 161.

112 Sabben-Clare, *Winchester*, pp. 38–9.

113 Tyerman, *Harrow*, p. 405.

114 Walford, *Life in Public Schools*, pp. 208, 216–17.

115 John Rae, 'Tom Brown's Porsche days', *The Times*, 31 July 1987.

116 Paxman, *Friends*, pp. 168–9, 171, 332.

4

1 Mumsnet discussion, 'I send my child to private school because ...?' 12 July 2012.

2 Katie Gibbons, 'Stressed private school pupils get "disaster" training', *The Times*, 25 February 2014.

3 Richard Ford, 'Self harm and depression are on the rise in private schools', *The Times*, 5 October 2015.

4 Maxwell, C. and P. Aggleton (2013), 'Becoming accomplished: concerted cultivation among privately educated young women', *Pedagogy, Culture & Society*, 21(1), 75–93.

5 Data derived from the Millennium Cohort Study, authors' analysis, University of London, Institute of Education, Centre for Longitudinal Studies, *Millennium Cohort Study: Sixth Survey, 2015* [computer file]. Colchester, Essex: UK Data Archive [distributor], May 2017. SN: 8156, http://dx.doi.org/10.5255/UKDA-SN-8156-1.

6 Green, F., S. Machin, R. Murphy and Y. Zhu (2008), 'Competition for Private and State School Teachers', *Journal of Education and Work*, 21(5), 383–404.

7 Data from Table 15 of the *ISC Census and Annual Report 2018*; note that the ISC covers most but not all private schools, and the total transfer across Britain may therefore be greater.

8 Davies, P. and N. M. Davies (2014), 'Paying for quality? Associations between private school income, performance and use of resources', *British Educational Research Journal*, 40(3), 421–40.

9 Amanda Cashmore, 'Leading £25,000-a-year private St Paul's Girls' School is slammed for serving baked potatoes and beans as AUSTERITY DAY lunch', *Mail Online*, 22 June 2018.

10 Lucy Higginson, 'Luxury hotel or boarding school dorm?', *Daily Telegraph*, 30 October 2017.

11 Peter Stanford, 'Boarding schools face a steep learning curve', *Daily Telegraph*, 13 February 2016.

12 James Gale and James Gillespie, 'Elite schools upstage the West End', *Sunday Times*, 10 September 2017.

13 *Guardian* editorial, 9 September 2017.

14 Ben Chu, 'Private schools catering to the global elite are spending lavishly because of their huge UK tax breaks – it has to stop', *Independent*, 10 May 2016.

15 Belfield, C. and L. Sibieta (2016), *Long-Run Trends in School Spending in England*, London, Institute for Fiscal Studies, IFS Report R115; Belfield, C., C. Crawford and L. Sibieta (2017), *Long-run comparisons of spending per pupil across different stages of education*, London, Institute of Fiscal Studies; Independent Schools Council (2016), ISC Census 2016; Department for Education (2014), '*Boarding schools. An opportunity to improve outcomes for vulnerable children*', https://www.bl.uk/collection-items/boarding-schools-an-opportunity-to-improve-outcomes-for-vulnerable-children.

16 The audited accounts of schools that are charities can be seen through the Charity Commission, at https://www.gov.uk/government/organisations/charity-commission. Also, some schools post accounts on their websites. However, the accounts do not always separately itemise donations. Moreover, not all private schools are charities, and sometimes the accounts are not open to the public. Asset valuations are affected by property prices, which vary across the nation.

17 This figure applies to all schools covered by the Independent Schools Council, ISC Census 2013, ISC.

18 Tom Bateman, 'Independent school students gain extra time for exams', *BBC News* website, 10 February 2017.

19 Anna Davis, 'Exam marking blunders hit state pupils harder, says private school head', *Evening Standard*, 12 November 2015.

20 Emma Seith, 'Exam appeals system "loaded in favour of pupils in private schools", says Labour', *TES*, 17 December 2017.

21 Paul Mason, 'Private schools know how to game university privilege – state-educated kids don't have this privilege', *Guardian*, 30 November 2014.

22 Boliver, V. (2013), 'How fair is access to more prestigious UK universities?', *British Journal of Sociology*, 64(2), 344–64.

23 Krueger, A. B. and D. M. Whitmore (2001), 'The effect of attending a small class in the early grades on college-test taking and middle school test results: Evidence from Project STAR', *Economic Journal*, 111(468), 1–28.

24 Fredriksson, P., B. Oeckert and H. Oosterbeek (2013), 'Long-Term Effects of Class Size', *Quarterly Journal of Economics*, 128(1), 249–85.

25 Jackson, C. K., R. C. Johnson and C. Persico (2016), 'The effects of school spending on educational and economic outcomes: evidence from school finance reforms', *Quarterly Journal of Economics*, 131(1), 157–218.

26 See, for example, Rivkin, S. G., E. A. Hanushek and J. F. Kain (2005), 'Teachers, schools, and academic achievement', *Econometrica*, 73(2), 417–58. The picture is further clouded because it is likely that the benefits of small class sizes vary across age, gender and ability. For example, studies have found that small classes are especially beneficial for lower-ability pupils, possibly because these pupils do not normally attract sufficient attention from teachers in larger classes – but here, too, the evidence is far from definitive. For a British example, see Dearden, L., J. Ferri and C. Meghir (2002), 'The effect of school quality on educational attainment and wages', *Review of Economics and Statistics*, 84(1), 1–20. Also see Gibbons, S. and S. McNally (2013), *The Effects of Resources Across School Phases: A Summary of Recent Evidence*, LSE, Centre for Economic Performance, Discussion Paper No. 1226.

27 Sacerdote, B. (2011), 'Peer Effects in Education: How Might They Work, How Big Are They and How Much Do We Know Thus Far?', in E. A. Hanushek, S. Machin and L. Woessmann (eds), *Handbook of the Economics of Education*, vol. 3, 249–77.

28 Fortuina, J., M. van Geela and P. Veddera (2016), 'Peers and academic achievement: A longitudinal study on selection and socialization effects of in-class friends', *Journal of Educational Research*, 109(1), 1–6.

29 Antecol, H., O. Eren and S. Ozbeklik (2016), 'Peer Effects in Disadvantaged Primary Schools Evidence from a Randomized Experiment', *Journal of Human Resources*, 51(1), 95–132.

30 Lavy, V., O. Silva and F. Weinhardt (2012), 'The Good, the Bad, and the Average: Evidence on Ability Peer Effects in Schools', *Journal of Labor Economics*, 30(2), 367–414.

31 The Total Difficulties Score, computed from twenty items in the Strengths and Difficulties Questionnaire, which is a behavioural screening instrument for three- to sixteen-year-olds.

32 Maxwell, C. and P. Aggleton, 'Creating cosmopolitan subjects: the role of families and private schools in England', *Sociology*, 50(4), 780–95.

33 ISC Census 2017.

34 Mark Peel, *The New Meritocracy: A History of UK Independent Schools, 1979–2015*, Elliott and Thompson, London, 2015, p. 123.

35 Andrew Adonis, *Education, Education, Education. Reforming England's Schools*, Biteback, London, 2012, p. 157.

36 Hanushek, E., S. Link, and L.Woessmann (2013), 'Does school autonomy make sense everywhere? Panel estimates from PISA', *Journal of Development Economics*, vol. 104, pp. 212–32.

37 Micklewright, J., J. Jerrim, A. Vignoles, A. Jenkins, R. Allen, S. Ilie, E. Bellarbre, F. Barrera and C. Hein (2014), *Teachers in England's Secondary Schools: Evidence from TALIS 2013*, Department for Education, Research Report.

38 Verschelde, M., J. Hindriks, G. Rayp and K. Schoors (2015), 'School Staff Autonomy and Educational Performance: Within-School-Type Evidence', *Fiscal Studies*, 36(2), 127–55; Brian John Caldwell (2016), 'Impact of school autonomy on student achievement: cases from Australia', *International Journal of Educational Management*, 30(7), 1171–87.

39 Proportions obtained from the PISA 2015 survey data for schools, authors' analysis. See OECD (2016), *PISA 2015 Results* (Volume II): *Policies and Practices for Successful Schools*, PISA, Paris, OECD Publishing, p. 114.

40 Ann West and David Wolfe (2018), *Academies, the School System in England and a Vision for the Future*, LSE Education Research Group, Clare Market Papers No. 23.

41 GB Parliament, House of Commons Education Committee (2015), *Academies and Free Schools: Fourth Report of Session 2014–15. Report, Together with Formal Minutes Relating to the Report* (HC 258) [online], http://www.publications.parliament.uk/pa/cm201415/cmselect/cmeduc/258/258.pdf [28 April 2015]; Jon Andrews (2018), *School*

performance in academy chains and local authorities – 2017, London Education Policy Institute.

42 Camilla Turner, 'Private school parents "think they're buying exam success"', *Daily Telegraph*, 10 April 2018.

43 Mark Peel, *The New Meritocracy: A History of UK Independent Schools, 1979–2015*, Elliott and Thompson, London, 2015, p. 3.

44 Jess Staufenberg, 'Ofsted: Small private school leaders don't know how to improve teaching', *Schools Week*, 12 October 2017.

45 Bryson, Alex and Francis Green (2018), 'Do Private Schools Manage Better?'; *National Institute Economic Review*, 243 (February).

46 Bloom, N., R. Lemos, R. Sadun and J. Van Reenen (2015), 'Does Management Matter in Schools?', *Economic Journal*, 125(584), 647–74.

47 P. Auerbach, *Socialist Optimism. An Alternative Political Economy for the Twenty-First Century*, Palgrave Macmillan, New York, 2016, pp. 346–50.

48 Robert Whelan, 'End the private school arms race', *Daily Telegraph*, Letters, 22 February 2009.

49 https://www.gov.uk/cma-cases/independent-schools-exchange-of-information-on-future-fees; Rebecca Smithers, 'Slap on wrist for private schools in fees cartel', *Guardian*, 27 February 2006.

50 Elliott, Caroline, Palitha Konara and Yingqi Wei (2016), Competition, Cooperation and Regulatory Intervention Impacts on Independent School Fees, *International Journal of the Economics of Business*, 23:2, 243–62.

51 Richard Garner, 'For now, things may be politically peaceful for independent schools, but trouble lies ahead …', *TES*, 18 November 2017.

52 Sally Williams, 'Is this the end for private schools?', *The Times*, 16 April 2016.

53 Authors' analysis of the DfE's schools databases for 2010 and 2017: see www.gov.uk/government/statistics/schools-pupils-and-their-characteristics-january-2010 and www.gov.uk/government/statistics/schools-pupils-and-their-characteristics-january-2017.

5

1 David Donnison (1970), *The Public Schools Commission: Second Report*, Her Majesty's Stationery Office, London, 1970.

2 This applies to the schools affiliated to the Independent Schools Council, *ISC Census and Annual Report 2018*: https://www.isc.co.uk/research/annual-census.

3 Green, F., J. Anders, M. Henderson and G. Henseke (2017), *Who Chooses Private Schooling in Britain and Why?*, Centre for Research on Learning and Life Chances (LLAKES), London, Research Paper 62.

4 Anna Davis, 'Increase in private education fees is driving out middle-class families', *Evening Standard*, 5 May 2016.

5 Power, S., A. Curtis, G. Whitty, T. Edwards and S. Exley (2009), '*Embers From The Ashes*'? *The Experience Of Being An Assisted Place Holder*, The Sutton Trust, London.

6 Report by Nicola Woolcock, 'Send your child to private school and get free flights', *The Times*, 2 May 2017.

7 Authors' calculations from data provided in the ISC Census; figures apply to schools covered in the census; the figures in other private schools, not part of the ISC, will be lower.

8 Julie Henry, 'Private schools "abuse their charity status" by giving discounts to richer families', *Observer*, 3 June 2018; Nicola Woolcock, 'Top school gives fee discounts to £120,000 couples', *The Times*, 19 September 2016.

9 R. Straus, 'The 5 sneaky (but perfectly legal!) ways Britain's richest parents dodge the taxman to help pay private school fees', *Mail Online*, 21 February 2014.

10 Green, F., J. Anders, M. Henderson and G. Henseke (2017), *Who Chooses Private Schooling*.

11 Mumsnet forum, 12 February 2013.

12 Green, F., J. Anders, M. Henderson and G. Henseke (2017), *Who Chooses Private Schooling*.

13 Ibid.

14 Ibid.

15 Interview with anonymous headteacher, part of research for ESRC LLAKES Centre project: 'The effects of private and quasi-private schooling on society', described in Wilde, R., F. Green, P. Taylor-Gooby and S. Wiborg (2016), 'Private Schools and the Provision of "Public Benefit"', *Journal of Social Policy*, 45(2), 305–23.

16 Green, F., J. Anders, M. Henderson and G. Henseke (2017), *Who Chooses Private Schooling*.

17 *Evening Standard*, 5 March 2014.

18 'The "made it" list', *The Times*, 4 December 2014.

19 Irene Fox, *Private Schools and Public Issues: The Parents' View*, Macmillan, London, 1985.

20 Ibid., p. 157.

21 Ball, S. J. (1997), 'On the cusp: parents choosing between state and private schools in the UK: action within an economy of symbolic goods', *International Journal of Inclusive Education*, 1(1), 1–17.

22 West, A., P. Noden, A. Edge, M. David and J. Davies (1998), 'Choices and Expectations at Primary and Secondary Stages in the State and Private Sectors', *Educational Studies*, 24:1, 45–60.

23 Benson, M., G. Bridge and D. Wilson (2015), 'School Choice in London and Paris – A Comparison of Middle-class Strategies', *Social Policy & Administration*, 49(1), 24–43.

24 Foskett, N. and J. Hemsley-Brown, 'Economic Aspirations, Cultural Replication and Social Dilemmas – Interpreting Parental Choice of British Private Schools', in G. Walford (ed.), *British Private Schools. Research on Policy and Practice*, Woburn Press, London, 2003, pp. 188–201.

25 Luke Harding, 'How the Russians Came to Hogwarts', *Guardian*, 7 May 2013.

26 Green, F., S. Machin, R. Murphy and Y. Zhu (2011), 'The Changing Economic Advantage from Private Schools', *Economica*, 79, 658–79.

27 Green, F., G. Henseke, Samantha Parsons, A. Sullivan and R. Wiggins (2018), 'Do private school girls marry rich?', *Longitudinal and Life Course Studies Journal*, 2018 online.

28 *Guardian*, 31 July 2012.

29 *Evening Standard*, 3 December 2015.

30 A. Swift, *How Not to Be a Hypocrite. School Choice for the Morally Perplexed*, Routledge, London, 2003.

31 Ball, 'On the cusp'.

32 *Daily Telegraph*, 1 October 2013.

33 *The Economist*, 2 February 2013.

34 *Daily Telegraph*, 5 September 2015.

35 Benson et al., 'School Choice'.

36 Joris Luyendijk, 'How I learnt to loathe England', *Prospect Magazine*, November 2017.

37 *Evening Standard*, 3 December 2015.

38 Mumsnet forum, 27 July 2012.

39 Authors' own analysis of the British Social Attitudes Survey in 2009, 2011 and 2013.

6

1   Graeme Paton, 'Private school pupils "increasingly dominating" British life, says Michael Gove', *Daily Telegraph*, 10 May 2012.

2   Tim Ross, 'Nick Clegg: promoting "communist" policies for university access', *Daily Telegraph*, 22 May 2012; Nicholas Cecil, 'Milburn blasts professions for excluding poorer people', *Evening Standard*, 30 May 2012.

3   Matthew Parris, 'Schools that sell privilege can't be charities', *The Times*, 9 June 2012.

4   'Privileged education, public benefit and charitable status', *The Times*, 12 June 2012 (Newton); Alan White, ' "Gove is stuck on a Scottish moor, firing off rockets" ', *New Statesman*, 2 July 2012 (Hands); 'The enemies of social mobility,' *Independent*, 15 June 2012 (Ian Richards, Martin Callaghan); 'Public schools', *The Times*, 11 June 2012 (Benyon); 'The beneficiaries of privilege will never tackle social mobility', *Guardian*, 25 May 2012 (Bob Holman).

5   Owen Gibson and Matthew Taylor, 'State pupils don't get sporting chance, says British Olympic chief', *Guardian*, 3 August 2012.

6   'Raise state schools to Olympic standard', *Daily Telegraph*, 3 August 2012; 'Gold standard', John Moule, 'Striving and thriving', *The Spectator Guide to Independent Schools*, September 2012, pp. 3, 6.

7   Wendy Berliner and Richard Adams, 'Ofsted chief accuses private schools over help for poor', *Guardian*, 3 October 2013.

8   'Private Good', *The Times*, 3 October 2013.

9   For a flavour of what responses there were, see, 'Off Message', *ft.com*, 12 November 2013; 'Empty rhetoric on private schools' grip on top jobs', *Guardian*, 15 November 2013.

10 Matthew Parris, 'Kick open the doors to private education', *The Times*, 14 December 2013.

11 David Kynaston and George Kynaston, 'Education's Berlin Wall', *New Statesman*, 31 January 2014; Michael Gove, 'Our segregated education system perpetuates inequality and holds our nation back', *New Statesman*, 14 February 2014.

12 'Across the great divide', *Guardian*, 4 February 2014.

13 'Investing in teachers and quality facilities will raise school standards', *Daily Telegraph*, 5 February 2014 (Pitcher, Holl, Mullen); 'State v private', *The Times*, 5 February 2014 (Hudson).

14 'Fantasies shaping children's futures', *Guardian*, 6 February 2014.

15 Andrew Sparrow, 'Report condones "closed shop" of Britain's elite', *Guardian*, 28 August 2014; Graeme Paton, 'Declare the social mix of your staff, firms told', *Daily Telegraph*, 28 August 2014.

16 'Elitism and a skewed view of Britain's diversity', *Guardian*, 30 August 2014.

17 Graeme Paton, 'Ofsted chief: private schools "must justify their tax breaks"', *Daily Telegraph*, 3 September 2014.

18 Richard Harman, 'Stop this smearing: private schools are a boon to Britain', *The Times*, 29 September 2014.

19 'Is it right that public schools have charitable status?', *Observer*, 30 November 2014.

20 Julie Burchill, 'Born to be famous', *Spectator*, 26 July 2014.

21 Rowena Mason, 'You're full of bull: Blunt's broadside at MP', *Guardian*, 20 January 2015.

22 Bryan Appleyard, 'Red hot', *Sunday Times*, 12 April 2015.

23 Ben Quinn and Mark Tram, 'Lewis hits back in school party "elitism" row', *Guardian*, 28 January 2016.

24 John Plunkett, 'Working-class actors don't land best roles because "it's fashionable to sound posh"', *Guardian*, 1 March 2016.

25 'Privilege is the reason for posh actor posse', *Guardian*, 2 March 2016.

26 Hannah Ellis-Petersen, 'Do not blame arts for problems with social mobility, says Hytner', *Guardian*, 30 January 2015.

27 Matthew Parris, 'Posh boys from elite schools deserve to be sneered at', *The Times*, 28 May 2016.

28 Matthew Parris, 'Complain all you like: it won't stop me sneering', *The Times*, 1 June 2016.

29 Matthew Parris, 'Bog-standard elitism', *The Times*, 15 June 2016.

30 Robert Shrimsley, 'A frightfully British purge of the posh', *Financial Times*, 4 June 2016.

31 'Social mobility and private education', *Guardian*, 7 June 2016.

32 Peter Wilby, 'Eton's provost: "Social mobility is improving, but real change is slow"', *Guardian*, 26 July 2016.

33 Julie Robinson, 'You may dislike private schools, and that's just fine, but don't get your hopes up that the new-look Cabinet will be their demise', *Daily Telegraph*, 19 July 2016.

34 June Armitage, 'Tycoon attacks "terrible waste" of state pupils' Olympic talent', *Evening Standard*, 25 August 2016; Freddie Whittaker, 'Independent schools "uneasy" as employers urged to ask job applicants for education background', *Schools Week*, 2 September 2016.

35 'A simple system to ensure that all pupils are educated by their ability', *Daily Telegraph*, 12 September 2016.

36 'Down with the dismal concept of meritocracy', *Guardian*, 14 September 2016.

37 Michael Gove, 'Put VAT on school fees and soak the rich', *The Times*, 24 February 2017.

38 Sarah Harris, 'Fury at Gove's calls for 20% VAT to be levied on private school fees to tax the "global super-rich"', *Mail Online*, 25 February 2017.

39 'Free school meals and VAT on school fees: top marks for Labour', *Guardian*, 7 April 2017.

40 John Stevens and Emily Kent Smith, 'Backlash over Corbyn's plan to charge VAT on school fees', *Daily Mail*, 7 April 2017; 'Free lunch folly', *Daily Mail*, 7 April 2017.

41 'Half-Baked', *The Times*, 7 April 2017.

42 Richard Vaughan, 'Ministers row back on private school threat', *The i*, 13 September 2017.

43 Simon Johnson, 'SNP's decision to charge Scottish private schools business rates "will cost taxpayer double"', *Daily Telegraph*, 17 December 2017.

44 Simon Johnson, 'SNP "treating Scottish private school parents like super-rich" after minister claims they can afford fee rise', *Daily Telegraph*, 17 January 2018; Scott Macnab, 'Scottish Budget 2017: Private schools hit with £5m rates hike', *Scotsman*, 14 December 2017; Derek Healey, 'Dundee High School rector calls on MSPs to keep rates relief for independent schools', *Courier* (Dundee), 7 February 2018.

45 *Independent Education Today* website, 3 March 2018.

46 *Daily Telegraph*, 16 June 2018 (report by Christopher Hope).

47 Amanda Cashmore, 'Leading £25,000-a-year private St Paul's Girls' School is slammed for serving baked potatoes and beans as AUSTERITY DAY lunch', *Mail Online*, 22 June 2018; Sian Griffiths, 'Private schools shun tough GCSEs', *Sunday Times*, 24 June 2018.

48 Sarah Baxter, 'Mr and Mrs Posh are still winning the class war', *Sunday Times*, 24 June 2018.

49 Robert Verkaik, *Posh Boys: How the English Public Schools Ruin Britain*, Oneworld, London, 2018, p. 340.

50 Clive Davis, 'Should we "euthanise" the private schools', *The Times*, 30 June 2018; Andrew Marr, 'Posh boys still get the top jobs', *Sunday Times*, 8 July 2018.

51 Hannah Richardson, ' "Glass floor" protecting middle classes from social slide – report', BBC website, 26 July 2015; Peter Wilby, 'A "glass floor" for middle-class dimwits', *New Statesman*, 31 July 2015.

52 'A class apart', *The Economist*, 22 October 2016.

53 'Elevator malfunction', *The Economist* ('Bagehot'), 9 December 2017.

54 David Kynaston, 'Private schools are blocking social mobility', *Daily Telegraph*, 30 October 2013; 'Better education for all', *Daily Telegraph*, 31 October 2013.

55 Janet Daley, 'Maoist class war wrecked our state schools', *Sunday Telegraph*, 17 November 2013; 'Mobility starts at school', *Daily Telegraph*, 28 August 2014; Charles Moore, 'It's true, grammar schools are not about equality – that's why we should build more of them', *Daily Telegraph*, 17 October 2015.

56 Fraser Nelson, 'Purge of the posh', *Spectator*, 4 June 2016.

57 Will Hutton, 'There is much more still to do to get poor students into higher education', *Observer*, 17 August 2014; Deborah Orr, 'Lemmy gambled and won', *Guardian*, 2 January 2016; Polly Toynbee, 'Free to dream, I'd be left of Corbyn', *Guardian*, 4 August 2015; Owen Jones, 'Our private school elite's dominance is not just unfair – it damages us all', *Guardian*, 25 February 2016; Bryan Appleyard, 'In from the Cold War', *Sunday Times*, 3 September 2017. For Hutton, see also his *How Good We Can Be: Ending the Mercenary Society and Building a Great Country*, Little, Brown, London, 2015, pp. 117–19, 191–2.

58 David Mitchell, 'Seriously – do teachers in private schools really expect our applause?', *Observer*, 3 February 2013.

59 Robert Webb, 'I don't mind if our politicians went to posh schools', *New Statesman*, 30 January 2015.

60 Melissa Benn, 'I returned to my father's school to say why private education must go', *Guardian*, 31 May 2016; Fiona Millar, 'Private schools: we need full disclosure about their affairs', *Guardian*, 8 October 2013.

61 David Kynaston, 'How class impacts on education', *Guardian*, 19 June 2014.

62 'Private schools should make a real contribution to society in return for charitable status', *Guardian*, 26 November 2014.

63 See for instance two letters in the *Guardian*: 15 November 2013 (Ron Glatter, Open University) and 20 June 2017 (Michael Pyke, Paying for State Education).

64 Nick Clegg et al., *Commission on Inequality in Education*, Social Market Foundation, 2017, pp. 8, 66–7.

65 'Schools of thought', *New Statesman*, 14 February 2014 (Williams); 'Elitism and a skewed view of Britain's diversity', *Guardian*, 30 August 2014 (Green); 'Elephant in the room of education policy', *Guardian*, 10 May 2016 (Colley); 'No place for private schools', *Observer*, 12 June 2016 (Wigglesworth).

66 Tim Lott, 'Why I want to see all private schools abolished', *Guardian*, 22 April 2017.

67 http://www.ucl.ac.uk/ioe/news-events/events-pub/oct-2017/ what-if-furthering-social-mobility-through-education

68 Liz Thomson, '"I hope I'm not being too old-gittish"', *New Statesman*, 21 October 2016.

69 *The Pledge*, Sky News, 31 May 2018.

70 Ellie Mae O'Hagan, 'Let's restrict the number of privately educated people in Britain's elite', *Guardian*, 7 August 2017.

71 'Give state pupils a leg-up', *Observer*, 19 June 2016.

72 Peter Wilby, 'Classroom to boardroom', *New Statesman*, 20 March 2015.

73 Peter Wilby, 'My idea to break the stranglehold of the public school gang', *Guardian*, 18 September 2012.

74 Peter Wilby, 'My small column in the Guardian is now a play at the Old Vic: let the message be heard', *Guardian*, 15 September 2015.

75 Peter Lampl, 'No privilege required', *Financial Times*, 8 September 2012.

76 Authors' interview with Sir Peter Lampl, 28 March 2018.

77 Matthew Parris, 'Keep open the doors to private education', *The Times*, 14 December 2013; 'Social mobility', *The Times*, 19 December 2013 (Seldon); Anthony Seldon, 'Open the private schools to the poor', *New Statesman*, 7 February 2014; Anthony Seldon, 'Open our elite schools to the poorest pupils', *Daily Telegraph*, 6 May 2014.

78 Shaun Fenton, 'Theresa May should fund private schools to take on poor students', *Daily Telegraph*, 3 August 2016.

79 ISC Press Office, 'Joint funding could see 10,000 free new independent school places every year', 9 December 2016.

80 Richard Adams, 'Private schools in England propose 10,000 free places', *Guardian*, 9 December 2016.

81 Richard Garner, 'Ministers in secret talks to bring back direct grant schools', *Independent*, 18 October 2016.

82 Andrew Adonis, 'Education's Berlin Wall is falling at long last', *The Times*, 26 June 2012.

83 Andrew Adonis, *Education, Education, Education: Reforming England's Schools*, Biteback, London, 2012, p. 256.

84 Andrew Adonis, 'Academies can make the difference', *New Statesman*, 7 February 2014.

85 Adonis, *Education, Education, Education*, pp. 148–9, 156–62.

86 Kynastons, 'Berlin Wall'.

87 Warwick Mansell, 'Worlds collide: can private schools ever hope to pass on their "DNA"?', *Guardian*, 18 August 2015; Wilby, 'Classroom'.

7

1 ISC, *Manifesto 2017*, https://www.isc.co.uk/media/4092/68538-4.pdf

2 Oxford Economics, 2014, *The Impact of Independent Schools on the British Economy. A Report Prepared for the Independent Schools Council*, Oxford Economics, Oxford.

3 Nicola Woolcock, 'Private schools boost economy by £12bn a year', *The Times*, 3 April 2014; Irena Barker, 'Private schools contribute almost £12 billion a year to British economy, report finds', *TES*, 2 April 2014.

4 The argument is the same as for universities: see Siegfried, J. J., A. R. Sanderson and P. McHenry (2007), 'The economic impact of colleges and universities', *Economics of Education Review*, 26(5), 546–58.

5 Biggar Economics (2016), *Economic Impact of Scottish Independent Schools*, A report to the Scottish Council of Independent Schools.

6 David Turner, *The Old Boys: The Decline and Rise of the Public School*, Yale University Press, London, 2015, p. 264.

7 Sakellariou, C. (2017), 'Private or public school advantage? Evidence from 40 countries using PISA 2012-Mathematics', *Applied Economics*, 49(29), 2875–92. In this study, some private school advantage in the UK was evident even after taking account of background and of the selective peer groups in schools (communication from author).

8 Turner, *Old Boys*, p. 272.

9 Bryson, Alex and Francis Green, 2018, 'Do Private Schools Manage Better?', *National Institute Economic Review*, 243 (February).

10 Anna Leszkiewicz, 'Don't worry, Old Etonian Damian Lewis calls claims of privilege in acting "nonsense!"', *New Statesman*, 20 April 2017.

11 Turner, *Old Boys*, p. 271.

12 Peter Wilby, 'Elite private headteacher: "The children we educate will create a fairer society"', *Guardian*, 13 June 2017; Anna Davis, 'Private school pupils should be taught how lucky they are, says London headteacher', *Evening Standard*, 19 September 2017.

13 Malcolm Tozer (2017), review of Mark Peel, *The New Meritocracy: A History of UK Independent Schools 1979–2015*, in *History of Education*, 46:1, 128–30.

14 Brighouse, H. and A. Swift, 'The place of educational equality in educational justice', in K. Meyer (ed.), *Education, Justice and the Human Good*, Routledge, London, 2014, p. 15.

15 Independent Schools Council (2015), *ISC Census and Annual Report 2015*, ISC, p. 3.

16 Charlotte Santry, 'Exclusive: Private schools boss condemns "anti-privilege mood"', *TES*, 18 May 2018.

17 http://www.scis.org.uk/information-for-parents/why-choose-an-independent-school/

18 Christopher Ray, letter to *The Times*, 25 February 2017, reproduced at: http://expressiveparents.com/charitable-status-and-independent-schools/

19 Laura McInerney, 'Let the Private Schools Take 25% at Random', https://lauramcinerney.com/2013/07/02/let-the-private-schools-have-25-at-random/.

20 Kevin Fear, 'Response to Michael Gove', https://head.nottinghamhighblogs.net/2017/02/26/response-to-michael-gove/.

21 See Fig. 2.4 in OECD (2012), *Public and Private Schools: How Management and Funding Relate to their Socio-economic Profile*, OECD Publishing.

22 Richard Harman, 'HMC statement in response to Report from Social Mobility and Child Poverty Commission', 28 August 2014, https://www.hmc.org.uk/blog/statement-hmc-chairman-richard-harman-resopnse/(sic)

23 Jim Pickard, 'UK Schools expand their operations abroad', *Financial Times*, 2 September 2013; Greg Hurst, 'Eton borrows £45m for boys who can't pay', *The Times*, 13 August 2015; Julian Thomas, 'This constant bashing of independent schools needs to end', *TES*, 11 December 2017.

24 ISC (2017), *Celebrating Partnerships*, Issue 2, p. 24.

25 Power, S., G. Whitty and E. Wisby (2006), *The Educational and Career Trajectories of Assisted Place Holders*, The Sutton Trust, London; Power, S., S. Sims and G. Whitty (2013), *Lasting Benefits. The Long-term Legacy of the Assisted Places Scheme for Assisted Place Holders*, The Sutton Trust, London.

26 Freddie Whittaker, 'Private schools take 1% of pupils from very disadvantaged backgrounds', *Schools Week*, 28 November 2017; ISC (2017), *Celebrating Partnerships*, Issue 2, p. 24.

27 Davies, P., J. Noble, K. Slack and K. Bigurs (2010), *Fee remissions and bursaries in independent schools*, The Sutton Trust, London; Wilde, R., F. Green, P. Taylor-Gooby and S. Wiborg (2016), 'Private Schools and the Provision of "Public Benefit"', *Journal of Social Policy*, 45:2, 305–23.

28 Julie Henry, 'Private schools "abuse their charity status" by giving discounts to richer families', *Observer*, 3 June 2018.

29 Freddie Whittaker, 'Private schools take 1% of pupils from very disadvantaged backgrounds', *Schools Week*, 28 November 2017.

30 Straw, S., S. C. Bamford and K. Martin (2016), *Evaluation of The SpringBoard Bursary Foundation: Year 3*, Slough, NFER.

31 Wilde et al., 'Private Schools'.

32 Julie Robinson, 'Increasing hostility towards private education', *Daily Telegraph*, 21 June 2016; letters, *Guardian*, 25 April 2017; Independent Schools Council (2017), *ISC Census and Annual Report 2017*, ISC, p. 2.

33 See, for example, Lord Lexden, speaking in the House of Lords short debate 'Independent Schools: Variety and Diversity', 4 March 2015.

34 Independent Schools Council (2018), *ISC Census and Annual Report 2018*, ISC, p. 21.

35 Joe Nutt, 'State and independent school partnerships must be more than joint concerts and swimming galas', *TES*, 2 April 2018.

36 Wilde et al., 'Private Schools'; ISC, *Celebrating Partnerships*, 2017, Issue 2, p. 22; Rosemary Bennett, 'Private schools will keep charitable status', *The Times*, 13 September 2017.

37 This rough figure is calculated from the estimates of the total raised per school given in the ISC Censuses, for 2016, 2017 and 2018.

38 Wilde et al., 'Private Schools'.

39 BBC Radio 4, *Across the Red Line*, 10 March 2018.

40 Janet Murray, 'Why I sent my child to private school', *Guardian*, 23 July 2012.

41 Mumsnet conversation, 27 July 2012; https://www.mumsnet.com/ Talk/education/1526214-I-send-my-child-to-private-school-because

42 Gibbons, S. and S. Machin (2006), 'Paying for primary schools: Admission constraints, school popularity or congestion?', *Economic Journal*, 116:510, C77–C92.

43 Samuel R. Lucas, 'Effectively Maintained Inequality: Education Transitions, Track Mobility, and Social', *American Journal of Sociology*, vol. 106, no. 6 (May 2001), pp. 1642–90.

44 Turner, *Old Boys*, p. 278.

45 Murray, 'Why I sent my child'.

46 Clegg, N., R. Allen, S. Fernandes, S. Freedman and S. Kinnock (2017), *Commission on Inequality in Education*, the Social Market Foundation, London.

47 Dadsnet, 5 October 2014, 30 September 2014; Mumsnet, 15 February 2015.

8

1 The majority (57 per cent) of those who agreed indicated that they 'strongly agreed' with the statement. The poll surveyed online a sample of 2,000 respondents aged eighteen and older on 14–15 March 2018; weights were deployed to ensure national representative proportions according to standard demographic variables.

2 As an example of how governments want to use private schools to help state schools, see Department for Education, May 2018, 'Schools that work for everyone. Government consultation response'.

3 Martin Stephen, *The English Public School*, Metro Publishing, 2018, p. 275.

4 Sally Weale and Caelainn Barr, 'Initiative to persuade universities to recruit more students from state schools is stalling', *Guardian*, 2 February 2018.

5 Gorard, S., V. Boliver, N. Siddiqui, P. Banerjee and R. Morris (2017), 'Which are the most suitable contextual indicators for use in widening

participation to HE?', Working Paper, School of Education and School of Applied Social Sciences, Durham University, Durham; Boliver, V., C. Crawford, M. Powell and W. Craige (2017), *The use of contextual information by leading universities*, London, The Sutton Trust; Boliver V., S. Gorard, M. Powell and T. Moreira (2017), *Mapping and evaluating the use of contextual data in undergraduate admissions in Scotland*, an *Impact for Access* project funded by the Scottish Funding Council; Boliver V., S. Gorard and N. Siddiqui (2017), 'A more radical approach to contextualised admissions', in *Where next for widening participation and fair access?* Higher Education Report, HEPI Report 98.

6 A similar proposal is advanced by Harry Brighouse in his 2000 Fabian pamphlet *A Level Playing Field: The Reform of Private Schools*, London, Fabian Policy Report 52, p. 16.

7 Xavier Greenwood and Richard Adams, 'Revealed: the £21bn wealth built up by Oxford and Cambridge', *Guardian*, 29 May 2018.

8 Ibid., p. 13.

9 A. Courtois, *Elite Schooling and Social Inequality: Privilege and Power in Ireland's Top Private Schools*, Palgrave Macmillan, London, 2018.

10 Richard Vaughan, 'Employers must offer jobs to state school students over Old Etonians', *iNews*, 30 April 2018.

11 ISC Census 2017.

12 Will Dahlgreen, 'Wide support for tackling private school exemptions', *YouGov UK*, 27 February 2014. https://yougov.co.uk/news/2014/11/27/strong-public-support-tackling-private-school-tax-/

13 Minutes of Taunton Deane Council Meeting, 6 February 2017; Freddie Whittaker, 'Council launches investigation into benefits of private schools', *Schools Week*, 3 March 2017; Amy Cole, 'Taunton Deane Borough Council agree to start a forum to discuss private schools' "community benefit"', *County Gazette*, 9 February 2017.

14 Hilary Osborne and agencies, 'Private schools to save £522m in tax thanks to charitable status', *Guardian*, 11 June 2017. An earlier estimate for 2014 by Labour MP Simon Danczuk put the savings figure somewhat higher, at £150 million per year (Holly Watt and Graeme Paton, *Daily Telegraph*, 24 November 2014).

15 Camilla Turner, 'Private schools abandon charitable status in bid to avoid "huge pressure" to deliver "public benefit"', *Daily Telegraph*, 27 April 2018.

16 Scottish Government 'Review of the Barclay Report of Non-Domestic Rates', http://www.gov.scot/Publications/2017/08/3435; Daniel Sanderson, 'Scottish Budget 2017: Business rate rise for private schools "will be passed to parents"', *The Times*, 15 December 2017; SCIS Press Statement, 14 December 2017; ISC statement following Scottish Government's response to Barclay Review, https://www.isc.co.uk/media-enquiries

17 'Independent schools: variety and diversity', House of Lords debate, 4 March 2015.

18 The Labour Party expected about £1.5 billion based on estimates from a Fabian review essay of 2010. Our rough estimate is higher than the Labour Party figure because it uses 2018 average school fees; our estimate also assumes a 5 per cent drop in numbers as some parents switch to the state sector.

19 Debate on 'Education and Society', House of Lords, 8 December 2017, *Hansard*, vol. 787.

20 Eleanor Busby, 'Levy on independent schools "should be set to bring in more disadvantaged pupils"', *TES*, 3 December 2017.

21 Laura Hughes, 'Labour's plan to tax private school fees to pay for free school meals in tatters', *Daily Telegraph*, 6 April 2017.

22 This estimate assumes that the price elasticity of demand is -0.26 – the best estimate at the age seven stage, computed in Blundell, R., L. Dearden and L. Sibieta (2010), *The demand for private schooling: the impact of price and quality*, Institute of Fiscal Studies, London.

23 Melissa Benn, *Life Lessons: The Case for a National Educational Service*, Verso Books, London, 2018.

24 Interview communication from Sir Peter Lampl, 18 March 2018.

25 The Sutton Trust, *Open Access: Democratising Entry to Independent Day Schools*, update March 2015. https://www.suttontrust.com/research-paper/open-access-democratising-entry-independent-day-schools/

26 Broughton, N., O. Ezeyi, C. Hupkau, N. Keohane and R. Shorthouse, *Open Access. An independent evaluation*, Social Market Foundation, June 2014.

27 Greg Hurst, 'One in ten private places must go to disadvantaged pupils, heads say', *The Times*, 5 May 2014.

28 Anthony Seldon, *Schools United: Ending the divide between independent and state*, Social Market Foundation, January 2014.

29 Independent Schools Council, *Manifesto 2017*; Julie Robinson, ISC Response to the government's consultation on its Green Paper 'Schools that work for everyone', December 2016.

30 Richard Adams, 'Private schools in England propose 10,000 free places', *Guardian*, 9 December 2016.

31 Fiona Millar, 'The Sutton Trust's "radical" idea for schools is anything but', *Guardian*, 12 June 2012.

32 Interview with Peter Lampl, 28 March 2018.

33 Fiona Millar, 'When private schools fail, why should the state bail them out?', *Guardian*, 11 February 2014.

34 Laura McInerney, 'There's a better way for private schools to help the state sector', *Guardian*, 11 December 2016.

35 Benn, *Life Lessons*.

36 Interview with David Wolfe, 10 May 2018.

37 Richard Garner, 'As many as 100 independent schools could join the state sector within a decade as free schools or academies', *Independent*, 22 January 2014.

38 John Claughton, 'Is education the solution to social mobility?', *iSS Magazine*, 1 October 2017.

39 This estimate of the number of switching pupils again assumes that private schools' unit costs are roughly three times state spending per capita, and that the best estimate of price elasticity is given in Blundell, R., L. Dearden and L. Sibieta, *The Demand for Private Schooling*; the fee increase, the numbers switching and the addition to the government's education budget would all become lower if schools retrench and lower their unit costs. If the minimum proportion of state school pupils in the private schools was set at only 25 per cent, the additional cost comes down to around £200 million, while if the minimum was set at 50 per cent the additional cost could be closer to £600 million.

40 John Dickens, 'Proposals for pioneering "low cost" private school in England revealed', *Schools Week*, 17 February 2017; James Tooley, 'A chain of low cost private schools for the UK: a demonstration model of the viability and efficacy of free markets in education', Institute of Economic Affairs, https://iea.org.uk/wp-content/uploads/2017/04/Koch-Tooley-final-edited.pdf

41 Geoffrey Walford (2011), 'Low-fee private schools in England and in less economically developed countries. What can be learnt from a comparison?', *Compare*, 41:3, 401–13.

42 'Can a £52-a-week private school work in the rich world?', *The Economist*, 12 May 2018.

43 The Sutton Trust, *Open Access*.

44 Anthony Seldon (2001), *Public and Private Education: The Divide Must End*, the Social Market Foundation, London.

45 *ICS Census and Annual Report, 2018*, p. 10.

9

1 Gordon Brown in conversation with David Kynaston, 10 December 2014; authors' interview with Alan Milburn, 23 May 2018.

2 John Rae, *The Public School Revolution: Britain's Independent Schools, 1964–1979*, Faber and Faber, London, 1981, p. 74.

3 Charlotte Santry, 'Private schools boss condemns "anti-privilege mood"', *TES*, 18 May 2018.

4 Reeves, A., S. Friedman, C. Rahal and M. Flemmen (2017), 'The Decline and Persistence of the Old Boy: Private Schools and Elite Recruitment 1897 to 2016', *American Sociological Review*, 1–28.

5 Interview with Andrew Adonis, 14 May 2018.

6 Ben Quinn, 'Outrage at "lavish" spending by City of London Corporation', *Observer*, 19 November 2017.

7 Owen Jones, *The Establishment: And How They Get Away with It*, Allen Lane, London, 2014.

8 'Quango queen takes on the public schools', *Daily Telegraph*, 2 November 2007.

9 Alasdair Palmer, 'Private schools are at the mercy of the Charity Commission's prejudice', *Daily Telegraph*, 10 October 2009.

10 Graeme Paton, 'Private schools attack "politically-motivated" charity rules', *Daily Telegraph*, 12 January 2010.

11 Jessica Shepherd, 'Private schools win case over showing benefit to society', *Guardian*, 14 October 2011.

12 Stephen Lloyd, 'Where does the independent schools case leave us now?', *Civil Society*, 24 October 2011.

13 Interview with Andrew Adonis, 14 May 2018.

14 The Wellington Community, *What's on*, Summer 2018.

15 Libby Purves, 'There's more to life than revising for exams', *The Times*, 2 April 2018.

16 John Rae, *The Old Boys' Network: A Headmaster's Diaries, 1972–1988*, Short Books, London, 2009, p. 92.

17 *A+ Education* (South-east, Spring 2018); *angels & urchins*, Spring 2018; *Guardian*, 17 February 2018; Sophie Grubb, 'Win sixth form place at coveted Oxford school', *Oxford Mail*, 22 March 2018.

18 Louis Wise, 'Russia by way of Glasgow', *Sunday Times*, 24 July 2016.

19 Frances Gibb, 'Why it pays for a trainee to be posh', *The Times*, 15 February 2018; Nicola Woolcock, 'When public school kids get locked up', *The Times*, 15 February 2018.

20 Peter Wilby, '"The last thing a chief inspector should be is a crusader," she says. Oh really?', *Guardian*, 6 February 2018.

21 Jenni Russell, 'It's a cosy myth that anyone can reach the top', *The Times*, 28 August 2014.

22 Anne McElvoy, 'I teach at Stanford, I launched a tech company and I still don't have a smartphone – life is good', *Evening Standard*, 19 May 2015.

23 John Ahier and John Beck, 'Education and the Politics of Envy', *British Journal of Educational Studies*, December 2003 (51/4), pp. 321, 323, 325.

24 Judith Woods, 'One student's gain is another's loss – that can't be right', *Daily Telegraph*, 27 October 2017.

25 Chris Ramsey, 'University admissions: "equal opportunity" should not mean punishing pupils from good schools', *Daily Telegraph*, 2 November 2017.

26 Jones, *Establishment*, p. 101.

27 British Social Attitudes Survey 2010, authors' analysis.

28 Alex Matthews, 'Tesco worker's son, 16, who was raised in one of Britain's most impoverished areas follows in footsteps of Princes William and Harry by winning a place at Eton', *Mail Online*, 5/6 December 2017.

29 E. P. Thompson, *The Poverty of Theory and Other Essays*, Merlin Press, Balbriggan, 1978, pp. 35–91.

30 Saskia Papadakis, 'Elites and their Teachers', *Discover Society*, 3 April 2018.

31 Simon Barrow, 'The inheritance of privilege', *The Economist*, 14 February 2015.

32 Laura McInerney, 'Follow the Indian model', *New Statesman*, 7 February 2014.

33 Pasi Sahlberg, *Finnish Lessons: What Can the World Learn from Educational Change in Finland?*, Teachers College Press, New York, Census 2011, pp. 22–4, 96, 121–3.

34 Jon Henley, 'Free and fair: How Finland came up with the answers', *Guardian*, 13 February 2018; 'Finland's story shows equality is a better route to happiness than rapid growth', *Observer*, 18 March 2018.

35 Sahlberg, *Finnish Lessons*, p. 24.

POSTSCRIPT: MOVING AHEAD?

1 Dan Kennedy, 'Too posh for Tinder', *The Times*, 4 August 2018; Simon Johnson, 'Private school pupils three times as likely to appeal exam results after SNP introduces charges', *Daily Telegraph*, 11 August 2018; Carol Midgley, 'Beggared yourself with school fees?', *The Times*, 12 September 2018; Sian Griffiths, 'Private schools lure state maths teachers to foreign offshoots', *Sunday Times*, 16 September 2018; Suzanne Moore, 'Classy Cerys Matthews has the common touch', *Guardian*, 18 September 2018; Olivia Rudgard, 'Graduate career schemes "biased towards private school students"', *Daily Telegraph*, 24 September 2018; Pippa Crerar, 'Money-laundering crackdowns on public schools and law firms', *Guardian*, 1 November 2018; Rosemary Bennett, 'Eight schools send more to Oxbridge than 2,800 rivals', *The Times*, 7 December 2018; Rupert Neate, 'The rich get their own inflation index – and won't like what it says', *Guardian*, 11 December 2018; Sian Griffiths, 'Ruby Wax tells private pupils to visit poor children', *Sunday Times*, 6 January 2019; Joshi Herrmann, 'Why we're trying to help level the Oxbridge playing field', *The i*, 10 January 2019; Kiran Samrai, 'One 16-year-old isn't the problem with private education – Britain's system of inequality is', *Prospect*, 23 January 2019; William Sitwell, 'You 'avin' a laff?', *Daily Telegraph*, 29 January 2019; Jack Malvern, 'School challenges right of (fair)way', *The Times*, 30 January 2019; Caroline Roux, 'Forget Latin, it's all about fine acoustics and a sea view', *Daily Telegraph*, 11 February 2019; Nicola Woolcock, 'School heads clean toilets and wash dishes after budget cuts', *The Times*, 5 March 2019; Independent Schools Council (2017). *ISC Census and Annual Report 2019*.

2 Melissa Benn, *Life Lessons: The Case for a National Education Service*, Verso, London, 2018, pp. 131–5, 137–8.

3 Lee Elliot Major and Stephen Machin, *Social Mobility and Its Enemies*, Pelican, London, 2018, pp. 147, 208.

4 Sam Friedman and Daniel Laurison, *The Class Ceiling: Why It Pays to Be Privileged*, Policy Press, Bristol, 2019, pp. 229–38.

5 Clare Foges, 'Better to smash the class ceiling than rage at it', *The Times*, 28 January 2019.

6 *The Economist*, 15 September 2018.

7 'The elite that failed', *The Economist*, 22 December 2018.

8 Andrew Denholm, 'Economists issue dire warning over future of Edinburgh private schools', *Herald*, 18 February 2019.

9 Rosamund Urwin, 'Westminster School wants brains, not fees', *Sunday Times*, 7 October 2018; *TES News*, 25 November 2018, 6 December 2018; Camilla Turner, 'Cut scholarships and fund less well-off pupils instead, says head of £32,000-a-year school', *Daily Telegraph*, 7 January 2019, 'Private school bursaries are being used to top up fees of middle-class children, leading head says', *Daily Telegraph*, 26 January 2019.

10 '"Folly" of imposing VAT on private schools', *The Times*, 18 October 2018; Lynne Davidson, 'Chancellor Philip Hammond has scrapped VAT on private schools ahead of the Budget as borrowing figures show an 11-year low at £4.1bn', *Sun*, 20 October 2018; Joe Murphy and Nicholas Cecil, '70 per cent of Britons against Budget idea to raid pension savings', *Evening Standard*, 26 October 2018.

11 Pippa Allen-Kinross, 'Looked-after children to get mentors and cut-price fees from private schools', *Schools Week*, 4 December 2018; Nicholas Watt, 'Private schools should help children in care, says government', *BBC News*, 7 August 2018.

12 Haroon Siddique, 'Labour calls for an inquiry into GCSE changes "gamed by private schools"', *Guardian*, 31 December 2018; Camilla Turner, 'Private school pupils who take IGCSEs have better chance of getting top marks, exam watchdog admits', *Daily Telegraph*, 13 March 2019.

13 www.conservativehome.com, Dominic Raab, 'Unleashing the Great British Underdog', 11 March 2019.

14 Alice Thomson and Rachel Sylvester, '"Why not offer an Oxbridge place to the best 100 pupils in each area?"', *The Times*, 16 March 2019.

15 Joe Murphy and Charlotte Edwardes, 'Michael Gove: I'd like to make sending children to private school seem eccentric', *Evening Standard*, 1 March 2019.

16 Alex Renton, 'Old school ties can't last forever', *Spectator*, 2 February
    2019; Anne McElvoy, 'Public school toffs versus the Bash Street
    Kids', *Evening Standard*, 31 January 2019; Janice Turner, 'Revisiting
    the 7 per cent problem', *New Statesman*, 1 February 2019; 'Privates
    on parade', *Private Eye*, 8 February 2019; Allison Pearson, 'Selective
    schools could spell the end of private education', *Sunday Telegraph*,
    3 February 2019; Kate Clanchy, 'The unfairness of fee-paying schools
    affects all our lives', *Guardian*, 26 January 2019 (fuller version online,
    25 January 2019); Jamie Whyte, 'Illiberal and irrelevant', *Standpoint*,
    March 2019; Hugo Rifkind, 'Unjust, elitist: please let my kids in', *The
    Times*, 2 February 2019; Harry Mount, 'Why parents will always turn
    to St Custard's', *Catholic Herald*, 1 March 2019; Maggie Fergusson,
    'Closing time?', *Tablet*, 2 February 2019; Dominic Sandbrook,
    'Aiming to rein in the privileged', *Sunday Times*, 3 February 2019;
    Miranda Green, 'The great divide', *Financial Times*, 16 February 2019.

17 *Quad*, 18 February 2019. https://www.alumni.ox.ac.uk/quad/article/
    unfair-private-schools.

18 Higher Education Policy Institute blog, 2 February 2019.
    https://www.hepi.ac.uk/category/blog/page/2/.

19 Book review, *TES*, 10/2/201. https://www.tes.com/news/book-review-
    engines-privilege-britains-private-school-problem; our response:
    'We stand by our book: private education should be reformed'.
    https://www.tes.com/news/we-stand-our-book-private-education-
    should-be-reformed .

20 *Reasons to be Cheerful* podcast, episode 71; Ed Miliband, 'Private
    school reform is needed if society is ever to become equal', *Metro*, 4
    February 2019.

21 'Revisiting the 7 per cent problem', *New Statesman*, 1 February 2019.

22 'Private schools present obstacles to social mobility that must be
    overcome', *Guardian*, 13 February 2019.

23 Sadie Nicholas, 'Sneered at for sending our children to private
    school', *Daily Mail*, 13 February 2019.

24 Damian Whitworth, 'Can Westminster ditch elitism with charity –
    and six schools in China?', *The Times*, 5 October 2018.

25 Question from floor, posed at LSE launch: https://www.lse.ac.uk/
    lse-player?id=4609.

26 Tin Hinson, 'Investigating private schools: not just the fees that are
    unfair', *Bristol Cable*, 29 April 2019.

Acknowledgements

We warmly thank the following who found time to discuss with one or other or both of us the private school question: Andrew Adonis; Melissa Benn; Tim Brighouse; Solomon Elliott; Patrick Fullick; Peter Lampl; Lee Elliot Major; Laura McInerney; Alan Milburn; Charlie Samuda; David Ward; David Wolfe; Annalisa Zisman. Others who have pointed us in helpful directions include Harry Brighouse, Sam Freedman, Nick Hillman and Pasi Sahlberg. Golo Henseke has helped enormously with some of the data analysis, and, together with Jake Anders and Morag Henderson, has greatly contributed to our understanding of private schools in the twenty-first century.

The following kindly read and commented on all or part of the book in draft form: Paul Auerbach; Melissa Benn; Mike Burns; Alison Culverwell; Rose Elgar; Daniel Green; Toby Green; Sara Kinsey; George Kynaston; Lucy Kynaston; Laura McInerney; Harry Ricketts; Martin Thom; David Warren.

The responsibility for the book, including any errors of fact or interpretation, remains entirely ours.

In addition, Francis Green gratefully acknowledges support from the Economic and Social Research Council for funding through the LLAKES Research Centre at UCL Institute of Education; and David Kynaston is grateful to Amanda Howard (Superscript Editorial Services) for typing up his tapes. We are both grateful to Richard Collins for copy-editing; to Catherine Best for proofreading; to David Atkinson for compiling the index; to our agent Georgia Garrett and her assistant Madeleine Dunnigan; and to Michael Fishwick, our editor at Bloomsbury, and his colleagues Sarah Ruddick and Lilidh Kendrick.

Index

A Note on the Type

The text of this book is set Adobe Garamond. It is one of several versions of Garamond based on the designs of Claude Garamond. It is thought that Garamond based his font on Bembo, cut in 1495 by Francesco Griffo in collaboration with the Italian printer Aldus Manutius. Garamond types were first used in books printed in Paris around 1532. Many of the present-day versions of this type are based on the *Typi Academiae* of Jean Jannon cut in Sedan in 1615.

Claude Garamond was born in Paris in 1480. He learned how to cut type from his father and by the age of fifteen he was able to fashion steel punches the size of a pica with great precision. At the age of sixty he was commissioned by King Francis I to design a Greek alphabet, and for this he was given the honourable title of royal type founder. He died in 1561.